Literature, History and Identity in Northern Nigeria

Literature, History and Identity in Northern Nigeria

Edited by

Ismaila A. Tsiga
M. O. Bhadmus

Safari Books Ltd
Ibadan

Published by
Safari Books Ltd
Ile Ori Detu
1, Shell Close
Onireke
Ibadan.
Email: safarinigeria@gmail.com
Website: www.safaribooksng.com

© 2015, Ismaila A. Tsiga; M.O. Bhadmus

First Published 2015

All rights reserved. This book is copyright and so no part of it may be reproduced, stored in a retrieval system, or transmitted, in any form or by any means, electrical, mechanical, electrostatic, magnetic tape, photocopying, recording or otherwise, without the prior written permission of the author.

ISBN: 978-978-8431-87-9

Dedication

This book is dedicated jointly to Professor Abubakar Adamu Rasheed, the Vice-Chancellor, Bayero University, Kano, and Professor Abdul-Rasheed Na'Allah, the Vice-Chancellor, Kwara State University, Malete, for their enormous contribution to the development of literature, history and identity in Northern Nigeria.

TABLE OF CONTENTS

Dedication .... *v*
Foreword .... *xi*
Acknowledgements .... *xiii*
About the Contributors .... *xv*
Introduction .... *xix*

PART ONE: LITERATURE, HISTORY AND IDENTITY

Chapter One:
    Literature, History and Identity: Theories, Contents and Perspectives 1
    Abdul-Rasheed Na'Allah

Chapter Two:
    Traversing the Worlds of Literature, History and Identity: Life Writing in Northern Nigeria.. 13
    Ismaila A. Tsiga

PART TWO: LITERATURE AND HISTORY

Chapter Three:
    'Without A Spare Tyre ...': The Interstices of Literature in Northern Nigeria... 55
    John Sani Illah

Chapter Four:
    Theatre and Resistance in the Age of Colonial Imperialism: Ahmed Yerima's *Attahiru* and *Ameh Oboni: The Great* as Paradigm................................. 73
    Olalekan Ishaq Balogun

Chapter Five:
　　Literature and History: Celebrating the
　　Heroism of Attahiru in Ahmed Yerima's
　　Attahiru.. 87
　　　Jeremiah Methuselah

Chapter Six:
　　Trans-Fictional Migration and Inter-Textual
　　Re-Interpretation: The Grimm Brothers'
　　Tales in Muslim Hausa Literature..................... 101
　　　Abdalla Uba Adamu

Chapter Seven:
　　The Influence of Arabic on Nigerian
　　Literature: A Study of Some Selected
　　Works of Abubakar Imam 129
　　　Jamiu Muhammad Yunusa

Chapter Eight:
　　Sa'adu Zungur: A Literary Historian's
　　Glimpse.. 141
　　　Ibrahim A.M. Malumfashi

Chapter Nine:
　　From the Written to the Oral: A Survey
　　of Hausa Prose Fiction on Radio...................... 159
　　　Sabiu Alhaji Garba

Chapter Ten:
　　A Historiographic Survey of Ilorin Music....... 175
　　　Femi Abiodun

PART THREE: LITERATURE AND IDENTITY

Chapter Eleven
　　Literature and Identity in Northern
　　Nigeria. 193
　　　Yakubu A. Nasidi

Chapter Twelve
Identifying a People Through Literature: A Study of the Literary Tradition in the Ilorin Emirate... 207
Hamzat I. AbdulRaheem

Chapter Thirteen
Self-Exploration and Split Identity in Northern Nigerian Novels: A Reading of Labo Yari's *Man of the Moment*............................ 223
Zainab Muhammad Kazaure

Chapter Fourteen
Vocality, Voicelessness and the Woman's Identity in Kanchana Ubgabe's *Soulmates*........ 237
Foluke Aliyu-Ibrahim

Chapter Fifteen
Changing Trends and Interface Between Oral Literary and Film Communication for Ethno-National Identity and Development: The Tiv Typology....................... 251
Godwin Aondofa Ikyer

Chapter Sixteen
Films and Matrimonial Harmony: An Assessment of the Impact of African Magic Movies on Audience from North-Central Nigeria... 265
Saudat Salah AbdulBaqi

Chapter Seventeen
Prose and Identity in Northern Nigeria: The Antecedents, Contexts and Implications for Literature in Northern Nigeria.................... 281
Suleiman A. Jaji

Chapter Eighteen
    The Use of Language in Two Kannywood
    Films.. 299
          Aliyu Isa Suleiman

Chapter Nineteen
    In Search of Identity: The Emerging Male
    and the Emergent Female in Zaynab
    Alkali's *The Initiates*.. 331
          Audee T. Giwa

Chapter Twenty
    Contemporary Northern Nigerian Female
    Writings and the Question of Blame:
    A Reading of Bilkisu Abubakar's Novels... 341
  Aisha Umar Mohammed and Abdullahi Muhammad

Chapter Twenty-One
    'Identity Crisis': The Dearth of Children's
    Literature in Northern Nigeria.................... 353
    **Aishat Ize Yusuf, Ruth Obaude Owenmeh and
        Vincent Uzoma P. Agulonye**

Foreword

Literature, History and Identity in Northern Nigeria is a unique collection of articles on literature in northern Nigeria. The articles have been carefully selected from the papers presented at the 7th Conference on literature in northern Nigeria at Bayero University, Kano, that was organised in collaboration with the Kwara State University, Malete, from 3rd – 6th December 2012. While the last book, a collection of essays on the 2011 conference, *Gender Politics: Women's Writings and Films in Northern Nigeria,* is gender specific, this collection is deliberately comprehensive and far ranging, with its bundle focus on literature, history and identity.

Within this discourse, the theme of identity invariably becomes not only the signified, but equally the signifier, especially in the cultural melting pot of northern Nigeria. Identity is a product of literature and history, but at the same time produces literature and history. This causal relationship makes the title of this collection of essays on literature in northern Nigeria contemporary and apt for our present challenges and prospect as a people. We are a product of our cultural practices, arts, aesthetics and history, as they all assist us, not only in negotiating existence and self-realisation, but in determining fundamentally what we are as a people in the greater scheme of being and knowing; what the philosophers of antiquity call 'ontology' and 'epistemology'.

Equally, the literature of northern Nigeria in its various forms, which this book represents, will continue to be relevant and necessary, specifically to the grand scale of Nigerian and world literature. Of course, literature will always be literature; but it will invariably continue to have historical and cultural resonance in spite of attempts by some to deny this tendency under the assault of colonialism, modernism and globalisation.

The conferences on literature in northern Nigeria are, therefore, predicated on the need to recognise, protect and celebrate the specificity of this brand of literature in relation to the global practice of arts and aesthetics; and as part of our shared common heritage of humanity in the 21st century.

This collection of essays, like those before it, on literature in northern Nigeria, is an affirmation of the continuing interests and relevance of the conference on literature in northern Nigeria. It is, therefore, my pleasure and honour to recommend this book to all scholars of literary studies and particularly to those with special interest in the northern Nigerian field of cultural practice.

This foreword will, however, be incomplete without recognising and commending the singular effort of Professor Shuaib Oba Abdulraheem in founding the Conference on Literature in Northern Nigeria in 1989 and continuously participating in the subsequent ones. I equally appreciate the collaborative initiatives of my fellow Vice Chancellor, Professor Abdul-Rasheed Na'Allah, the VC of KWASU, Malete, whose university now joins BUK in organising the conference on alternate years for scholarly harvest, such as this book.

Professor Abubakar A. Rasheed
Vice Chancellor
Bayero University, Kano
22nd April 2014.

Acknowledgements

Our gratitude goes to the Vice Chancellors of Bayero University, Kano, and the Kwara State University, Malete, Prof. Abubakar A. Rasheed and Prof. Abdul-Rasheed Na'Allah, respectively; for supporting the 'Literature in Northern Nigeria Conference' and sponsoring this publication.

We equally acknowledge the immense contributions of our colleagues on the Local Organising Committee for the conference: Prof. Sa'idu B. Ahmad, Prof. Zaynab Alkali, Prof. Attahiru Dawood, Prof. Isa Mukthar, Dr. Sadiya Sani Daura, Dr. Hamzat Abdulrahim and Dr. Femi Abiodun.

Similarly, we thank all the contributors, particularly the lead paper presenters, and the other numerous people who have given assistance in one way or another towards this publication. In particular, we wish to thank Prof. Yakubu Nasidi, who died suddenly a short time after the conference. His paper, which is included in this publication, was probably the last critical work he presented at a public forum. We pray for the repose of his soul, while expressing our heartfelt sympathy to his family for the loss.

Malama Ralia Maijama'a proofread the final manuscript of this book for which we are grateful.

We thank you all.

Professor Isma'ila A. Tsiga
Prof. M.O. Bhadmus
5th May 2014

About the Contributors

1. Professor Abdul-Rasheed Na'Allah is the Vice Chancellor, Kwara State University, Malete.
2. Professor Ismaila A. Tsiga teaches in the Department of English and Literary Studies, Bayero University, Kano.
3. Professor John Sani Illah teaches in the Department of Theatre and Film Arts, University of Jos.
4. Dr. Olalekan Ishaq Balogun teaches in the Department of Creative Arts, School of Postgraduate Studies, University of Lagos, Akoka.
5. Dr. Jeremiah Methuselah teaches in the Department of English and Drama, Kaduna State University, Kaduna.
6. Professor Abdalla Uba Adamu teaches in the Department of Mass Communication, Bayero University, Kano.
7. Dr. Jamiu Muhammad Yunusa teaches in the Department of Languages and Literary Studies, Kwara State University, Malete.
8. Professor Ibrahim A. M. Malumfashi teaches in the Department of Nigerian Languages and Linguistics, Kaduna State University, Kaduna.
9. Sabi'u Alhaji Garba teaches in the Department of Nigerian Languages, Usmanu Danfodiyo University, Sokoto.
10. Dr. Femi Abiodun teaches in the Visual and Performing Arts Department, Kwara State University, Malete.

11. Professor Yakubu A. Nasidi** teaches in the Department of English and Literary Studies, Ahmadu Bello University, Zaria.

12. Dr. Hamzat I. AbdulRaheem teaches in the Department of Languages and Literary Studies, Kwara State University, Malete.

13. Zainab Muhammad Kazaure teaches in the Department of English, Jigawa State College of Islamic and Legal Studies, Ringim.

14. Foluke R. Aliyu-Ibrahim teaches in the Department of English, Faculty of Arts, University of Ilorin, Ilorin.

15. Godwin Aondofa Ikyer teaches in the Department of English, Federal University, Dutsin-Ma, Katsina State.

16. Dr. Saudat Salah AbdulBaqi teaches in the Department of Mass Communications, University of Ilorin, Ilorin.

17. Dr. Suleiman A. Jaji teaches in the Department of English and Literary Studies, Ahmadu Bello University, Zaria.

18. Aliyu Isa Sulaiman teaches in the Department of Nigerian Languages and Linguistics, Kaduna State University, Kaduna.

19. Dr. Audee T. Giwa teaches in the Department of English and Drama, Kaduna State University, Kaduna.

20. Aisha Umar Mohammed and Abdullahi Muhammad teach in the Department of Modern European Languages and Linguistics, Usmanu Danfodiyo University, Sokoto.

21. Aishat Ize Yusuf, Ruth Obaude Owenmeh and Vincent Uzoma P. Agulonye are postgraduate students in the Department of English and Literary Studies, Bayero University, Kano.

* All titles and addresses refer to those given by the contributors in December 2012, when the papers were presented.

** Sadly, Prof. Nasidi suddenly passed away on Friday, 10th May 2013, at the mosque on the main campus of Ahmadu Bello University, in Samaru, Zaria, while he was saying his Jumu'ah prayers. May the Lord forgive his faults and bless his soul, amen.

Introduction

Literature's bosom friend is arguably history, with identity, probably, being one of their truest offspring. For instance, the might of Bayajidda is unmistakable in the narratology of legends on the origin of the Hausa states, even while the mythic content of the tale holds the historical seat of a people's roots and beginning. The classical works of philosopher-thinkers – such as Plato, Aristotle and Horace, equally attest to the brotherhood, even if some form of tension between literature and history sometimes exists, especially in the formation of character and identity. The articles in this collection, in one way or another, grapple with this ancient and at the same time contemporary concern, with regard to literature in northern Nigeria.

This book has three parts: Part one presents an overview of the running theme, in which Na'Allah explores the theoretical relationship between literature, history and identity in northern Nigeria, using the proverbial story of the blind man that holds a lamp while walking alone in the night. Similarly, Tsiga undertakes a stunning survey of the relationship between literature, history and identity in northern Nigeria, chronicling the development of life writing in the region dating back three hundred years, in a long bibliographical essay.

Part two focuses on the relationship between literature and history in northern Nigeria and begins with the article in which Illah investigates the theme. He uses the image of the bus to underscore the point he makes concerning the uniqueness of northern Nigerian literature, which continues its journey, even without a spare tyre. Equally in this part, Balogun discusses

Yerima's *Attahiru, Ameh Oboni: The Great* as theatres of colonial resistance; just as Methuselah also examines the heroism celebrated in Ahmed Yerima's *Attahiru*. Adamu revisits the trans-fictional use of the Grimm Brothers' tale in the early published Hausa written narratives, while Yunusa and Malumfashi examine similar historical concerns in Abubakar Imam and Sa'adu Zungur, respectively. This part concludes with Garba assessing the transformation of the written Hausa prose narratives into radio broadcasts; while Abiodun examines in a historiographic survey the various forms and composition of Ilorin music.

In what might have been the scholar's last conference article before his sudden death, Nasidi, in Part three, opens the debate on literature and identity in northern Nigeria, eloquently theorising on the relationship with Foucault, his favourite philosopher. AbdulRaheem illustrates how the literature of the people of Ilorin is their identity marker, while Kazaure investigates the split character in Labo Yari's *Man of the Moment*. Ibrahim explores identity in marriage between migrants and natives in Kanchana Ugbabe's *Soul Mates,* while Aondofa investigates globalisation and indigenous television. Using Tiv film typology, like Aondofa, Sulaiman examines the use of diction in characterisation in the film industry. The third of the contributors on the film industry, AbdulBaqi, uses films shown on DSTV's African Magic channels to investigate matrimonial harmony in North Central Nigeria. Jaji revisits the antecedents and prospects in the relationship between prose and identity in northern Nigeria. Giwa offers a detailed investigation of Zaynab Alkali's *The Initiates* on gender politics. Similarly, Muhammad and Muhammad are concerned with identity and the gender politics in Bilkisu Abubakar's *To Live Again* and The *Woman in Me*. The last article in the book, jointly written by Yusuf, Anwonmeh and Agulonye, offers the only viewpoint on children's literature in northern Nigeria.

Altogether, the articles in this book, thus, present fresh perspectives and advance novel arguments concerning the inseparable links, which, like in other parts of the world, bind literature, history and identity in northern Nigeria.

Ismaila A. Tsiga
Muhammed O. Bhadmus
November 15, 2014

PART ONE:
LITERATURE, HISTORY AND IDENTITY

Chapter One

Literature, History and Identity: Theories, Contents and Perspectives

Abdul-Rasheed Na'Allah

There was a Hausa language storybook, *Makaho Mai Fitila*, published in the *boko* script (as against the local *ajami* script), when I was a young elementary school pupil in Sakkwato. The story was about the blind man who carried a lamp whenever he walked on the streets in the night. One day a boy who came across him was stupefied; hence, he stopped him and asked why the blind man was carrying the lamp, since he could not see. The blind man replied that it was in order to ensure that people like the young man, who "truly had no eyes", did not bump into him *(Fitilan nan da na riqa, ba don kaina ba ne, domin irin ku ne, marasa hankali, da ba ku da ido, kada ku hau ni).*

It would appear that this simple story, even though written in the Roman script, had brought together the traditional African and, in particular, the Hausa cultural meaning of history and identity into literature. Reading the *Primary Reader* as a child, I learnt through this story of the encounter between the elderly man and the boy that the wisdom of the elders must merge with the zeal of the youths, in order to ensure the survival of the society. The story is like many other African folktales, in which the motives (motifs) give a strong didactic message for the sake of the society.

If history is defined as a 'story of humanity', of how individuals narrate their own stories (since it leaves everyone to tell what he or she chooses of the events of his or her life), it is, therefore, the people who decide what sort of energy to let into their collective record. The oral traditions of Africa are mainly of historical essence, from praise poetry to myths, epics and legends; and even including some proverbs. Identity through names and naming in Africa are rudiments of history and culture; and there seems to be no greater guide to literary resources than the traditional names of family, ethnicity and nation states. Indeed, these represent the truest compositions in literature, history and identity (Okpewho, 1979). For example, the Bayajida story in Hausa, although mythical, gives a historical essence to the origins of the Hausa people. Similarly, the story of Queen Amina of Zazzau, as a legend, has a major didactic effect; it would always connect a historical point and the people to certain places and issues.

Yet, to us in Africa, these are commonplace; history and historians are common people; the oral singers (*mawaqa or alulu gbomi eko*), whether in the King's palace or in the village square, are common people (Na'Allah, 2010). Surely, history and history performance, however enormous, seem to belong to the ordinary in Africa, but are equally available to the exploits of the rich and the royal. Of course, these materials are loved, respected and quite popular; yet, they are products of the commoner and the society treats them as such.

The epic poems of Homer (the Iliad and the Odyssey), without question, are presented as history with a very high literary quality and are given dignified status, just as we give our African myths (Isidore Okpewho; 1979; Thomas Hale, 1998). However, one could observe that many readers of Homer do not make much effort to distinguish between what is the truth and what is mythical in the poems. Indeed, most of the cultural references that have today become major pillars, supporting claims of the superiority of the European civilisation, derive from myths and legends. The European writers had so often presented them with audacity and allusion to the truth, thereby leading the rest of the world over time to not only 'capture' them, but also propagate them further.

The French School of Thought is about literature and its national and historical essence; and to date, most historical French thinkers have favoured the high historical point in their analytical dialectics. Even Foucault and Derrida, postmodernist thinkers linked to deconstructionism, have in their ways, showed that they consider history at a high point of relevance. Germany's Heidegger would not even treat any literary and theoretical composition devoid from history; indeed, he always prefers in DASAI a holistic approach. Among the celebrated magic of William Shakespeare is the historical nature of his drama; many historians still refer to him as a credible source when they adumbrate certain stories of the British royalty. In the same vein, Mao's Cultural Revolution in China had a major connection with history for its success, as writers of the era celebrated culture from its different historical points, not simply as an activity of momentary essence. Most writers of the Mao era combined literature and history, thereby making it a major characteristic of that era's literary expression.

Historical Fiction and Literary Fiction are, thus, some of the forms in which writers use history as a major platform for their creativity. To study a past event and use it as raw material for a fictional work, or render an experience with which the artist is familiar into a fictional account, have often shown remarkable success.

In almost all Nigerian communities, despite our rootedness in the oral tradition, writers have not always given history and literature a uniquely legendary status in our literary lives, like Homer, perhaps because we feel ashamed of our past. Are we suffering from colonial bondage and the mentality of the 'primitivist', as Cesaire calls it in *Discourse on Colonisation* (nd)? However, identity is the "sense of self", according to Anne Holden Ronning (2012), who also argues as follows:

> I would thus define cultural identity as the result of a process whereby individuals or groups evaluate consciously or subconsciously their own situation in society, and attempt to establish a sense of self-esteem and self-confidence,

which enables them to accept their own place in life and society. It involves an acceptance of our difference from others whilst forming a new belonging.

The key phrases, "sense of self-esteem," "self-confidence," "place in life and society", deserve special attention as they underline the essence of the arguments. Commenting on postcolonial literature of countries of Africa, South America and Asia, Ronning (2012) further offers the following insight:

> This literature, using language as the medium of expression, investigates the relation between histories as context for an understanding of identity. Theories of post-colonialism and multiculturalism provide us with tools for interpretation, also in a global context. The titles of some books and articles on postcolonial theory and literatures illustrate the line of thought which has become dominant, and which focuses on questions of identity: Brydon and Tiffin's *Decolonising Fictions* (1993); Linda Hutcheon's article "Circling the Downspout of Empire" in Adam and Tiffin's, *Past the Last Post: Theorizing Post-Colonialism and Post-Modernism* (1991); Tiffin and Lawson's *De- scribing Empire* (1994), and Salman Rushdie's *Imaginary Homelands* (1992).

Here is Ronning's (1997) specific example of how literature portrays identity:

> As such literature is, therefore, particularly well suited as a basis for the study of cultural identities. One text where this becomes obvious is Bbarati Mukherjee's Jasmine (1991). In this fictional autobiography, Mukherjee analyses the life of the protagonist, Jasmine, in India, where her marriage brings her into conflict with a rigid caste and gender discrimination system. After she emigrates to the US and remarries there, she finds that an equally problematic kind of racial discrimination not only becomes apparent, but also makes life in many ways equally difficult and complex for herself and her family. Finally, Jasmine comes to terms with the fact that she will always be different, and accepts that her independence as a woman is dependent on her

understanding and appreciating her own cultural identity. ("Literature as an Empowerment of Identity")

Literary theories or any theory at all, is about the cultural history and identity of a people. It is pertinent, therefore, that we discuss literature from northern Nigeria based on theories derived from local African traditions.

In particular, Hausa rhetorical and literary corpuses involve a process of cultural arrangement that makes every composer conscious of two important requirements: an affirmation of societal truth, even when vigorously re-examining it, and an avowal of the consequence of deviance from it. Although the poetics is a community-wide cultural perspective, every composer, critic and the consumer of art often consciously engage these binary yardsticks to ensure that the society continues to project acceptable ethics, truth and other forms of community morality. In other words, literature is a platform for creative talent, community survival and cultural strength.

Obviously, postmodern literary ideologues with their pessimistic societal values, which often reject any idea of an affirmed truth, would have a problem understanding the Hausa composer's eagerness to satisfy his community's poetics. For instance, this is how the Hausa state an important oral theory:

> *Wanda bai ji bari ba,*
> *Ya ji hoho.*
>
> Whoever would not listen to, "Stop it",
> Would listen to, "Serves you right"!

There are, obviously, some problems in rendering the Hausa cultural theory into English. "Stop it", and "serves you right" do not fully translate into "bari" and "hoho", respectively. The two words are like cause and effect in Hausa rhetorical expressions. Critics of any literature reflecting the Hausa and most northern Nigerian communities, thus, must understand this dual framework in order to be able to interpret the literary compositions appropriately.

In this regard, furthermore, to explain what Hausa poetics is not, perhaps we should remember the structuralist and post-structuralist Derrida. While interpreting and criticising a text, he often adopts a strategy of a "double mode of reading", in which he shows a lack of synthesis between a text and the philosophy it claims to represent. Jonathan Culler puts this better, when he says about Derrida:

> Attentive to the ways in which texts implicitly criticise and undermine the philosophies in which they are implicated, he carries on a double mode of reading, showing the text to be woven from different strands, which can never result in a synthesis but continually displace one another. (Structuralism and Since, 1955)

While analysing the language and structure of a text, Derrida often concentrates strongly on the text's internal effect. As he discusses Edmund Husserl's views about the origin of geometry in his *L'Origine de la Gãometrie* (1962), for example, Derrida says that language and writing, which Husserl claims will make geometry an ideal subject, contain within them problems they should solve (157). Furthermore, in *Of Grammatology,* Derrida further says that speech also possesses the characteristics of writing, and he discusses the possibility of "inverting the hierarchy" and "orienting a theory of language not on speech but on a generalised writing" (158).

Derrida's constant effort at deconstructing the text would not play well in the Hausa "bari" and "hoho" traditions. This is not because there may be no paradox or contradictions inherent in the life of a composer or even in his or her text, but because the exercise of 'deconstruction' must not be seen as jeopardising community ethics, its layers of truth, its aspirations and other cultural orientations. There are challenges all the time to community values and sometimes composers cast paradigms and recast them to accommodate new views or developments. However, a 'good literature' is that which creates a good person and enhances a useful community. It is not necessarily a literature that shifts the community or its people from the base of its values of goodness and cultural harmony.

Perhaps, Jaigbade Alao captures this view better in an Ilorin oral song:

> Awi talaiwi won ni ile aye nyi
> Ile aye o yi sibikankan
> Ibi ojo n yo ni tin yo
> Ibi orun ti n wo ni tin wo
> Ile aye o yi sibi kankan
> Awon enia inure ninpawada!
>
> We had only spoken a little when they interrupted saying that the world was changing
> The world isn't changing to anywhere/anything
> The day rises where it rises
> The sun sets where it sets
> The world isn't changing to anywhere/anything.
> Only the people [its occupants] are changing their behaviours!

Among other things, Alao insists that 'good' and 'bad' have recognisable yardsticks, and no one needs another person to remind him or her in which of the two categories his or her actions belong. The song also reinforces the society's belief that truth is constant and that, whereas human beings continue to change to satisfy their selfish interests, nothing would change about what is humane or charitable, and what constitute inhumane or uncharitable behaviours.

The poetics of 'bari' and 'hoho', while not asking for Derrida's 'double mode of reading', allows both the poet and his/her critics to protect the society from 'uncultural' and 'unethical' behaviours. The writer in Hausa is, like the oral performer, a custodian of humane cultural behaviour, who constantly defines the society from the rhetoric of inclusion and wisdom of community and individual responsibility. *Mr. Spider* in the oral fable did not farm, but stole from other people's farms, hence, he was condemned to remain naked forever. However, in instances where *Mr. Spider* escapes punishment during variations in performances, the oral singer or writer must search the cultural upheavals and locate the failure from the context of the societal reality.

The philosophy embedded in 'bari' includes the affirmation of value preoccupations of the society and its cultural norms, and challenges any abuses, miscalculations, or mismanagement as they may occur. Thus, the phrase, "*Wanda bai ji bari ba*", also includes those who the blind man in the *Makaho Mai Fitila* story claims have no eyes. The eyes are not just for seeing the paths to walk on, but for seeing what is beautiful and what is ugly, the *mai kyau* and *mara kyau* of life. Indeed, it is a constant refrain of the poetics of "the society must survive" and that of "the society is a platform for growth."

To identify with the 'bari' and 'hoho' of the society is to defend the society's laws, protect its sanity and uphold its pride. With the arrival of every new concept, theory or life, the challenge is to probe it and grade it according to the society's need for growth, peace and survival. This agrees with the critical theory, which provides that literary dialectics, abstract or concrete, must meet the test of the ever-important society. The 'bari' concept also implies that the writer or artist has a responsibility to warn the society against destructive tendencies, relieve people of their fears, educate them, entertain them and engage them in the fruitful process of the society's regeneration and rebirth. *Bari* and *hoho* go together: the writer's work constantly shows the repercussion of abandoning the path of good, the ways of the society's socio-cultural growth.

Thus, one discovers that the story in the book of *Makaho Mai Fitila* (The Blind Man with a Lamp), which was narrated at the beginning of this paper, will find clearer understanding, even in the strangest part of the world, if put under the surgical knives of 'bari' and 'hoho.' The same should be true of written works, such as Ibrahim Tahir's *The Last Imam,* Zaynab Alkali's

The Stillborn, or the poems in *Wakokin Hikima,* by the group of poets from Kano.

It is on this note also that one should hand over the surgical knife to the critics of African literature and pray for them to be able do their job well.

REFERENCES

- Anne Holden Ronning (2012), "Literature as an Empowerment of Identity", http://www.ifuw.org/seminars/1998/Literature.pdf (accessed 2/12/12).
- Ashcroft. Bill et.al. (1989), *The Empire Writes Back,* London: Routledge.
- Brydon, Diana (2000), *Postcolonial Critical Concepts in Literary and Cultural Studies.* New York: Routeledge.
- Cesaire, Aime, Discourse on Colonisation, n.d.
- Culler,
- Derrida,
- During, Simon (1990), "What Was the West?: Some Relations Between Modernity, Colonisation and Writing", Sport 4.
- Grinker, Richard, et al. (eds.) (2010), *Perspectives on Africa: a Reader in Culture, History and Representation.* Malden, MA: Wiley-Blackwell.
- Hale, Thomas (1998), *Griots and Griottes: Masters of Words and Music,* Bloomington: Indiana University Press.
- Hutcheon, Linda. (1991), "Circling the Downspout of Empire: Post-colonialism and Postmodernism."
- Muecke, Stephen. (1992) *Textual Spaces. Aboriginiality and Cultural Studies,* Kensington: University of NSW Press.
- Na'Allah, Abdul-Rasheed (2010), *African Discourse in Islam, Oral Traditions and Performance,* London and New York: Routledge.

References

- Okpewho, Isidore (1979), *The Epic in Africa: Towards a Poetics of Oral Performance.* New York: Columbia University Press.
- Ronning, Anne Holden. (1997) "A Question of Empowerment: the Black African Woman's Answer." Proceedings from the Sixth Nordic Conference for English Studies.
- Ronning, Anne Holden. (2012) "What is the Connection Between Literature and History?" http://www.wisegeek.com/what-is-the-connection-between-literature-and-history.htm (accessed 2/12/2012)

Chapter Two

Traversing the Worlds of Literature, History and Identity: Life Writing in Northern Nigeria

Ismaila A. Tsiga

When life writers write to chronicle an event, to explore a certain time period, or to enshrine a community, they are making 'history' in a sense. But they are also performing several rhetorical acts: justifying their own perceptions, upholding their reputations, disputing the accounts of others, settling scores, conveying cultural information, and inventing desirable futures, among others. (Smith and Watson, 2010:13)

History describes what people do... while biography reveals who they are. (Parke, 2002:6)

In introducing the major concerns of this chapter – and, by extension, this book - the above quotations, also, summarise the central arguments that underscore the validity of literature in upholding the history and identity of its society of origin. More significantly, the quotations project life writing as a unique literary artefact, which invokes history, in a manner normally unavailable to other genres in literature, for the construction of individual and collective identity: social, ideological and regional.

In Africa in general, history has always been an issue in modern literary discourse, largely because of its inseparable relationship with the forces that fashioned the continent's present economic and societal circumstances. The past, whether as a focal theme or background influence, has frequently determined the course of contemporary African imaginative writing, always throwing irresistible challenges and offering new prospects. Life narratives in particular are unique cultural mutations that expound their society's clustered subjectivity, even while they project it further, and their overall effect is vital in constructing group touch and solidarity, like the feelings of 'northern-ness' among the northern Nigerians.

In exploring these assertions, this chapter chronicles the development of life writing in northern Nigeria from available sources in the seventeenth century to the contemporary period, with particular emphasis on the collective import of the individual texts in constructing the region's history and identity. "It might be said," Sacks (1987:110) has argued a long time ago, "that each of us constructs and lives a 'narrative', and that this narrative is us, our identities."

Nation-ness and Identity

Northern Nigeria has often inspired a particular consciousness among its people, largely owing to the region's ancient history and transcending social values, in contemporary times. Much of this consciousness is transmitted through established social institutions and norms, including written expressions in different disciplines, which invoke notable historical landmarks and cultural tropes to create the concept of the 'Northern subjective'. After all, at the collective level, 'nationality', 'nation-ness' and 'nationalism' are, actually, "cultural artefacts of a particular kind" (Benedict 2006:4), whose roots lie deep within the psychology of 'cultural imaginings'. They are identity feelings nurtured on sentiments of particular group values and the illusion of a shared ethos, revealing, in the words of Seton-Watson (1977:5), that a significant number of people in the community, have now come to "consider themselves to form a nation, or behave as if they formed one." Such 'nations', as scholars also point out, are normally distinguished not by their measure of authenticity, but as much by their finite boundaries, which define the in-group from outsiders, as "by the style they are imagined" in the minds of the members of the group (Benedict, 2006:6).

In other words, individual members of any national or sub-national group, like that of the northern Nigerians, perceive their membership within the prism of certain shared values, as well as through the silent affirmation of such perception in their thoughts and regular interactions. The nation, as such, is always a 'large-scale solidarity', a social construct, wrought out of the collective faith and emotions of its constituent groups and sustained by its ideals of a collective destiny. It is the overt articulation of the aggregate consciousness and beliefs of the constituent elements, bound together by webs of its fraternity. That appeared to have been the crux of the speech delivered by the Premier, Sir Ahmadu Bello, on attainment of self-government by the Northern Region in March 1959, just preparatory to national independence in 1960:

> The Northern Region, as it is today, is the product of three main factors: Geography, History and Character of the people. I need not expand on this, but I must emphasise that these three factors have produced a real feeling of unity amongst the people who inhabit our Region. We have divergences in custom, religion and language. But we have emerged and progressed out of the stage in the life of a People where such differences constitute a barrier to unity. We have sought for unity, not uniformity. (Abdulkadir, 2004:3)

Herein lies the foundations of what Kwanashie (2002 : vi) calls 'the One-North phenomenon', that "idea of the unity and distinctiveness of the North within Nigeria." Indeed, as Bhabha (1990:19) concludes, a nation is but a soul, "a spiritual principle [defined by] *the possession in common of a rich legacy of memories* [and a] *present-day consent, the desire to live together,* the will to perpetuate the value of the heritage that one has received in an undivided form (emphasis added).

In this process, no cultural tool whets the abounding fraternity in the minds of the individual members more sharply than literature, with its array of creative gears and social tropes, which can always be called upon to construct a structured past, model the present and collective dreams into the indeterminate future. There is always a strong correlation between the stories a community tells and its sense of itself, for it is the stories that describe its environment, explain its social relations and define its position within the world. Thus, Eakin (2008:2) notes that, "When it comes to our identities, narrative is not merely *about* the self, but is rather in some profound way a constituent of part of self" (original emphasis).

Stories are strong cultural monuments that preserve the society's past and offer a glimpse of the meaning of its everyday life; they are a systematic interpretation of its communal thought, representing its rightful aspirations, identity, fears and values. This seems to inform Brennan's (1990:47) assertions that every study of nationalism is also a '*cultural* study' (original emphasis), "and specifically the study of imaginative literature is in many ways a profitable one for understanding the nation-centredness of the post-colonial world." For, as he concludes,

> "Nations…are imaginary constructs that depend for their existence on an apparatus of cultural fictions in which imaginative literature plays a decisive role (Brennan, 1990:49)."

Life-Writing in Northern Nigeria

More pointedly, this explains the distinctive role of life writing in northern Nigeria as a living witness and special discourse in the construction of the literature, history and identity of the people of the region. In consonance with the rest of the world, the "autobiographical genre of literary writing", Adegoju (2012:128) notes in a recent report, "has been widely acclaimed to be a site for identity construction and a form of cultural expression in Africa."

In critical treatises, scholars now loosely employ 'life writing' as an omnibus terminology to cover all forms of expressions of subjectivity concerning individuals. They range from the traditional life narratives of autobiography, biography, diary, letters, memoir and travel stories to the most recent forms of life presentation made possible by developments in modern information and communication technology, like autobiography, digital life story and ecobiography.

In fact, in their recent study, Smith and Watson (2010:253-86) have offered a glossary of sixty genres of life writing, which centre on documenting the historical and cultural evolution of the subject and his relational surrounds, especially his close associates and the dominant issues of their time. Considered in any of its myriad forms, life writing, thus, mirrors the society's values in a unique fashion, through locating its individual subject firmly within specific coordinates of time and a particular geographical space, while preserving the macro scene for the indefinite future. What's more, the creative (fictive) elements are ordinarily ignored by the reading audience, thereby conferring special truth value on the entire narrative, no matter how embellished it may appear in relation to the historical situation it reconstructs.

These issues seem to have inspired Usman's (2013:213) plea directed at the northern Nigerian establishment elders in particular:

> "One should emphasize here the need for elders, especially public figures, in all works of life, to strive to put together their thoughts on paper for the benefit of future generations."

He had voiced the appeal while speaking at the public presentation of a book on the life of one of the most respected ministers of the old regional government of northern Nigeria, *Humility and Service: The Life of Alhaji Ibrahim Biu* (Yerima, 2004). Usman, who was to give validity to his own call by acting fittingly, published his autobiography, *Hatching Hopes* (2004), later that year and, subsequently, a memoir about his writing career, *My Literary Journey* (2013). At the public presentation of the autobiography, Alkali (2013:171-2) was to echo the author's earlier plea more elaborately:

Let us sit down and commit into writing our biographies and autobiographies so that others will learn from the experience of those who have good and decent stories to tell. And we have many untold stories of many great men and women, both living and dead... (Emphasis added).

In fact, a few years before then, Kurfi (2004:xi) had advanced similar arguments to justify writing his own autobiography, which he said he had written, among other reasons, in order "to fill the gap which dearth of recording by northern leaders has created, of the commendable roles they played in making Nigeria what it is today – in economics, politics, military, civil and security services – unlike their counterparts in the South who have written copiously about their exploits." Through writing the autobiography, the personal story of the writer, thus, transforms into that of the whole society with which everyone can identify, thereby further reinforcing group solidarity and upholding the sense of a collective past and tenets. "A contemporary phenomenon has emerged in autobiographical writing", Adegoju (2012:128) quotes Howard (2006:8) to have observed.

"Elements of one's self-identity have been projected on to the many, with which others can identify; a transfer has taken place from [the] personal to [the] universal."

This situates the advice by another prominent national elder, Alhaji Adamu Chiroma, well in context, when he implores the senior citizens to write and document the past for posterity. In the preface to the autobiography of yet another quintessential northern elder, *Pull of Fate: The Autobiography of Magaji Dambatta* (2010), Chiroma beseeches the old people for more written life stories, while admonishing that, "those who miss reading them cannot have a full history of the past" (vii).

However, far from being a recent phenomenon, evidence suggests that the act of writing lives through formal inscription of subjectivity in northern Nigeria goes back more than three hundred years, making it one of the oldest forms of literary expression available from the region. In effect, life writing accounts in the areas that constitute contemporary northern Nigeria closely mirror the evolution of the territory's written history, beginning from its contact with Islam through the ancient caravan routes of the Kanem Borno Empire in the Seventh Century, to British colonial conquest and the subsequent developments that followed since independence in 1960. Altogether, five periods could be discerned in the evolution of life writing in northern Nigeria:

i. precolonial;
ii. colonial;
iii. independence;
iv. civil war; and
v. the contemporary.

Life-Writing in Precolonial Northern Nigeria

Life-writing scholarship does not usually devote much attention to precolonial Africa, largely because the old societies in the continent were assumed to have been non-literate; hence, could not have produced serious inscribed literature, especially in the sub-discourses that constitute life-writing. However, in the case of northern Nigeria, as in many areas of North and Sudanic Africa, recent research has indicated that this is not quite correct. On the contrary, although the precolonial period recorded low life-writing activity in these regions, documents now emerging firmly confirm that there were a few significant attempts at subjectivity expression. That such expressions were not many was chiefly due to the availability of only scanty records pertaining to the time and the modes of literary expression prevalent among the small circle of the *literati*.

In fact, in the specific instance of northern Nigeria, it used to be thought that there were no serious life-writing activities preceding the Sokoto Caliphate scholars, until Bobboyi and Hunwick (1989) reproduced an old copy of the definitive Arabic poem, "*Qasidah Kha'iyyah*" in *Sudanic Africa,* written by the famous Katsina scholar, Sheikh Muhammad Al-Sabbagh Al-Kashinawi (b. 1585AD), popularly known as Dan Marina. The researchers were to follow up on the article with a more detailed presentation during an international seminar on Islam and the history of learning in Katsina (Tsiga 1997), elaborating fully about how they found a copy of the poem in the private collection acquired from the family of the late Kano Islamic scholar, Malam Umar Falke (d.1962), for the library of the Northwestern University, Evanston, Illinois, USA. The poem, which was composed on 24th Safar 1070 AH (10th November 1659 AD), as dated by the poet himself in the last stanza, chronicles an incident involving a man within the area of Katsina, but its main thrust is the person of the 17th Century Emir of Katsina, Muhammadu Uban Yari, popularly known as "Karyagiwa" (*'karya-giwa'* in Hausa language literally meaning 'breaker/strangler of the elephant'), the title first adopted by Emir of Katsina, Aliyu in 1419AD (Yari, 2007:xi).

Bobboyi and Hunwick (1997:123) have offered further explanations concerning the man, Magani, whose act of apostasy provoked the incident the poem relates; he was also nicknamed "'Mai-Amfanin-Baki' – 'the one possessed of a useful mouth (or speech)' and by extension 'the honey-tongued' or 'the slick talker'." Apparently, Magani had succeeded in attracting a small group of followers when he made the false assertion that he was a prophet, before his activities were reported to the emir. Such a claim would normally be considered a very serious breach of the faith in Islam, although it had been made by a few other individuals well before then, beginning quite early in the history of the religion. Once Emir Karyagiwa received formal complaints against Magani, however, he asked for the man and his followers to be summoned; they were later tried before him by the group of scholars and jurists learned in Islamic Law. Sheikh Dan Marina, who was among the scholars who witnessed the trial (and, probably, helped with evidence from the holy books) now thought the event worth documenting, casting the emir as a hero of justice and Islamic leadership to be celebrated. Presented here are the opening stanzas that relate the events as they occurred:

1. Inform on my authority at the Shaykhs in Islam what occurred in an age of youth (?).
2. A trustworthy Imam, Karyagiwa, our wellbeloved, a helper of Islam, standing tall for the religion.
3. Gave victory to Islam, the religion of Muhammad, and strengthened it, putting an end to the claim of one puffed up with pride.
4. The pig of filth arose claiming the prophethood of the messengers of God among the abatikh.
5. The Amir-al-Mumin, the father of guidance, imposed on him the fixed penalty of the Sharia among those subdued by the sword (al-barayikh).
6. He hastened to listen to the complaints of him who raised them, receiving them from Ibn Yusuf who was shouting (?).
7. He called all the Muslims to his palace and brought them together, both young and old.
8. He consulted them as to what should be done in the matter of the accursed one. Death, they said with one accord (?).
9. They slaughtered them in front of him, through the grace of the Messenger of God, pride of the matatikh.
10. We were greatly pleased at that. No happiness is there like it, except in the abode of eternity on the day of taking the yawabikh.
11. After this, there remained no claimant to prophecy in our land for fear of the sword's exemplary punishment (Bobboyi and Hunwick, 1997:127).

The poem then goes on to explain the person of Amir Karyagiwa, praise him and pray to God for his safe guidance.

Scholars point at this particular poem as a rich source of information concerning the person of Karyagiwa, who is the subject, his style of governance and the society's state of affairs, including its social organisation and advancement in scholarship. In the latter regard, Kani (1997:29) identifies Sheikh Dan Marina specifically as "one of the celebrated scholars in Hausaland" to gain prominence during the period. Far more significant for this context, is the information Kani drops in his further comments that Dan Marina is credited with the writing of many scholarly works, including *"A biographical work on the history of the Ulama of Yorubaland.* [Unfortunately,] the non-availability of such an important work had prevented the students of history from reconstructing the history of Yorubaland in the seventeenth century" (emphasis added). The present context does not allow for more detailed investigations, but the information that Sheikh Dan Marina had actually recognised the need for writing the biographical account of the Yoruba *Ulama'* (and even undertaken the project) confirms the linkages among the intellectuals in the Islamic societies at the time and the level of awareness for life writing among the seventeenth century scholars.

Thus, it would not be a surprise to cite another example of a later precolonial life writer, Nana Asma'u Usman Danfodiyo (1793 – 1865), the famous scholar of the Sokoto caliphate and one of the female intellectual giants of Africa in the nineteenth century. Nana Asma'u, as she was fondly known, was the daughter of Usman Danfodiyo, the celebrated leader of the caliphate. Having literally grown up with learning, she had studied under great scholars, as attested to by the academic depth and variety of her writings. Mika'ilu (1999:x) reports that so far about ninety of her published works have been discovered by researchers in Arabic, Fulfulde, Hausa and Tomashek, the languages spoken by the prominent scholars within her locality in her time. Sixty-two of these works are featured in a special book of *The Collected Works of Nana Asma'u* (Mark and Boyd, 1999). The most remarkable issue in this instance is that thirty-one of the sixty-two works in the collection are personal writings of good literary quality, comprising eight panegyric odes about Muhammad (SAW), the Prophet of Islam, and twenty-three elegies, dedicated to preserving the memory and exploits of different individuals, with whom she interacted.

Odes dedicated to outstanding figures in the Islamic religion had been an old phenomenon in Hausa land so much that by the thirteenth century *Madhu* poetry, as it was more popularly identified, had become an established medium for literary and religious campaigns. It was used principally to explain certain matters in rhythmic form and celebrate some outstanding personalities and their various roles in history, while holding them up as notable examples to the present followers. Hiskett (1975:43) also considers the *Madhu* poems important in Muslim Hausa social life because they provide emotional satisfaction in worship and "relief from the dry rituals of orthodoxy."

Thus, Nana Asma'u's "Yearning for the Prophet," for instance, runs into three hundred and sixteen stanzas, out of which ninety-nine are devoted to the prophet's person, his birth in the city of Makkah, childhood, maturity, early prophethood and migration to Medina. The aim of the poem, as well as that of the seven other panegyric odes she wrote about him, was to explain his message and at the same time document his life within the Islamic perspectives. It should be noted that one of her older teachers, Muhammad Tukur, had in 1789 published, among others, a book of similar *Madhu* in Arabic, *Bushara,* which comprised one poem of 1200 stanzas (Tsiga, 2011:84). Nana Asma'u was to write another seventy-stanza ode in similar fashion in Hausa language to document the life of her own "father, his companions, siblings, children, servants, judges, scholars around him and the Muezzins that called prayers at his mosque" (Tsiga, 2011:85). Sixteen other poems record the personal history of members of her family who got deceased during her lifetime, including the one she composed in memory of her late husband, "Elegy for Gidado." The oldest of the elegies is the "Elegy for Abd Allah", which was written to commemorate the life of her father's brother, the 'Tall Arabist', as he was nicknamed on account because of his physical height and scholarship. Abdullahi Danfodiyo was reported to have read 20,300 works in his life (Augi 1993:54) and written countless works, including the full-scale compendium on governance, *Diya'a al-Hukkam*, which he dedicated to the Emir of Kano during his sojourn to the city in 1807.

Another set of two poems, "Elegy for Bello" (composed in two versions in Arabic and Fulfulde) and "Bello's Character," celebrate Nana's own elder brother who died in 1837, Muhammad Bello, with whom she was exceptionally close. Bello was the pillar of her life, having taught her many books directly and served as her mentor, companion and confidant while they were together; but it was his person that the two poems now depict. Certainly, they make much value in mapping Bello's "learning, un-worldliness, level-headedness, uprightness, preparedness, intelligence and resourcefulness," while omitting to mention his noble birth, personal prestige or high social standing as the Caliph that succeeded Sheikh Usman Danfodiyo. This appears to be a deliberate oversight, which leads Mark and Boyd (1999:53) to conclude that, "from Asma'u's omissions we learn much about her perceptions and values."

Viewed from another perspective, the poems, thus, offer a deep commentary on the ideals and principles of life in the society that shaped her vision. So far no particular life writers among the precolonial scholars in Hausa land have been discovered to have focussed attention on their own individual lives or made narrative capital out of their private exploits, although Umar and Hunwick (1997) have written about the Arabic memoir that recorded the British conquest of Kano, as witnessed by a North African youth who settled in the city in 1902. On the contrary, the old scholars had always narrated the personal stories of others who did well in the community, extolling their virtues and upholding their achievements. One can only read their own identity and character in-between the lines in the narrations, as it were, as they applaud the admirable qualities of the subjects upon whom they report. Miller (1997:10) describes this as a special technique in which "writing about others and otherness becomes a kind of self-writing, as the narrator examines similarities, differences, connections and gaps, and situates herself in relationship to them."

The precolonial writers had adopted this style consciously in conformity with their societal ethics, which "considered literary writing a moral and intellectual duty to the community, but not an opportunity for personal glorification" (Tsiga, 2011:78). In fact, they would have been embarrassed by the principal aims of writing modern self narratives: recounting about the self, describing personal achievements, defending one's position in life or somehow glorifying oneself into history. "What right has a human being to boast?", Sheikh Danfodiyo (1978:22) admonishes in one of his popular intellectual works written in 1806, *Bayan Wujub Al-Hijra 'Ala 'L-'Ibad*. "His beginning is sperm and his end is corpse. He cannot sustain himself nor ward off his own death."

This explains why the northern Nigerian precolonial scholars did not care to write any notable self narratives; no doubt, the ethics of their society would have shunned such accounts for being unscholarly and unabashed self celebration. Even serious narratives devoted to telling the life of others were uncommon; the only full length work from the period to come to light so far is "*Tarikh Mustafa Al-Torodi*", which sketches the life of one of the great intellectuals at the old Jami'ah (University) at Salame, to the northeast of Sokoto. Al-Torodi, a one-time scribe to Sheikh Usman Danfodiyo (Bello, 1994:2), had been among the *Ulama'* who were sent out to teach in the local communities for the intellectual advancement of the people soon after the coming into being of the Sokoto caliphate in 1804, in realisation of Caliph Muhammad Bello's assertion that, "everything has a support and foundation, and the support for [Islam] is knowledge" (Al-Hajj, 1994:2). Once the decision was taken to establish a university, therefore, Sheikh Al-Torodi was posted there to take charge, as captured in the biography written by one of his former students, Abdallah Al-Qadi Al-Hajj. Bello (1994), who discovered a copy of the original Arabic work in Sokoto, translated it into English, edited and published it as *Islamic Education in 18th Century Nigeria: Tarikh Mustafa Al-Torodi*.

Unfortunately, "in the course of the struggle between the French and the British imperial forces over who should get the larger territory in the caliphate, the French invaded Salame, burned a certain portion of the town and took away with them valuable books" (Bello, 1994:4). It is a great act of history that Al-Hajj's book survives to provide the most detailed profile available yet on the person of one of the archetypal teachers of the caliphate, explaining in the process the qualities that attracted the student to undertake the writing of the biography of his teacher with such passion and sense of duty:

> *He had a patience and gentleness which other scholars among those that I met did not have. I attached myself to him for over twenty years and never saw him scowling at any of his students, companions and relations; nor meeting anybody, free or slave, with bad language or action. He tolerated the folly and antipathy of ignorant and obstinate persons and returned only good to them. This is what I and others who associated with him know of his qualities.* (Bello, 1994:24)

Northern Life-Writing in the Colonial Period

It was left to the second phase in the history of life-writing in northern Nigeria to herald the really personal narrative, following the British conquest and the imposition of colonial rule on the vast territories, which were, subsequently, put together to form the region. Colonialism and the developments in technology had introduced new economic systems and with them a corresponding pattern of social relations that undermined the identity of the people, through the institutionalisation of new thoughts and values. The old cultures were undergoing tremendous change and a new social order was fast emerging, whose spread was being championed by the new administrative institutions being established throughout the region and the English-medium schools, which were socialising the youths into a totally different way of life.

Two groups of self-narratives appeared to have resulted from this consciousness, with the first comprising subjects concerned with the early period of the colonial contact and the second those whose life was more involved with the late years of the colonial government. Within the first group are also two types of narratives: (i) those concerned with the rapidly changing social and cultural landscape and its overall consequence on the people's disappearing past; and (ii) similar works written by more educated subjects, who had greater awareness of the social effects of colonialism, a few of them even having visited Europe or America. The writers in the first subgroup had watched their 'good old world' disappearing quickly, to be replaced by another totally different one, which was now evolving through contact with the colonial masters and global developments in science and technology. Sometimes prompted by white anthropologists and cultural researchers from Europe and America, some of them wanted to capture the passing world for the future generations before it completely disappeared. The result was the production of life-narratives with a heavy amount of anthropological details that cast the individual autobiographer less as an individual than a representative of the old society.

Such works, which Olney (1973:34) refers to as "anthropological autobiography", include *Baba of Karo: A Woman of the Muslim Hausa* (1955), a narrative account dictated by the subject to the American scholar, Mary F. Smith, during her research visit to Kano. Another example is the narrative of Alhaji Mahmudu Koki, a former Arabic teacher, Alkali and chief assistant to Dr. Bargery when the latter compiled the first Hausa dictionary. The old man, like Baba above, had also dictated his book in Hausa to Neil Skinner, who translated and edited it for publication. In the end, *Alhaji Mahmudu Koki: Kano Malam* details the life of a man who saw it all, as it were, having been "born into the civil war of Aliyu and Tukur...saw the coming of the British; knew Waziri Gidado and Resident Temple; lived to see the end of British rule and the Nigerian Civil War and, above all, had close contact with rulers and innovators, both Nigerian and British" (Skinner, 1977:1). No doubt, the narrative is a compendium on nearly a century of the tumultous years of northern Nigeria's history, as witnessed directly by the narrator himself. It is, in particular, an invaluable literature on the region's socio-economic history and a unique resource for all investigations relating to the recent forces that shaped the region's present identity.

The second subgroup concerned with the disappearing past consists of works in which the life-narrative is a means to achieving many aims, among which were to preserve their cultural past, cry out over their position as colonials and decry the new direction the nation was taking. For example, Benjamin Akiga (1965:2) in *Akiga's Story: The Tiv Tribe as Seen by One of Its Members*, admits to writing his book in order to record the passing social structure of his Tiv society, because "it is not every elder who is well versed in Tiv lore." There is, therefore, the fear that the elders will disappear, "and the knowledge they possess... is in danger of being totally lost because of the tremendous social changes currently in Africa" (Olney, 1973:34). In this regard, by way of yet another example, Malam Hassan and Malam Shuaibu shed all pretence of habouring personal motives in writing their recollections that constitute the *Chronicle of Abuja* (1952), whose publication they admit is aimed primarily at capturing the dying social history of their beloved old city and preserving the way of life of its people.

Alidou (2004:337), writing in respect of Hausaland, considers these writings as a form of 'resistance literature', the second force against the British invasion that threatened to erase the people's history from collective memory and triggered the desire of the *literati* to produce historical texts and chronicles in order to document the reign of renowned emirs, important historical events that marked their reigns and also life [in the precolonial] era... the Chronicle of Kano...for example, covers the history of the town of Kano from the period of its legendary leader Bagauda to the reign of the Emir Muhammadu Bello. Other chronicles include the Chronicle of Sokoto, completed in the 1920s and authored by Abubakar Dan Atiku, the Chronicle of Zaria, which provides an historical account of Zazzau, and the Chronicle of Katsina, which offers a list of the rulers of the town up to 1807. The same period also produced...historiographics of other towns and important historical events that affected non-Hausa kingdoms as shown in the work of Hausa malams from the area.

This appears to be pronounced even more extensively with the biographies documenting the lives of some of the old traditional rulers who held office during the colonial period, like Usman Dalhatu's *Malam Ja'afaru Dan Isyaku: The Great Emir of Zazzau* (2002). In particular, Labo Yari's 351-page biography, *Muhamman Dikko, Emir of Katsina and His Times, 1865 – 1944*, explains in detail the impact of the new ways on the northern societies and traditional leadership institutions. As Kurfi (Yari, 2007:xi) notes in the foreword to the book, Alhaji Muhammadu Dikko was "one of the greatest, indeed an icon, of the late 19th and first half of the 20th century." His story says much about the history and identity of the northern Nigerians during the colonial times: "Dikko scored 'First' amongst Emirs of northern Nigeria in several fields...the first to visit England, perform Hajj, ride on a car, fly in an aeroplane and open a school for girls...establish native treasury...departments of education, medical, agriculture, veterinary and works in the native administration."

He was to be succeeded by his son, Sir Usman Nagogo, whose reign was to bring events to the end of the colonial period, as narrated in his life story, *Usman Nagogo: Biography of the Emir of Katsina Sir Usman Nagogo*, written by Imam and Coomassie (1995). Thus, in preserving examples of the northern traditional leadership, these biographies offer a deeper insight into the evolution of the contemporary northern Nigerian society, especially since it came under British colonial control. Furniss (1995:iv), a professor in the University of London and renowned scholar on northern Nigeria who wrotes the foreword for the book, recalls that in Nagogo in particular, "there emerges a picture of the ideal perception of an aristocratic leader in northern society and…the style of the northern Nigerian aristocracy during the first half of this century and the British colonial culture of administrators with whom they worked."

Indeed, the credit for much of this success actually goes to the early crop of northern bureaucrats, who put their knowledge of the society to good use in guiding the policies of the British administrators, while upholding the traditional values of the society in their official duties. The lives of some of these dedicated officers who began their career under the colonial government have now been captured in biography books, which present moving narratives about their pioneer efforts and portray other dimensions in the history and identity of the Northern Region. Among such biographies is *Integrity and Service: The Life and Times of Ahmadu Coomassie*, which tells the story of "the first northerner to become a senior civil servant, and as the Permanent Secretary, Ministry of Education of Northern Nigeria…was one of the principal actors in the establishment of Ahmadu Bello University" (Coomassie and Sani, 2008:ix). Another example is *Mukhtar's Musa Daggash: The Story of a Shuwa Arab Boy*, which tells the personal history of the former Federal Permanent Secretary who was "imbued with an admirable spirit of selfless and dedicated service to God and to… country" (Mukhtar, 2002:vii). General Yakubu Gowon, who wrote the foreword to the two biographies, as the former Head of State who knew both civil servants well and even worked with them briefly before their exit from service in the mid sixties, reflects about their generation:

> Historians, political scientists and other scholars would argue endlessly as to the reasons behind such dedication. Was it their training in the colonial tradition; was it the nationalist fervour that pervaded the years leading up to independence; or was it the inherent qualities of the

African imbued with religious fervour, which produced such examplary characters? Whatever the answer might be, Nigeria produced a crop of civil servants whose record has never been equalled yet (Mukhtar, 2002:vii).

No doubt, as Parke (2002:2) observes, "The primary urges to celebrate, commemorate and immortalise the impulse of life against death have continued to be among the chief motives for writing lives."

Independence Life-Writing in Northern Nigeria

In this chronological study, the richest harvest yet of life-writing from northern Nigeria was to be in respect of the independence politicians and bureaucrats, some of whom still feature as subjects in recent publications. It is now [2012] fifty years since Sir Ahmadu Bello, the Sardauna of Sokoto and legendary Premier of Northern Region, published his landmark autobiography, *My Life* (1962), in which he documents not only his own life, but also that of his beloved region, its people, operations and political philosophy. "I have not written this book through any wish to obtain further publicity, or because I like writing about myself", the Sardauna is quick to point out in the preface, "but because I have been persuaded to write the story of my life as it may throw some light on the development of my country during a time of change and progress in Nigeria and Africa as a whole." After all, he affirms, "I have lived through practically the whole period of the British Colonial occupation of northern Nigeria and the final achievement of self-government and independence."

Certainly, *My Life* chronicles an exceptional life, which is viewed firmly within the author's regional perspectives of northern Nigeria, as summarised below:

> He addresses fifteen policy issues, including "our attitude to Federation" (p.228), "future of Emirs" (p.229), "principles of democracy in this Region" (p.230), "the 'political' parties" (p.231), "the Oppositions in the Regions" (231), "votes for women" (p.232), "Republic being formed in Nigeria"

(p.233), "African Unity" (p.234), "the armed forces" (p.235), "need for many years to come of skilled technical help" (p.236), "capitalism", "Communism" (p.236), and how "we are determined to manufacture as much as we can in this country from our own primary products" (p.237). In short, "I have taken you through my life, from the little waterside village of Rabah to the office of Premier of Northern Region." he concludes (Tsiga, 2012:59).

"Whether one regards Ahmadu Bello as a sub-nationalist, a nationalist, or a trans-nationalist is less important than the fact that he is crucial to an understanding of Nigerian political history", Paden (1986:6) asserts while introducing his monumental biography, *Ahmadu Bello, Sardauna of Sokoto: Values and Leadership in Nigeria,* which analyses the Sardauna within the context of northern regional values, against Nigerian and world politics. "Not to understand Ahmadu Bello is not to understand Nigeria, whether one agrees with him or not." Paden justifies this opinion in his 800-page study, which strongly substantiates the views advanced by the Sardauna earlier in *My Life*, thereby further unfolding the history, values and identity of the Northern Region more effectively, even as he discusses his principal subject. Similarly, his overall assessment of the northern political theatre is that "apart from the Sardauna, the two major 'establishment' figures are Abubakar [Tafawa] Balewa and Kashim Ibrahim" and the "three opposition leaders…Aminu Kano, Ibrahim Imam and J. S. Tarka" (Paden, 1986:361-2).

It is instructive that Balewa is also the subject of an 888-page biography, *A Right Honourable Gentle Man: The Life and Times of Sir Abubakar Tafawa Balewa* (1991), written by Trevor Clark, who knew him quite well. A veteran who joined HM British Colonial Administrative Service in Nigeria in 1948, Clark had worked in different capacities, including holding the office of Deputy Secretary to the Executive Council in the governor's office in the Northern Region at Kaduna. Explaining his motivation to document the history of Balewa, the man, his region and values in the book's introduction, Clark (1991:xi) remembers him as "one of the great men from Africa and better men of our century"; "someone uniquely honest in public life and politics. His murder in 1966, perpetrated in the arrogance of ignorant brutishness, appalled and affronted me, as it did countless others." No wonder Clark considers the biography as "Historical revision... being corrected", concluding strongly thus:

> The younger generation, which has often had the benefit of being educated or giving public service in states far from their places of birth, has now come to recognise that their fathers' story before independence was not as shameful as the early revisionists asserted; they too admit that Abubakar truthfully was one of their country's greatest sons, and one of their nation's few genuine founders ... In the customary Hausa words, sadly commemorating those departed in true faith and fear, Allah Ya ji kansa, amin (p.818).

The latter tribute at once attracts attention to the quality of the contribution the 'opposition leaders' also gave in shaping the region's history and identity in the early years of independence. Thus, Feinstein (1987:365) calls Malam Aminu Kano the 'Conscience of the Nation' whose great achievement, which he shared with many world revolutionaries in history, like Ghandi, Tolstoy and Ruskin, was "to convince those they touched to find a synthesis between humankind's goals and the actions and attitudes needed to achieve them." Feinstein's biography of the leader of the northern opposition chronicles how he was able to do just that, making him unique in the nation's politics and in the struggle for the uplift of the common people. In presenting *African Revolutionary: The Life and Times of Nigeria's Aminu Kano*, Feinstein (1987:xiii) further recognises how the written story, as the printed word, can "serve as bond between his ante-mortem work and its post-mortem significance." In fact, "Serendipitous, it might also contribute in some degree to the overall durability of his influence." Other related examples of such narratives of some of the significant opposition figures who worked with Aminu Kano are Tanko Yakasai's autobiography, *Tanko Yakasai, The Story of a Humble Life: An Autobiography* (2004) and that of Magaji Dambatta, *Pull of Fate: The Autobiography of Magaji Dambatta* (2010). Dambatta was the last surviving member to tell his own story among the founding fathers of the Northern Elements Progressive Union (NEPU), the revolutionary platform that brought Malam Aminu Kano to fame.

In similar vein, Tersoo Mnenga captures the life of another opposition figure and father of Tiv independence politics, in his biography, *J.S. Tarka: The Life of a Charismatic Leader* (2009), which builds on Hembe's insightful analysis published earlier, *J. S. Tarka: The Dilemma of Ethnic Minority Politics in Nigeria* (2005). "We have seen from the Tarka-Tiv case that the 'ideology of tribalism' is an efficient tool for producing 'tribal' or local level political leadership in Nigeria", Hembe (2005:437) concludes in upholding the quality of Tarka's contribution to Tiv, regional and national politics, "but that it works against the emergence of [a] strong national leadership at the federal level"; a situation which is always "wrongly used by the ruling elites to entrench themselves in power."

The Civil War and Northern Nigerian Life-Narratives

Surely, the 'ideology of tribalism' was behind the January 1966 military coup led by officers from the Igbo ethnic group that ended the life of the Prime Minister, Sir Abubakar Tafawa Balewa, the Premier of northern Nigeria, Sir Ahmadu Bello, and most of the senior military officers from the north, including Colonels Maimalari, Largema, Kur Muhammed and Pam, and Lt. Col. Unegbe, who were all shot in cold blood, together with many other political and military officers from other regions considered to be their allies or friends. The 'ideology of tribalism' was to reach its peak with Ojukwu's secession bid and declaration of the Republic of Biafra, a situation that plunged the country into a bloody civil war until 1970.

Much has been written about the war, but the most lasting literature, and by far the greatest, is the collection of published life-narratives in which the soldiers recall their personal experiences about the politics of the period and the battle front, or feature as subjects in accounts published by academics, historians or journalists. Mainasara (1982) was the first among the northerners to write about the coup, in response to the published accounts of the 1966 coup plotters and the subsequent developments that led to the civil war, in his *The Five Majors: Why They Struck*. Within the same year, Garba (1982) was to publish his *Nigerian Revolution: Another View*. Others followed, subsequently, including Oluleye (1985), *Military Leadership in Nigeria;* Elaigwu (1986), *Gowon: The Biography of Soldier-Statesman;* Yar'adua (1991), *Jungle Expert (the biography of Col. John Yahaya Madaki);* Ogundipe, (2001), *The Hurricane: General Murtala Mohammed;* Farris, & Bomoi, (eds) (2004), *Shehu Musa Yar'adua: A Life of Service;* Kuju (2006), *Dan Suleiman: Pilot of Justice;* Tarfa (2007), *Profile in Courage*; and Ladi Adamu's researched tribute to her late father who achieved fame at the civil war battlefront, *Adamu Pankshin: A Soldier's Soldier (2007)*. Other related accounts include Opadokun's work, which details the life of the nation's topmost investigative officer at the time and former Inspector General of Police, *Aristocratic Rebel: The Biography of M. D. Yusufu* (2006); and Commissioner of Police Usman Faruk's autobiography, *From Farm House to Government House: The Path of Destiny* (2006).

By far the most valuable publication in this regard is the official book of the Nigerian military on the war, *The Nigerian Civil War 1967 – 1970: History and Reminiscences* (Momoh, 2000), which includes 700 pages of short memoirs by more than fifty senior officers who participated in the war and a detailed analysis of their personal perception of the circumstances. In particular, the narratives of the northern officers captured in the collection provide, yet, the most detailed sketch of the northern history and identity as a major ideological influence on their participation in the war, like in this reflection by Col. M. Abdu:

> I was opportuned to be in Kaduna when the crisis started in 1966...But all that we noticed later [was that] there were elements of fear instilled in our people here in the north when an aircraft came in the night dropping some bombs. We got so frightened and we thought that, whether we liked it or not, it was high time for us to stand up and protect our country. There was an advertisement in the newspaper requesting for those who wanted to join the army quickly and participate in blocking the rebels from crossing into northern Nigeria. This was what gave birth to my joining the army in 1967. (Momoh, 2000:201)

On the whole, it should be pointed out here that the civil war was a watershed in the country's history in many ways and the collection of narratives relating to the lives of the various personalities from northern Nigeria who came to prominence during the period offers a significant contribution in documenting the history and identity of the region.

Contemporary Life-Writing in Northern Nigeria

Contemporary life-narratives in northern Nigeria constitute the greatest treasure trough, in terms of their quantity, variety and value, in documenting the individual and collective history and doctrine of the northern societies. In telling their individual stories, they offer a direct commentary on the people's intellectual growth and their changing pattern of individual awareness and self-conception. Six broad subgroups can be identified within this category, beginning with narratives about (i) the lives of politicians; (ii) public officers (including bureaucrats) (iii) artists and literary writers; (iv) traditional rulers; (v) professionals (journalists, medical doctors, lawyers and judges, academics, religious leaders, businessmen); and (vi) private citizens in their personal attempts to document certain lives. A few examples are highlighted below:

(i) Narratives of Politicians

In 1978, nearly a decade after the civil war, in which the government announced that there was 'neither victor nor vanquished', the military stepped down and handed over power to the civilians to begin the Second Republic. President Shehu Shagari, a quiet public officer who immediately took office, was until then, in the words of his biographer, David Williams (1982: xiii), "Perhaps the least well known...of any statesman of his rank." This prompted the writing of the biography, *President and Power in Nigeria: The Life of Shehu Shagari,* which the author said was "an attempt to present Nigeria's President as an individual who has had a long and varied public career; not as a representative of a party, of a class, or of an ethnic group." However, the notable differences between the politicians that had previously crippled the nation's politics soon came to the fore again with a few more complications, which, ultimately, led to the overthrow of the government by the military at the end of 1983. Many life-narratives have been written to document these crises, including such odd events as the tragic ideological conflict, which resulted into the murder of the Political Adviser to the Kano State Governor under the platform of the revolutionary People's Redemption Party, as recorded in the collection of biographical assays, *The Example of Bala Mohammed: His Life, Commitment and Assassination* (Ibrahim, 1981). On the other hand, President Shagari's long detention by the military and subsequent release without trial, made him feel obliged to write his own personal story, *Beckoned to Serve* (2001), in which he reviews his life all over again, carefully explaining his own viewpoint on every matter the military had accused him of earlier. Equally revealing is *The Life and Politics of Solomon Lar* (Magnate, 2003), which chronicles the personal history of one of the famous opposition figures during Shagari's presidency. Today there are many of such narratives about the contemporary politicians, including those who came into the limelight in recent years, like Michael Obi's *Ibrahim Mantu: Lesson in Tolerance* (2004), the biography of the former Deputy Senate President.

(ii) Narratives of Public Officers

Much is revealed about the evolution of the Nigerian public service and its contemporary operations in the narratives of its retired officers, such as Ahmadu Kurfi's *My Life and Times: An Autobiography* (2004), which gives an insider account of a career civil servant with a special consciousness for the contribution of the northern Nigerians to the development of the country under the colonial government, during the First Republic and in the subsequent years. In seeking "to record for posterity...crucial events in Nigeria of which I was an eye witness", among the four principal reasons for writing the autobiography, Kurfi also hopes "to fill a gap which dearth of recording by northern leaders has created, of the commendable roles they played in making Nigeria what it is today" (p. xi). The biography of the late Makaman Nupe, *Breaking the Myth: Shehu Musa and the 1991 Census* (Yahaya and Dan-Ali, 1997) offers another such testimony. At the other end of the spectrum is the account by one of the most recent civil servants to leave office, Usman's *Hatching Hopes* (2006), which chronicles the experiences of the retired Federal Permanent Secretary and reviews the state of the national civil service as it crosses over into the twenty-first century.

(iii) Self-Narratives of Artists and Literary Writers

As argued at the beginning of this presentation, artists and literary writers provide a unique insight into the realities of their society and epoch through their writings, a fact that is further demonstrated by the tone and direction of their life narratives. In this regard, the most outstanding example that readily comes to mind is *The Abubakar Imam Memoirs* edited by Abdurrahman Mora (1989), which describes first-hand the efforts of the literary icon, who started his career as a teacher, wrote many Hausa story books and became the first editor of the Hausa newspaper, *Gaskiya Ta Fi Kwabo* in 1938. Imam's literary prowess in Hausa was legendary, and, although he died in 1981, until now his publications command the highest respect among Hausa readers. The memoirs reflect the author's personal dedication, the difficulties of the literary terrain when he started writing and, above all, the social realities and direction of public thought at the time.

(iv) Life-Narratives of Traditional Rulers

For a variety of reasons – cultural, historical, political and religious – traditional rulers continue to be a force to reckon with in Nigerian social life in contemporary history, although lacking in constitutional support. In northern Nigeria in particular, the people revere their chiefs and emirs at all levels as symbols of their culture and history, which is why life writing featuring the rulers is invaluable in giving in-depth knowledge about relations within the individual societies and the collective functions of the traditional institutions. For example, much is revealed about the changing policies of successive governments – colonial, independent, civilian and military - concerning the traditional institution and its ability to adapt to the successive political and social changes that took place in the country over the years through the biographies of two of the longest-serving and most respected emirs in northern Nigeria, Sultan Abubakar III and Ado Bayero, the Emir of Kano. Shehu Malami's *Sir Siddiq Abubakar III: 17th Sultan of Sokoto* (1989) and Omar Farouk Ibrahim's *Prince of the Times: Ado Bayero And The Transformation of Emiral Authority in Kano* (2001), explain how the traditional authorities had frequently been caught up in the cross currents of the country's changing socio-political situations and their special effort to mediate between the labyrinths of demands by the layers of governments above them, while struggling to keep the respect of their people through quality leadership. This is further upheld by Hamidu Alkali in his well-researched biography of Alhaji Junaidu, the famous Waziri of Sokoto, *The Chirf Arbiter: Waziri Junaidu and His Intellectual Contribution* (2002).

(v) Life-Narratives of Professionals

Undoubtedly, the largest treasure of life-narratives that reflects the evolution of northern Nigeria's history and identity in contemporary times is that written by the region's different professionals. This has been occasioned, among other factors, by the explosion in education since independence, dramatic changes in the economy and the awareness to use commemorative writings for ideological reasons in order to, among other reasons, "entirely circumvent the finitude of human life", as Parke (2002:1) describes it. So much has been published in this regard that the narratives now cover practically every field of endeavour, making them an invaluable resource, as suggested by the cursory examples drawn below:

(a) *Journalists:* Among the self-narratives of the journalists that reflect particular periods in the country's history is Eugenia Abu's collection of essays, *In The Blink of An Eye* (2007). Initially written over many years of her career, the essays now collectively provide an interesting insight into the journalism profession in Nigeria in general, with particular reference to television and the female perspectives. Similarly, Muhammad Sanusi Umar's recent biography, *Halilu Ahmed Getso: The Radio Talk* (2012), offers interesting perspectives on the development of the radio broadcast industry, especially in northern Nigeria. Hausa radio journalism in particular dates back to the Second World War and today, one hundred local stations and at least fifteen international radio houses employ it in regular broadcasts, with the BBC Trust rating its Hausa Service to reach an estimated 23.5 million adult listeners every week. (Garba, 2011:7).

(b) *Medical Doctors:* Many self-narratives have been published regarding the medical profession in Nigeria that at the same time reflect the milestones achieved in medical and social history in northern Nigeria. Among the latest is that of the Ahmadu Bello University's renowned professor of medicine, Idris Mohammed, whose lament against the "slow-down, stasis and eventual decline in the quality of medical education and health care" in Nigeria prompted him to look back at "an eventful career" of thirty-five years in his book, *Academics, Epidemics and Politics* (2008). Although he takes pain in the preface to emphasise that "This is not an autobiography", the first chapter is, significantly, titled "The Early Years", with the story beginning, "I was born in Gombe Town in 1942..."!

(c) *Lawyers and Judges:* Far more than the medical doctors, lawyers and judges have been more forthcoming with their life-narratives, either writing themselves or allowing others to write about them. Like in other professional areas, while telling their interesting life-stories, these narratives constitute a long report on the history and practice of law in Nigeria in general and northern Nigeria in particular, considering the calibre of cases handled by the different subjects. For example, Hauwa Imam's *A Judicial Path: Biography of Honourable Justice SMA Belgore* (2009), records an exceptional life that underscores the unity-in-diversity of the peoples of the North. Justice Belgore, an Ilorin indigene whose roots lie deep in Kebbi, had a tenure during which some of the most remarkable developments in the Nigerian judiciary took place. The book gives valuable insight into the country's judiciary, especially in relating the segment of the subject's career when he served as the Chief Justice of Nigeria, giving much insight into the changing patterns of the judicial landscape in the country. Among the most recent publications is Justice Usman Mohammed's remarkable memoir, published only this year [2012], appropriately titled, *My Passion for Justice,* in which he looks back upon his long years of service in the judiciary and its overall impact on his way of life.

(d) *Academics and Educationists:* The increasing number of narratives by or about academics, teachers and other educationists from northern Nigeria in recent years offers an interesting reflection on the growth of the education sector in the region, where the first full-fledged secondary school did not open until 1922 and there was no university until four years after independence. The few seed institutions have, of course, since multiplied into many more others, which today boast of an enrolment figure running into several millions across the education levels. For instance, Ali's book on the life of Professor Jibril Aminu, *Enduring Footprints* (1994), records the subject's historic struggles as an educational administrator, first in the university and later in the Federal Ministry of Education; and his outstanding achievements, like pioneering the education of the nomads. The biographical collection, *Beyond Fairy Tales: Selected Writings of Dr. Yusufu Bala Usman,* offers a moving tribute by former colleagues at the Abdullahi Smith Research Centre to the erudite Ahmadu Bello University scholar whose contribution to learning in northern Nigeria was legendary. Among the most recent in this regard is Professor Adamu Baikie's colossal book, *Against All Odds: An Autobiography* (2011), which chronicles his humble beginning in Kano to vast experiences in the seat of the Vice Chancellor in three universities in Nigeria and South Africa, among many other successes.

(e) *Religious Leaders:* One of the most remarkable examples of narratives concerning the life of religious leaders in contemporary Northern Nigeria is Sheikh Abubakar Mahmoud Gumi's popular autobiography, *Where I Stand,* which was in press when he passed away and was released posthumously two months afterwards. Sheikh Gumi was easily the most outstanding Islamic scholar in the region and the country as a whole, from independence until his death in September 1992. The autobiography traces his life history, from childhood lessons, on the Qur'an, along with other pupils in his father's school at home, to more formal studies in Sokoto, Kano and the Sudan, as well as his final career as the Grand Khadi of northern Nigeria. In paraphrasing Paden's comments cited above concerning the late Sir Ahmadu Bello, one could similarly say that, regardless of whether one agrees with him or not, understanding Sheikh Gumi is crucial to interpreting the forces that shape the practice of Islam in contemporary Nigeria, especially northern Nigeria.

(f) *Private Sector:* The emerging narratives involving personalities in the private sector, especially the finance industry, are both an indication of the division's growth in recent years and the availability of good resource on its contributions towards national development. One of the best examples in this regard is Hauwa Imam's biography of Alhaji Mohammed Bulama, a former Managing Director of the historic Bank of the North, *The Banking Guru* (2003). As its name suggests, the Northern Region Government had established the Bank of The North soon after independence, in order to boost private sector activities and the overall economic development of the region.

Conclusion

One could go on to list many more areas of activity in northern Nigerian life-narratives, but for the restrictions imposed by the present context. What is quite apparent is that, for obvious reasons, the past shall, for a long time to come, continue to fascinate the northern Nigerians, largely because of its significance in constituting their current history and identity. It would ordinarily appear surprising, for instance, that northern Nigerians would still celebrate with such passion the role played by the founding founders, especially those who served during the strategic period from the mid-forties to the 1966 coup, when a number of them were assassinated. A good example is that only recently, Abdulkadir (2004) published a colourful 'who is who' of these founding fathers, compiled into a single volume, *Work and Worship: Makers of Northern Nigeria*. The book contains biographical entries on 260 prominent northern elders, complete with their pictures and a brief on the offices they individually held.

However, as noted elsewhere (Tsiga, 2011), one cannot help but notice the almost total absence of the women in northern Nigerian life writing. Indeed, apart from Eugenia Abu's collection cited in (v) (c) above, the only full scale work so far available is Ladi Adamu's moving biography, *Hajiya Hafsatu: The Unsung Heroine* (2005), which was written in tribute to the subject's gallantry. It would be recalled that Hajiya Hafsatu, the wife of the northern Nigerian Premier, Sir Ahmadu Bello, was shot dead when she spread herself to protect her husband as the soldiers invaded their home on the night of the 1966 coup. Nonetheless, the recent effort by Hajara H. Kabir (2010), *Northern Women Development: A Focus on Women in Northern Nigeria,* reflects the new consciousness for documenting the lives and endeavours of the women, even though the heavy emphasis of the book on women in government and the wives of political office holders leaves out a lot on the 'real' story of women in northern Nigeria.

On the whole, the above examples uphold the validity of the claims made at the opening of the chapter that, in preserving and projecting the northern Nigerian history and identity into the indefinite future, no cultural discourse tells a more faithful and lasting story than literature, as demonstrated with specific reference to life-writing.

Bibliography

- Abu, Eugenia (2007), *In the Blink of an Eye*, Ibadan: Spectrum Books.
- Abdulkadir, A.T. (2004), *Work and Worship: Makers of Northern Nigeria*, Kaduna: De Imam Ventures.
- Adamu, Ladi S. (2007), *Adamu Pankshin: A Soldier's Soldier*, Kaduna: Adams Books.
- Adamu, Ladi S. (2005), *Hajiya Hafsatu: The Unsung Heroine*, Kaduna: Adams Books.
- Adegoju, Adeyemi (2012), "Autobiographical Memory and Identity Construction in Tayo Olafioye's *Grandma's Sun*", in Makokha, J. K. S. et al (eds.), *Style in African Literature: Essays on Literary Stylistics and Narrative Styles*, New York: Radopi.
- Akiga, Benjamin (1965), *Akiga's Story: The Tiv Tribe as Seen By One of Its Own Members*, transl. Rupert East, London: Oxford University Press.
- Ali, Sidi H. (1994), *Jibril Aminu: Enduring Footprints*, Lagos: Triumph Graphic Printers.
- Alidou, Ousseina (2004), "The Emergence of Hausa Literature", in Irele, F. Abiola and Simon Gikandi (eds.), *The Cambridge History of African and Caribbean Literature*, Cambridge: Cambridge University Press, Vol. I, pp. 329 – 356.
- Alkali, Hamidu, *The Chief Arbiter: Wazir Junaidu and His Intellectual Contribution*, Sokoto: Centre for Islamic Studies, Usmanu Danfodiyo University
- Alkali, Muhammad Nur (2013), in Bukar Usman, *My Literary Journey*, Abuja: Klamidas.

- Baikie, Adamu (2011), *Against All Odds: An Autobiography*, Zaria: Tamaza Publishing.
- Bello, Ahmadu (1962), *My Life*, Cambridge: Cambridge University Press.
- Berger, Roger A. (2010), "Decolonizing Autobiography", *Research in African Literatures*, Vol 41, No. 2, pp. 32 – 54.
- Bobboyi, Hamidu and John Hunwick, "Falkeina I: A Poem by Ibn Al-Sabbagh (Dan Marina in Praise of the Amir-al-Mumin Karyagiwa", *Sudanic Africa: A Journal of Historical Sources*, Vol. 2, pp.133-4. See also Tsiga (1997), pp.121-132.
- Boyd, Jean (1987), *The Caliph's Sister: Nana Asma'u, 1793-1865, Teacher, Poet and Islamic Leader*, London: Frank Cass.
- Boyd, Jean and Mack, Beverly (1999), *The Collected Works of Nana Asma'u, Daughter of Usman dan Fodiyo (1793 – 1864)*, Ibadan: Sam Bookman.
- Brennan, Timothy (1990), "The National Longing for Form", Bhabha, Homi K. (ed), *Nation and Narration*, Abingdon, Oxon: Routledge.
- Clark, Trevor (1991), *A Right Honourable Gentle Man: The Life and Times of Sir Abubakar Tafawa Balewa*, Zaria: Hudahuda.
- Dalhatu, Usman (2002), *Malam Ja'afaru Dan Isyaku: The Great Emir of Zazzau*, Zaria: Woodpecker Communications.
- Dambatta, Magaji (2010), *Pull of Fate: The Autobiography of Magaji Dambatta*, Zaria: Ahmadu Bello University Press.
- Elaigwu, J. I. (1986), *Gowon: The Biography of Soldier-Statesman*, Lagos: West African Publishers.
- Farris, J. W. & Bomoi, M. (eds.) (2004), *Shehu Musa Yar'adua: A Life of Service*, Abuja: Shehu Musa Yar'adua Foundation.
- Faruk, Usman (2006), *From Farm House To Government House: The Path of Destiny*, Zaria: Amana Publishers.

- Feinstein, Ian ([1973] 1987), *African Revolutionary: The Life and Times of Nigeria's Aminu Kano*, Enugu; Fourth Dimension Publishers.

- Foduye, Uthman Ibn [1806] (1978), *Bayan Wujub Al-Hijra 'Ala 'L-'Ibad*, edited and translated by F. H. El-Misri, Khartoum: Khartoum University Press.

- Garba, Sabi'u A. (2011), "Hausa in the Media", paper presented at the 24th Annual Conference of the Linguistic Studies Association of Nigeria, Bayero University, Kano.

- Gerard, Albert (1981), "1500 Years of Creative Writing in Black Africa", *Research in African Literatures*, Vol. 12, No.2, pp.147 -161.

- Graf, William D. (1984), "Nigerian Political Biographies", *Canadian Journal of African Studies/Revue Canadienne des Études Africaines*, Vol.18, No. 1, pp. 235-238.

- Gumi, Sheikh Abubakar Mahmoud, with I. A Tsiga (1992), *Where I Stand*, Ibadan: Spectrum Books.

- Hembe, Godwin Nyor (2005), J S Tarka: *The Dilemma of Ethnic Minority Politics in Nigeria*, Makurdi: Aboki Publishers.

- Ibrahim, Omar Farouk (2001), *Prince of the Times: Ado Bayero and the Transformation of Emiral Authority in Kano*, Trenton, New Jersey: Africa World Press.

- Ibrahim, Rufai (ed.) (1981), *The Example of Bala Mohammed: His Life, Commitment and Assassination*, Zaria: Gaskiya Corporation.

- Imam, Hauwa (2009), *A Judicial Path: Biography of Honourable Justice SMA Belgore* (2009), Ibadan: Safari Books.

- Imam, Hauwa (2003), *The Banking Guru, Ibadan:* Spectrum Books.

- Kabir, Hajara M. (2010), *Northern Women Development: A Focus on Women in Northern Nigeria,* Lagos: Print Serve.
- Kani, Ahmed M. (1997), "The Place of Katsina in the Intellectual History of Bilad al-Sudan up to 1800", Tsiga, I. and Abdallah, U. A. (eds.), *Islam and the History of Learning in Katsina,* Ibadan, Spectrum Books.
- Karo, Baba (1955), *Baba of Karo,* New York: Philosophical Library.
- Kuju, Matthews (2006), *Dan Suleiman: Pilot of Justice,* Lafia: Eggonnews.
- Kwanashie, G.M., (2002), *The Making of the North in Nigeria, 1900 – 1965,* Zaria: Ahmadu Bello University Press.
- Magnate, Josef (2003), *The Life and Politics of Solomon Lar,* Washington, D.C.: American Literary Publishers, Inc.
- Malami, Shehu (1989), *Sir Siddiq Abubakar III: 17th Sultan of Sokoto,* Ibadan: Evans.
- Miller, Mary-Kay F. (1997), "My Mothers/My Selves: (Re) Reading a Tradition of West African Women's Autobiography", *Research in African Literatures,* Vol. 28 No. 2, pp. 5-15.
- Mnenga, Tersoo (2009), *J.S. Tarka: The Life of a Charismatic Leader,* Abuja: Bakin Nigeria Publishing.
- Mohammed, Idris (2008), *Academics, Epidemics and Politics,* Ibadan: Bookkraft.
- Mohammed, Usman (2012), *My Passion for Justice,* Abuja: Capital Publishers.
- Momoh, H. B. et al. (eds.) (2000), *The Nigerian Civil War 1967 – 70: History and Reminiscences,* Ibadan: Sam Bookman Publishers.
- Mora, Abdurrahman, (ed.) (1989), *The Abubakar Imam Memoirs,* Zaria: Northern Nigerian Publishing Company.

- Mora, Muhammed Inuwa (ed.) (1996), *New Foundation: Preparing the Future Leaders*, Zaria: Northern Nigerian Publishing Company.
- Mukhtar, Yakubu (2002), *Musa Daggash: The Story of a Shuwa Arab Boy*, Ibadan: Heinemann.
- Ogundipe, Taiwo (2001), *The Hurricane: General Murtala Mohammed*, NPP: Topseal Communications.
- Opadokun, Ayo (2006), *Aristocratic Rebel: The Biography of M. D. Yusufu*, Lagos: Bonafidea.
- Paden, John (1986), *Ahmadu Bello, Sardauna of Sokoto: Values and Leadership in Nigeria*, London: Hodder and Stoughton.
- Parke, Catherine (2002), *Biography: Writing Lives*, New York Routledge.
- Renan, Ernest (1990) "What is a Nation?", in Bhabha, Homi K. *(ed.), Nation and Narration*, Abingdon, Oxon: Routledge, pp.8 – 22.
- Umar, Muhammad Sani, *Halilu Ahmed Getso: The Radio Talk*, Zaria: Ahmadu Bello University Press.
- Umar, M. S. and J.O. Hunwick (1997), "Your Humble Servant: The Memoirs of Abd Allah Al-Ghadamisi of Kano, 1903-1908, Part I: The British Conquest of Kano", *Sudanic Africa: A Journal of Historical Sources*, Vol. 7, pp. 60-96.
- Seton-Watson, Hugh (1977), *Nations and States: An Enquiry Into The Origins of Nations and Nationalism*, Boulder, Colorado: Westview Press.
- Shagari, Shehu (2001), *Beckoned to Serve*, Ibadan: Heinemann.
- Smith, Mary F. (1955), *Baba of Karo: A Woman of the Muslim Hausa*, New York: Philosophical Library.

- Smith, S. and Watson, J. (2010), *Reading Autobiography: A Guide to Interpreting Lives,* Minneapolis: University of Minnesota Press.

- Tarfa, Paul C. (2007), *Profile in Courage,* Ibadan: Spectrum Books.

- Tsiga, Ismail A. (2010), *Autobiography as Social History: Apartheid and the Rise of the Black Autobiography Tradition in South Africa,* Ibadan: Spectrum Books.

- Tsiga, Ismail A. (2011), "Ethics and Literary Tradition in Sokoto Caliphate: Elegiac Portraiture as Biography in the Poetry of Nana Asma'u Usman dan Fodiyo", *FAIS Journal of the Humanities,* Bayero University, Kano, Vol. 5 No. 2.

- Tsiga, Ismail A. (2008), "The Civil War and Autobiography in Nigeria: A Prolegomenon on the Emergence of a Sub-Genre", *Kakaki,* Vol. 8, pp. 59 – 82.

- Tsiga, "Another Intellectual History: Life Narratives and the Foundations of the Nigerian State", in Ahmad, S.B. and Abdussalam, I.K. (eds.) (2011), *Resurgent Nigeria: Issues in Nigerian Intellectual History,* Ibadan: University Press.

- Umar, Muhammad Sanusi, *Halilu Ahmed Getso: The Radio Talk,* Zaria: Ahmadu Bello University Press.

- Usman, Bukar (2006), *Hatching Hopes,* Abuja: Klamidas.

- Usman, Bukar (2013), *My Literary Journey,* Abuja: Klamidas.

- Usman, Yusufu Bala (2006), *Beyond Fairy Tales: Selected Writings of Dr. Yusufu Bala Usman,* Zaria: Abdullahi Smith Centre for Historical Research.

- Usman, Y.B. & Kwanashie, G.A. (eds.) (1995), *Inside Nigerian History 1950 -1970: Events, Issues and Sources,* Zaria: Ahmadu Bello University Press.

- Williams, David (1982), *President and Power in Nigeria: The Life of Shehu Shagari,* London: Frank Cass and Company.

- Yahaya, Isiaka Alada and Dan-Ali, Mannir Ali, *Breaking the Myth: Shehu Musa and the 1991 Census*, Ibadan: Spectrum Books.
- Yakasai, Tanko (2004), *Tanko Yakasai, The Story of a Humble Life: An Autobiography*, Zaria: Amana Publishers.
- Yar'adua, Abubakar S. (1991), *Jungle Expert*, New York: Civiletis International.
- Yari, Labo (2007), *Muhamman Dikko, Emir of Katsina and His Times*, 1865-1944, Katsina: Summit Books.
- Yerima, Haruna (2004), *Humility and Service: The Life of Alhaji Ibrahim Biu*, Kaduna: Millennium.

PART TWO:
LITERATURE AND HISTORY

Chapter Three

'Without a Spare Tyre...': The Interstices of Literature in Northern Nigeria

John Sani Illah

"The history which bears and determines us has the form of a war rather than that of language: relations of power, not relations of meaning."

The first conceptual problem concerning this topic is that of definition. What constitutes "Literature in Northern Nigeria"? Who writes it, produces it and consumes it? In the context of this discourse, one could simply take it to mean literature in English originating from northern Nigeria.

This, at once, excludes all other written forms of literature and oratures produced and consumed in other northern Nigerian languages in the region: Arabic, Hausa, Igala, Kanuri, Nupe, etc.; although it could enter into significant relationships with these residual or subordinate productions. Research evidence suggests, for instance, that the Hausa literary movement has produced significant works, which also inspire a vibrant literary activity: workshops, exhibitions, Readers' Clubs, and so on.

Obviously, the Nigerian literature in English mediates this kind of literature, just as it also assumes its characteristics, which arise from its history as an anti-colonial mode of assertion that exhibits the following characteristics:

(i) It is written in the English language.
(ii) It is on the curriculum of educational institutions at all levels.
(iii) It is normally subject to the laws of commodity production.

The Nigerian literary elite were among those invited to attend the "Conference of African Writers of English Expression" in Makerere in 1962. However, as Adrian Roscoe argues in *Mother is Gold*, an African (Nigerian) who decides to write in the language of the erstwhile colonial master is making a conscious historical and ideological choice and risks being judged as part of English letters as a whole.

This argument concerning the status of English in Nigeria's literary production, might appear outmoded and frilled at the edges now, but it remains an identity marker. For, as Foucault has suggested, literature, that innocuous series of imaginary words, is a form of warfare. Its main weapon, among others, is language. Those who win are those with access to its vortex. Those who have no access lose out. In effect, English language is an identity marker, as much as it is a minority language in Nigeria, contrary to its much touted status of a unifier. According to Eagleton (1976), any literature in English,

> From the infant school to the university faculty…is a vital instrument for the insertion of individuals into the perpetual and symbolic forms of the dominant ideological formation, able to accomplish the function with a "naturalness", spontaneity and experiential immediacy possible to no other ideological practice.

This is merely, prefatorily, to put us on notice that the proposition *Literature (in English) in Northern Nigeria* is emblematic of its given historicity and structuration. Hence, all the observable contradictions of the written Nigerian literature in English often insulated away in the wrapping sheets of our educational curricular will equally apply to it, as well as take their toll on it.

On the North and Northern Nigeria

The second controversial and problematic conception to address is: What is the North? What is Northern Nigeria? Where is the North? Furthermore, where is the North in Nigeria's literature in English?

At times, one would wish that the North or Northern Nigeria were a single geographical expression, describing the sprawling area from Ogori/Magongo in south western Kogi State to Lake Chad in the north-east; and from the Mambila Plateau in the south east to Illela on the border with Niger Republic in the north-western fringes. However, it is not. Today, the Nigerian Constitution (1999) has created even new fault lines, further triggering identity conflations and re-diffusion, by recognising the following as 'geo-political zones':

(i) North Central
(ii) North East
(iii) North West

Thus, are we still dealing with the old North, the old 'Northern Region', in cultural and identity terms?

Many northern scholars, especially of the 'Middle Belt' origin, including Jibo (2003), Egwu (2003), Dakas (2003 and Gambo (2007) have argued otherwise. They state that, in the face of the emergent cultural contestations and crises in northern Nigeria, the North Central Region, or ideologically put, the Middle Belt, is a geographically distinct area, constituted of dissimilar ethnic nationalities that did not simply fall, but were forcibly incorporated into the opprobrium of the colonialists. In other words, contrary to colonialist historiography, one should not conceive, present or misrepresent the North as one monolithic whole, whatever the parameters.

While this argument suits the ideological intentions of the colonialists, however, it would not serve the tasks of decolonisation, nation-building and development. There is no predetermining commonality in geography, culture and politics. Neither is there a predetermining fundamental difference involving these factors. Rather, the dissimilar histories and values cutting across centuries have helped to nurture today's North. 'Dissimilarity does not constitute difference.' As Abdullahi Mahadi argues,

> History has not arrived at its present time all of a sudden; it reached its present stage through a very slow and difficult evolutionary process, passing through so many millennia, phases of human development.

Therefore, as presently constituted, especially where our oral, non-written sources are part of our daily construction of history, we are unable to see the convolutions and affinities that existed a mere one hundred years ago. If we add this to other self-serving ideologies, it becomes clearer why we see and pursue difference and division, conflicts and crises, even though too, these are the ingredients for the construction of history. They are necessary and inevitable.

In the context of this discourse, therefore, the North and northern Nigeria have been deconstructed as given by colonial history and the constitution of the Federal Republic (1999). Beyond this, the North is a vast heritage. By the template of its evolution, many empires used to dot its landscape: the Hausa City-States, the Kwararafa Empire, the Borno Empire, the Igala Kingdom, the Nupe Kingdom and, more recently, the Sokoto Caliphate. These were not just kingdoms. They were epics, panegyrics, prototype characters, poetry and myth–making: horses on the move, swords at play, heads severed, human folly and travesty; kingdoms rising, kingdoms falling and burying their stories and totems, and so on.

History is the terrain and the halfway house of literature, incubating intrigue, motive, passion, love and hate; the canon–fodder of good plot, character and imagery. History is the bondage of consciousness; literature is the handgun for its liberation. However, the vast histories of northern Nigeria are largely unexplored in literature. Tedium, repetition and structured falsehoods currently veil the hidden dualities and pluralities as well as their triggering vestigia. The task before literature in Northern Nigeria is, therefore, how to reconfigure these to renew and rekindle our spirits with fresh nuance, innuendo and allegro. We need this elemental anagnorsis to challenge ourselves.

'Without a Spare Tyre...'

The discussion here begins by drawing attention to the epigrammatic metaphor in the title of this paper: "*Without A Spare Tyre...*" This is from Ibro's song "Makaho." Ibro is a popular new generation Nigerian music performer based in Kano. This generation of Nigeria's new musicians feature performers like 2-Face, D-Banj, Lagbaja, W4, Timaya, Ruggedman, TY Bello, P - Square, Idris Abdulkareem, African China, Infinity, Jeremiah Gyang, etc. It is a young generation that is versatile, eclectic and trado-modern. In this particular CD, Ibro combines into his song the trado-modern twists and vocal artistry of the street beggars with some current social material. One is able to recognise the traditional style of rendition, but the instrumentation is Western and hybridised with Afro-beat.

This song, "Makaho", became so popular in Nigeria that it rose to the top of the charts; FM stations and clubhouses constantly played it on the request of their many music lovers. "Makaho" is a road song, comedy and satire all rolled into one. It celebrates northern Nigerian road lore, in which the Mercedes 911 truck (Roka) features prominently as the major character.

It tells the story of some blind men who go on a crazy quest, in search of a philanthropist who would buy them their dream Mercedes 911 commercial truck, to lift passengers (not goods) from Kano to other cities across the country. They first approach Alhaji Lere, a businessman based in Kaduna. He scoffs at them; remarking that the 'bolts in my head have not gotten loose yet'. Next, they go to Dererebe, who copies CDs/VCDs. They tell him that they know he has money; hence, he should buy them the truck. He refuses, stating that driving is difficult enough for those who can see; much less those who cannot! Next, they meet an Igbo businessman, IK Motors, who also drives them away. Finally, they go to Alhaji Jalo, who agrees to buy them the truck! They choose their dream Mercedes 911, rejecting all the other brands of trucks, like Austin Power, Toyota, Corridor and Bedford.

That same day, the blind driver, Makaho, and his retinue of other blind staff, including the conductor, motor mate and their commission agent, together drive their truck into a Kano motor park, through a billowing of dust, since they cannot see their way well. They are ready for business. They overload the lorry with passengers, even as the blind driver, in a twist of irony, turns his head round to warn them not to overload the truck, since it has no spare tyre.

For those of us who travel on Nigerian roads, the image of a driver stranded on the road with his car jerked up and a flat tyre in his hand, flagging down a lift to the nearest roadside vulcaniser, is not a totally uncommon sight. He might be a family man travelling home for the Muslim Eid or Christmas. The wife and children would have to wait under a nearby tree. There is no surprise in that! In another hour, he would be back in a mini bus or riding a hired motorcycle, clutching the vulcanised tyre, ready to continue with the journey. Sometimes, however, that might not even be the last patch on this treacherous journey, the journey of life!

WB Yeats in his poem, "The Second Coming", celebrates this image of the blind leading the blind. Chinua Achebe's classic, *Things Fall Apart*, takes its title from this poem. Similarly, Wole Soyinka deals with the trappings of the road in the poem "Death at Dawn", and the play, *The Road*. The imagery of the Nigerian roads is further marked by sharp bends, potholes, broken down trailers on the highway, wheel cover vendors, road blocks, highway hawkers, etc.

However, the expressionist image of a man stranded on an arid landscape without a spare tyre, represents for me the interstices of literature in northern Nigeria. One, there is no significant subordinate backup literature in the Nigeria languages. Apart from Hausa, no other language in northern Nigeria enjoys a significant literary output. According to Yusuf M. Adamu,

> The Kano branch of ANA [Association of Nigerian Authors] made great efforts to organise and bring together all Hausa authors. In 1996, we attended the 16th annual convention of the national ANA in Kaduna, where we presented some papers and mounted an exhibition of Hausa books. ANA Kano donated about seventy new Hausa titles to the ANA National Library in Lagos. From then on, Hausa authors began to be accepted on the national literary landscape.

In terms of the Hausa novel, Abubakar Imam, Tafida Ibrahim Garba and, more recently, Ibrahim Sheme, stand tall. Muhammed Munkaila in his essay 'Language Manipulation in Hausa Political Poetry' in Charles Bodunde (2001) underlines Sa'ad Zungur, Tijjani Tukur, Aliyu Hassan and Aliyu Gombe as contributing immensely to the cause of poetry in Hausa. I have not followed the general fortunes of this Hausa literary movement. However, the explosive rise of the Hausa home video, as documented in the collection, *Hausa Home Video: Technology, Economy and Society* (Abdulla, 2004), creates an additional challenge for literary critics.

In similar vein, the other national languages in northern Nigeria are on the decline. As curricular events, only a gingerly attention is paid to them at our primary, secondary and tertiary levels of education, as they are hardly used for instruction. The colonial policy of discriminating against them has endured, while promoting English to their detriment. In fact, over two and half decades ago, Usman Adamu Binanci had decried a situation in which those who learnt their national language "in colleges and universities learnt it through the English Language." That was because the languages had no well-developed orthographies; even those that had established orthographies did not have significant literatures. More seriously, the national language policy lacks support infrastructure and is, to say the least, evasive in respect of its implementation and has no financial muscle.

No doubt, the hegemonic position of the English language in education, social and family life emasculates the national languages in Nigeria. Our attitudes also favour this hegemony, as parents often find it fashionable to encourage their children to speak English, even at home. Furthermore, in this era of globalisation, computerisation and miniaturisation, phones, ipads and softwares are not in the national languages and have contents we cannot really control. Since the young people are inseparably wired to these modern gadgets, they get weaned away from their material cultures daily, even as battered as the cultures are already.

Two, there is a massive disconnection between the vast heritages of northern Nigeria and their exploration and expression as literary themes. Thus, the conditions are rife for significant literatures from northern Nigeria. The region is in transition; the old values are in conflict with the new ways. There are implosive intimations in politics, commerce and ideology. This is what literature — that creative enterprise of wording our imaginary thought and consciousness, of re-narrating our history and heritage, for entertainment and moral re-arming – thrives on. However, there are gaps to fill; hence our plea against driving *'without a spare tyre'*!

On Literature, and Literature in Northern Nigeria

In spite of the foregoing, literature is an increasingly fractious enterprise. It is buffeted from all sides. According to Dubravka Ugresic,

> Today, no one does set out the difference between master and amateur, between good and bad literature. Publishers don't want to get involved; they are almost guaranteed to lose money on a good writer and make money on a bad one (of blog. Blogspot .com 2012/02).

In fact, many dismiss today's literature as 'trash' — novelettes, plays, collections, scribbled for promotion purposes by university academics. These are taken across the road to pirate publishers, without any editorial or peer review mechanisms and given glossy covers and pushed to students to read. Criticism too has not fared better:

Critics hold their fire, scared of being accused of elitism. Critics have had the rug pulled out from under them in any case. No longer bound by ethics or competence, they don't even know what they are supposed to talk about anymore. University literature departments don't set out the differences – literature has turned into cultural studies in any case. (of bog. blogspot. com 2012/02)

Media literary commentary is similarly franked: Niyi Osundare observes that not infrequently, review columns confront the reader with howlers, such as "the second paragraph of the poem", "This is X's second anthology of short stories" (for anthology, read collection). Sometimes the work is praised as "simplistic", when what the writer actually means is "simple".

Generally, these are not the days of grand literature – Shakespeare, Tolstoy, Trotsky, Goethe, Jane Eyre – the days when readers lazed in bed with huge novels, or sit in dimly lit libraries with Goethe's Faust (Volumes I & II) are gone. From Achebe's *Things Fall Apart* to the *Anthills of the Savannah*, Soyinka's *A Dance of the Forests* to *Death and the King's Horseman*, to Okigho and Okara, the literary enterprise is taunted with declining readership. This is the age of TV and the social media. If novels and plays could be consumed as text messages and chats, their fortunes would have improved. Even as curricular events, literary activities, like reading clubs, fan clubs, writers workshops, debating societies, dramatic societies no longer exist to support literature in schools. Students are happy to enter examination halls with quick summaries and question and answer series.

In the last thirty years, the authorities have skewed the educational policy of 60:40 ratio in favour of the sciences in student admission and staff recruitment; and budget support has taken its toll on the arts, especially literature. Teachers are not available. History graduates have been seen to teach literature at secondary and post-secondary levels. To read literature in the university is to take to a life of servitude in teaching. This policy has done significant damage to the arts, especially when candidates rejected from the sciences are dumped on the arts faculties.

Similarly, publishing houses are no longer willing to subsidise the publication of novels, plays and poetry. The claim is that the market is just not there. They are taking to printing exercise books; and on newsprint for that matter. In fact, beginning from about 1980, most of the international publishing houses have moved from Nigeria to South Africa and other countries. Book fairs and exhibitions have become irregular. These used to bring authors and readers together. Now, only pirated copies are on open displays at the open roadside book vendors' sheds, which are popularly called 'bend down bookshops', across Nigeria.

The state of the literary enterprise, in any epoch, is always measured by the health of this tripod. First, we have the authors/writers, who passionately connect with their material environment through the story telling process and thereby renew us with tears and laughter. Attendant upon these is the intermediary group of editors, critics and reviewers. Secondly, we have the publishing houses, which print and market what the authors write. Thirdly, there is the audience that who reads or watches them. Of course, there are other variables of sociology, education and political economy that sustain and mainstream this enterprise of literature. Once this tripod of authors, publishing houses and the readership is put in jeopardy, the whole structure of the literary production will hang in the balance. This is further explained by Raymond Williams (*Marxism and Literature* 1977), Terry Eagleton (*Criticism and Ideology* 1976) and Janet Wolf (The *Social Production of Art* 1993).

The literary enterprise in Nigeria has produced great moments. There are many literary associations to testify to the vibrancy of this enterprise – the Literary Society of Nigeria (LSN), Society of Nigerian Theatre Artists (SONTA), Association of Nigerian Authors (ANA), Nigerian Folklore Society, and so on. There are also awards and prizes to recognise excellence and creativity, like the LNG Prize for Literature. This enterprise has also produced great minds and great works, as well as new rankings in three generations as shown in the table below:

Fig. 1: First Generation of Nigerian Authors/Writers in English

S/No.	Name	Gender	Classification	Remarks
1.	James E. Henshaw	M	Dramatist	
2.	Dennis Osadebe	M	Poet	
3.	Christopher Okigbo	M	Poet	
4.	Gabriel Okara	M	Poet	
5.	Wole Soyinka	M	Dramatist / Novelist /poet	Nobel laureate
6.	Bekederemo Clark	M	Poet/Dramatist	
7.	Chinua Achebe	M	Novelist	
8.	Elechi Amadi	M	Novelist	
9.	James Aluko	M	Novelist	
10.	Cyprian Ekwensi	M	Novelist	
11.	Amos Tutuola	M	Novelist	
12.	Hubert Ogunde	M	Dramatist	
13.	Wale Ogunyemi	M	Dramatist	
14.	Zulu Sofola	F	Dramatist	
15.	Abubakar Imam	M	Novelist	

Fig 2: Second Generation of Nigerian Authors/Writers in English

S/No.	Name	Gender	Classification	Remarks
1.	Harry Garba	M	Poet	
2.	Shamsudeen Amali	M	Dramatist	
3.	Iorwuese Hagher	M	Dramatist	
4.	Kole Omotosho	M	Novelist	
5.	Bode Sowande	M	Dramatist	
6.	Femi Osofisan	M	Dramatist/poet	
7.	Flora Nwapa	F	Novelist	
8.	Buchi Emecheta	F	Novelist	
9.	Zaynab Alkali	F	Novelist	
10.	Niyi Osundare	M	Poet	
11.	Odia Ofiemun	M	Poet	

12.	Isidore Okpewho	M	Novelist/poet
13.	Sonala Oluhense	M	Novelist
14.	Festus Iyayi	M	Novelist
15.	Ibrahim Tahir	M	Novelist
16.	Chris Abah	M	Novelist
17.	Abubakar Gimba	M	Novelist
18.	Olu Obafemi	M	Dramatist
19.	Bode Osayin	M	Dramatist
20.	Ben Tomologu	M	Dramatist
21.	Tanure Ojaide	M	Poet
22.	Bandele Thomas	M	Novelist
23.	Hyginus Ekwuazi	M	Poet
24.	Emeka Nwabueze	M	Dramatist
25.	Akanji Nasiru	M	Dramatist
26.	Tess Onwueme	F	Dramatist
27.	Zikky Kofoworola	M	Dramatist
28.	Ben Okri	M	Novelist
29.	Tunde Fatunde	M	Dramatist
30.	Tunde Lakoju	M	Dramatist

Fig 3: Third Generation of Nigerian Authors/Writers in English

S/No.	Name	Gender	Classification	Remarks
1.	Eugeinia Abuh	F	Poet	
2.	Remi Raji	M	Poet	
3.	Da Silva	M	Novelist	
4.	Onokome Qkome	M	Novelist	
5.	Mohammed Umar	M	Novelist	
6.	Chinamanda Adiche	F	Dramatist	
7.	Sefi Atta	F	Novelist	
8.	Zainabu Jallo	F	Dramatist	
9.	Helon Habila	M	Dramatist	
10.	Victor Dugga	M	Dramatist	
11.	Emman Idegu	M	Dramatist	

12.	Emman Dandaura	M		
13.	Irene Salami –Agunloye	F	Novelist	
14.	Idris Okpanachi	M	Novelist	
15.	Bilikisu Abubakar	F	Novelist	
16.	Aliyu Kamal	M	Novelist	
17.	Adamu Kyuka	M	Novelist	
18.	Esiaba Irobi	M	Dramatist	
19..	Tracie Utoh-Ezeaghu	F	Dramatist	
20.	Blessing Ugochukwu	F	Novelist	
21.	Ojo Bakare	M	Dramatist	
22.	Ahmed Yermah	M	Dramatist	
23.	Adinoyi, Ojo Onukaba	M	Dramatist	
24.	Kaime Agari	F	Novelist	
25.	Jude Dibia	M	Novelist	

These classifications overlap and are not clear-cut. Those in the first and second generations continue to write. Of course, diachronic factors and variables of ideology play a part in who to list and where, but this is not the place for any controversy on the classification of Nigerian authors/writers in English. The point here, in the context of 'Literature in northern Nigeria', is that, out of the seventy authors listed above, only about twenty are of northern origin as defined. However, does this matter? Yes, it does.

For those, especially in our emergent national contexts, not familiar with the antecedent historical factors, it is a statistical anomaly. For other self-serving ideologies, this could be used to suggest that the North is not producing any significant literatures, even from areas where Christian missionary education took root very early. In the first generation, the future was bleak. In the second generation, the number is more of a token. More recently, as evident in the table, there appears to be a literary re-awakening from northern Nigeria.

From a mere formalist point of view, literature is only but a series of storylines, characters and imagery. Writing is a transaction of consciousness, as the writer can only depict what is in his routine consciousness. Hence, Achebe's *Things Fall Apart* is set in Umaofia and Okonkwo is his lead character. In Soyinka's *Death and the King's Horseman,* the characters, Elesin-oba, Iyaloja, index Yoruba history and mythology. That was why Edward Said, in *Orientalism,* dwells much on enabling people to narrate or re-narrate their experience and history. Once you are not writing your own story, or synopsising your own history, others will write you out or paint you according to what is homologous to their authorial ideology.

That is why history is strategic to literature. It gives it ambience. We get to know the historical fault lines, fall guys and class subterfuges in the making of any society by tracking the synoptic nuances textually and sub-textually. Adolpho Sanchez calls this process the 're-historising' of the present consciousness. Brecht, in *The Short Organum* refers to it as 'historification'. It allows us to deepen our empathy and exercise our individual license to expand the wilderness of the text. It is implosive, bringing in new images, new passions, new frames, adding value, re-engaging and re-experiencing history as intimation and collocation.

On the strength of the current literary insurgency from northern Nigeria, the literary elite, as presently constituted, need to re-invigorate the structure of literary production in northern Nigeria. These include paying visits to our schools, which are the training ground for identifying and honing talents. Writers must take time off to visit schools and talk with the students. Similarly, school libraries must be stocked with new relevant anthologies, collections and dramas, through book donations.

In the days past, school literary associations, debating clubs, drama societies and music clubs were used as the platform to mentor would be writers. In many public schools today, these have collapsed. Can the Literature in Northern Nigeria

Conference undertake it as a project to re-institute these associations in select schools, with prizes and awards? Fan clubs and reading societies should be encouraged to start off, with retired headmasters, principals and directors serving as the hubs.

As identified in the course of this presentation, publishing houses are strategic to the evolution of literature. They used to do it as a subsidy, giving back to the community, or as corporate responsibility. Gaskiya Corporation, Zaria used to play this role in the publication of novels in Hausa. They readily published Abubakar Imam and Tafida. The Ahmadu Bello University Press also made some attempts earlier, but did not sustain the support for literary production in northern Nigeria. What publishing options are available to would be writers?

The task before the Literature in Northern Nigeria Conference is, indeed, enormous. Even without a spare tyre, it is managing to limp along. However, as history teaches us, no literature can survive without the necessary support of its institutional social structures.

References

- Abdallah, U Adamu, Yusuf M. Adamu and Umar F. Jibril (eds) (2004), *Hausa Home Video: Technology, Economy and Society*, Kano: Centre for Hausa Cultural Studies.

- Adamu, Yusuf M. (2002), "Between the Word and the Screen: A Historical Perspective of the Hausa Literary Movement and the Home Video Invasion", *Journal of African Cultural Studies*, Vol. 15 No 2.

- Bertolt, Brecht (1977), *Brecht on Theatre: The Development of an Aesthetic*, John Willet (ed), New York: Hill and Wang.

- Daksa, C.J Dakas (2001), *The Minorities Question and Constitution in Nigeria: Toward a Concrete Guarantee of Minority Right Under the Nigeria Constitution*, Jos: League for Human Rights.

- Eagleton, Terry (1976), *Criticism and Ideology*, London: Verso Press.

- Egwu, Sam (2001), "States and Class in Nigeria: Context for Farming Middle-Belt Identity", in *The Right to be Different*, Jos: League for Human Rights.

- Gambo, M. Audu (2007), "A Historical Analysis of the Tarok – Hausa/Fulani Conflict in Wase LGA of Plateau State, 2002-2005" in Akinwumi O. et al (eds), *Historical Perspectives on Nigeria's Post–Colonial Conflicts*, Lagos: Historical Society of Nigeria.

- Gofwen, I. Rotgak (2004), *Religious Conflicts in Northern Nigeria and Nation Building: The Throes of Two Decades 1980-2000* Kaduna: HRM.

- Haroun, A. Adamu (1973), *The North and Nigerian Unity*, Lagos: Daily Times.

References

- Jibo, Nvendaga (2003), *The Middle Belt and the Federal Project in Nigeria*, Ibadan: JODAD Publishers.
- Mahadi, Abdulahi (2008): "Who is Afraid of History?" in *Gombe Studies*, the Journal of Gombe State University, Vol 1 No. 1.
- Mnamani, Chimaroke (2005), *Nigeria Central, the Middle Belt, Glue to the Nation, Jos:* Nigerian Union of Journalists.
- Munkaila, Mohammed (2001), "Language Manipulation in Hausa Political Poetry", in Charles Bodunde and Ekkehard Breitinger (eds) (2001), *African Languages and Literature in the Political Context of the 1990s*, Bayreuth: University of Bayreuth.
- Said, Edward (1979), *Orientalism*, London: Vintage.
- Sanchez Adolpho (1973), "Art and Society" in *Essays in Marxist Aesthetics*, Monthly Review Press.
- Usman, A. Binanci (1985), "Translation Problem in Cross –Cultural Communication: A Case for English–Hausa Translation", in Proceedings of the Nigeria Folklore Society, 5th Annual Conference, Zaria: Ahmadu Bello University Press.
- Williams, Raymond (1977), *Marxism and Literature*, London: Oxford University Press.
- Wolf, Janet (1993), *The Social Production of Art*, New York: Nyu Press.

Chapter Four

Theatre and Resistance in the Age of Colonial Imperialism: Ahmed Yerima's *Attahiru* and *Ameh Oboni: The Great* as Paradigm

Olalekan Ishaq Balogun

> "...imperialism (colonialism) is piracy transplanted from the seas to dry land, piracy organised, consolidated and adapted to the aim of plundering the human and natural resources of our people (127)."
> ---Amilcar Cabral---

In Africa, as in much of the rest of the Third World, the colonial enterprise not only undermined the sociopolitical reality of the people, but also subverted their cultural and religious values. Perhaps, after having read Cabral well, Ilyin and Motylev feel motivated to explain that,

> ...for nearly a century in Africa, two centuries in Asia, and three to four centuries in Latin America, the colonial countries were plundered of all their wealth, their most fertile lands were used to produce a single type of crop for the colonialists, and the obtained products were exported to the imperialist states (264).

Fanon also provides an apt summation in his description of the phenomenon: "colonialism is not a thinking machine, not a body endowed with reasoning faculties...it is violence in its natural state." (48) This 'violence', created by the displacement of existing sociopolitical structure and its replacement by foreign hegemony, was through methods that were at once deceptive and overwhelming in their impact. Colonial attitude towards the African natives was nothing but an abhorrence of their ways, intellect and beliefs; an attitude that was carried over even where foreign values were concerned.[1] Instead, the wealth of the colonies was sought with greed and annoying audacity. This attitude of denigration brings to mind Ayi Kwei Armah's proverbial bird, *chichidoodoo*, which hates excreta with passion, but feeds on maggot produced therein.[2] No doubt, conflicts arising from the encounter continue to plague the societies. Global crises have been blamed on the colonial encounter, which not only created a near eternal fracture of social cohesion in countries that once enjoyed relative peaceful coexistence, despite their minimal level of development.[3] This is despite the justification offered by some colonial apologists of the sordid condition of living and political imbalance that resulted in disillusionment among the populace, which continues to underline the fact of the negative consequence of the encounter.[4] As Cesaire aptly puts it,

> Wherever there are colonisers and colonised face to face, I see force, brutality, cruelty, sadism, conflict, and in a parody of education, the hasty manufacture of a few thousand subordinate functionaries, "boys", artisans, office clerks and interpreters necessary for the smooth operation of business (21).

---

1 Colonial attitude towards African natives readily subscribes to the theory of Ernest Gellner, which focuses on education as a means of subjugating people to a cultural hegemony, leading to their domination. See Gellner, Smith (1983), *Nations and Nationalism*, Oxford: Blackwell; 2nd edition, (2006); Smith, A.D. (1971) *Theories of Nationalism*, London: Duckworth; Fafunwa, A. Babs, *History of Education in Nigeria* (1974), London: George, Allen &Unwin; Daniel, John (1981) "The Culture of Dependency and Political Education in Africa", in Cohen, D. and Daniel (eds.) J. *Political Economy of Africa: Selected Readings*. London: Longman.
2 See Armah, Ayi Kwei (1968), *The Beautyful Ones Are Not Yet Born*, AWS 43, London: Heinemann.
3 See Ake, Claude (1981), *A Political Economy of Africa*. London: Longman; Ward, W.E.F "The Colonial Phase in British West Africa: Political Developments", in Ade Ajayi, J.F. & Espie, Ian (eds) (1965), *A Thousand Years of West African History*. Ibadan: University Press & Nelson, p 389; Rodney, Walter (1982), *How Europe Underdeveloped Africa*, Enugu: Ikenga Publishers; Akinjogbin, I.A and Osoba S.O. (1980), *Topics on Nigerian Economic and Social History*, Ile Ife: University of Ife Press.
4 See "Northern Nigeria: Background to Conflict", *in International Crisis Group: Africa Report No 168*, 20 December, 2010.

Given the genesis and spate of contemporary tribal and religious conflicts, especially in northern Nigeria, which is the focus of this paper, the encounter between the African natives and the colonisers continues to resonate with the tragic reality that Cesaire paints. As Isichei remarks, Nigeria's "confrontation with an alien culture, its conquest, and the experience of an alien rule, created...crises." (180) The creation of the colonial state, which was the direct result of the introduction and imposition of Indirect Rule by Lord Frederick Lugard, brought about disharmony in the precolonial Nigerian polities that were hitherto heterogenous societies with their respective endocentric engines of growth, coupled with corresponding politico-cultural institutions (Olorunleke 126).

That such history continues to hold relevance and its appropriation for dramatic purposes points to the role of literature and, more specifically, the theatre in engaging into the appropriate discourse in the society. Yerima's argument that, "History contains actions of human miseries and joy, sadness and laughter (which are) all basic tools for good quality tragedy, once a playwright knows how to use and explore them." clearly draws attention to this fact (p.48). The works of other dramatists, such as Soyinka, Clark and Rotimi as well as the later generation of dramatists, including Osofisan and Sowande focus on the colonial encounter and its aftermath, further demonstrate this.

Northern Nigeria Before Colonialism

Northern Nigeria is home to numerous ethnic groups and religious communities. They include historically important urban centres, like Kano, Sokoto, Zaria, and Maiduguri, despite the majority rural landscape. These cities have been famous centres of learning in the Islamic world for centuries, with the predominance of groups, such as the Hausa, Fulani and Kanuri among other roughly 160 smaller groups; majority of them Muslims and the smaller number animists and, later, Christians. Since the British colonisation in the early 1900s, these groups have crystallised into both "majority groups" and "minorities". Specifically, the Sokoto Caliphate traces its pre-eminence to the efforts of Shehu Uthman Dan Fodio whose jihad, aimed at purifying the Islamic practice in the region, ultimately led to the installation of a new righteous leadership.

Deriving cohesion from Islam and consisting of autonomous emirates, each with its own emir and system of administration, the new state had at its head the caliph, based in Sokoto, who doubled as both the political and spiritual leader. Under his leadership, the capitals and emirates witnessed the flourishing of trade, secured transport routes and attainment of considerable wealth[5]. The caliphate encompassed "the vast territories of the United Islamic States of West Africa, which extended from Gao on the River Niger in the west to Garoua near the source of River Benue in the East, and from the fringes of the rainforest south." (Shagari 10).

In the late nineteenth century, the British government established its control of southern Nigeria as a protectorate, with Lagos as a colony. In 1900, it began extending its control northward, proclaiming that region also a protectorate. Frederick Lugard, the High Commissioner of Northern Nigeria, gradually negotiated with the emirs to accept colonial rule. Some agreed as their kingdoms were already weakened by the internal crises resulting from a number of factors, including the end of the once lucrative Atlantic slave trade. However, those who resisted were defeated by force, from Bida in 1901 to Sokoto in 1906.

Attahiru: Martyrdom in the Protection of the Caliphate

As pointed out earlier, the Sokoto Caliphate occupied an important, though ambivalent, position in the consciousness of Muslims in northern Nigeria. Its history is a source of pride and its legacy gives a sense of community and cohesion, which includes unusually for West Africa, an indigenous African written text, the Hausa Ajami, which is still widely used. The caliphate also left behind a structure of political governance centered on the emirs and their inheritors. This condition was reinforced by the fact that Attahiru, the caliph at the time of the colonial conquest, did not surrender to the British rule, but fought to the death.

---

[5] Ibid.

Yerima's play, *Attahiru*, is, thus, a drama of resistance that captures the reality of Sultan Attahiru's heroic confrontation with the forces of imperialism. His martyrdom and heroism were entrenched in history by the fact that he ruled for just six months, which explains why his name and fame have become indelible in the unending story of the heroic struggle of the Africans against colonialism and in defence of their freedom, liberty and justice (10).

Sultan Attahiru's ascension to the caliphate in November 1902 as the twelfth Caliph of Sokoto and the Sarkin Musulumi was, according to Yerima, overshadowed by a major development in the history of Nigeria, notably the British military penetration of the hinterland to the North. The imperial might had earlier been felt through the defeat of indigenous resistance movements in Ijebuland (1892), Brass (1895), Ilorin and Bida (1897), Benin (1897), Arochukwu (1901-02) among others[6]. Sultan Attahiru was not unaware of this development — a fact the Sultan in Attahiru expresses at his coronation, amidst the euphoria of celebrations and hope for new prosperity in the caliphate:

> CALIPH: I am becoming the caliph at a time when the history of our lives is at a delicate balance. At a time when the white man is determined to upset the peace of our lives. But it is too early to dare enemies, or to look for one. I shall await their moves. But let us pray to Allah's hand in the matter. Let us pray for peace. Let us pray for our children. Let us pray for the growth of our lives and position in the Islamic world. Thank you all.(21)

While Sultan Attahiru, with the support of his council engages in resolving domestic disputes over market control and authority, such as the one involving Sarkin Zango and Sarkin Fatake, and their members who are mostly peasants and traders, as required of his exalted position, the signal of the impending clash between his authority and colonial imperialism with unprecedented results is given with the news of the removal of his representatives, the emirs of Bida and Kontagora, who

---
6 See Afigbo, A.E "The Colonial Phase in British West Africa: A Reassessment of the Historiography of the Period", in Ade Ajayi, J.F & Espie, Ian (eds) (1965), *A Thousand Years of West African History*. Ibadan: University Press & Nelson, p 389

are accused of high-handedness. His authority is further undermined by the new High Commissioner of northern Nigeria, who sends the message to him to choose new emirs to replace the ones deposed, but the choice can only be confirmed through colonial ratification. Lugard ridicules the Islamic religion further by referring to the deposed emirs as scoundrels and infidels. As Waziri retorts, "the greatest irony is that the selector of these good Muslims, is himself a white man, an infidel. A *kafir!*"(28).

Sultan Attahiru himself remains undaunted, even while the caliphate trembles at the thought of the likely brutal confrontation, as expressed by a few of the titled chiefs, who cite the unfriendly relationship with Zaria. The latter emirate, had nursed a grudge against the Sultan of Sokoto for not actively intervening to stop its falling to the onslaught of the Emir of Kontagora, thereby forcing the Emir of Zazzau to seek the friendship and support of the white man. However, the caliph seems indifferent to the looming shadow of imperialism, as he talks tough and sends a decisive letter stating in unequivocal terms the position of the caliphate under his authority as a true Muslim and leader of the faithfuls. The seriousness of the tone of the letter is not lost on Lugard who, in a meeting with his lieutenants, Colonel Morland and Willcocks, expresses his disdain for the way events are turning, despite his readiness to match the caliph strength for strength.

Nonetheless, underlying the motive of transgression on the African soil is no doubt the selfish interests of the European powers. The British incursion and frenzied desire to control the colony, by any means if necessary, is motivated by the presence of the French. As Willcocks observes:

Willcocks: My major worry is the French. They are moving closer to Sokoto through the north of Katsina.

Lugard: I have studied the situation myself. It means that we either fight and take Sokoto now, or the French would cross the Niger and join Sokoto and thereby cutting us off totally. This must never be allowed.

Morland:	Details Sir, I am hoping that if we have to take Sokoto, it will be swift and quick. We can't allow a long war or defeat.
Lugard:	Defeat? Never! Right now, the morale of our men is high. With the spoils of Zaria and Kano, they will fight even their fathers for the glory of Britain. (35)

As the drums of war sound at the background, faith and devotion to the great cause of Islam find their way into Sultan Attahiru's meeting with his son, Mai Wurno, and the spiritual teacher, Mallam. Against the perspective of spirituality that sets in, notwithstanding the prophecy that foretells the end of the century-reign of the caliphate established by Shehu Uthman Dan Fodio, Sultan Attahiru's composure reveals a character of immense grace and poise. Despite the series of revealing nightmares, which portend danger, he finds recourse in doing the bidding of Allah, standing up to challenge the desecration of the valued Islamic tenets by an unrelenting foe, who "raises dust on all fronts around Sokoto"(38) and who has already succeeded in breaking up the unity of the Caliphate built by his (Attahiru)'s ancestors and installing his own loyalists who openly question the Sultan's ruling. With the fall of the flag bearers under the Caliph, notably Yola, Zaria, Kano, Kontagora and Ilorin, resigning to fate is not a luxury that Sultan Attahiru should ignore; nor is the fear of the consequence too grim to entertain. Rather, it now becomes a duty to face up to the fate with mixed determination to succeed, like Caliph Atiku, Muazu, Umaru and Abdul-Rahman did, who were all caliphs before his time.

As the imperialist's final onslaught begins and Katsina tumbles, Sokoto under Sultan Attahiru, continues to be steadfast and determined, noting that "if Sokoto must fall, it will fall fighting, not with the Caliph and his people unwrapping their *Rawani* for the white man to see their bald heads."(47). After the bloody confrontation at Bebeji, noted for the heavy loss of lives, Burmi soon becomes the fiercest battle ground and the place history will meet with resilience, faith with duty and honour with fate, as the troops led by Sultan Attahiru clash with Lugard's band of imperial infidels. Not daunted by the colonialists' hurried enthronement of Prince Muhammad al-Tahir Aliyu as the new sultan — a move to divide the caliphate and undermine the authority of Attahiru— Muslim faithfuls and loyalists rally round in support of truth, symbolised by Sultan Attahiru, who now prophetically notes that, "it is not how long, but what you did while on the throne that people will remember."(61) Defeated by the superior forces of Lugard all right, Sultan Attahiru's heroism is, however, marked by the symbolism of the flag that is never allowed to plunge to the ground, as each falling Muslim defends it with his life and, indeed, all saying "no to colonial oppression at the cost of their lives."(61)

Ameh Oboni, the Great: Sustaining Hegemony Through Ritual Death

While Sultan Attahiru's heroism is won at the battle ground, Ameh Oboni's feat comes under darker and more brutal circumstances, which continue to draw attention to the treachery of the human mind. From the very beginning, he appears to be doomed to failure[7]. He becomes the King of Igala amidst a very terrible conflict of interest — conflict between spiritual and political duty, economic control and ritual sacrifice — mired by the colonial imperialist presence that is bent on toppling his rule, much as it had done in Benin, Itsekiri and Opobo land. The contradictions in the Attah's personality and the nature of the tragedy are portrayed by his subversion of the process of the coronation, albeit without really grasping the extent of the damage he is causing at the time to the monarchy that he is assuming control of. At a time of great trouble like this, when the society is being spurred on by the imperialists, who are not only cunning, but equally determined to have their way, the people themselves should not be divided along selfish lines and parochial interests, to the detriment of the fate of the entire collective.

---

[7] Yerima writes that "...Ameh Oboni was a very wronged tragic hero — the reluctant one— pushed by the wit of his people...". See "Author's Note", (2005), *Ameh Oboni: the Great*, Ibadan: Kraft Books Limited.

To make matters worse, the new Attah's problems are further compounded by the betrayal of some of his most trusted subjects, who now question the kind of Islam that he professes, having assumed the throne that had readily promoted the observance of various heathen practices. Taking advantage of such divided socio-cultural and political arrangement, D. J. Muffet, the colonial district officer, prepares for the monarch's dethronement. As the Attah wonders at the turn of events, one cannot help but sympathise with him:

> Attah: I became a Muslim in 1934 when I stayed with the great teacher, Mallam Audu, in Okene. When I became the Attah nine years ago, I knew that as a traditional ruler, I was the link with the past of my people and their spiritual presence. So, my knowledge of Islam projected this dual position. But in Kaduna, my kind of Islam is not accepted any more. They want me to discard my past, my tradition and live the life of what they call a true Muslim...that type who will be controlled by the so-called true Muslims of the core North. The ones the white man can trust, because in his white Rawani, he does not care for the excesses of the white man and his Queen. Because of what they have told the white man, he is no longer comfortable with me. And my son helped to fuel this dislike for me and our ways (27).

With such atmosphere of lack of cohesion and understanding between the king and his subjects, Muffet's preparation to overrun the empire and take control of its political structure and resources appears assured. The many petitions written to the governor-general against Ameh Oboni by his subjects provided the excuse to undermine his control. However, like Sultan Attahiru, his own reign is seen also as a fulfilment of destiny, the marked attainment by a special individual tasked by his ancestors, despite the foreboding background of colonial intrusion. Ohioga, tells him:

> Ohioga: The music must play out itself. The gods have chosen you for their sacrifice. Caution, my king. (23)

Despite this, one can fully understand the consternation of Ameh Oboni when Abutu informs him that the district officer has ordered policemen to bar him from entering his palace upon his return to Idah. He is amazed that Abutu, whom he made a councillor, can come to deliver such a disgusting message. Knowing that he appears to have been cornered from all sides, having seen the treachery of his people grow with each passing day, he prepares for the eventuality. Ameh Oboni can read the writing on the wall; he understands too well also that "in Igala land, a family masquerade, that he has become, does not dress up and refuse to come out to dance with its peers or else, he brings to shame the dressers and the family name, which he represents."(52) He also understands that no man wins judgement against his clan[8], that there is no need to concentrate on fighting the smoke, when the big fire rages, which is a succinct proverb to describe the antics of his people against him, with the tacit support of the colonial authority.

With nothing left to hold on to except his guts, he confronts the fear that gnaws at the heart of his people. He fully understands that "the white man's hands are steadfast and seem determined to push down the walls of the shrine."(44) In order to secure an eternal place for his children in the line of monarchy and their right to lay claim to the throne and, at the same time, rewrite his own tragic history of betrayal and defeat by the imperialist, he snatches victory from the hands of shame and defeat, by laying down his life as the ultimate sacrifice. He teaches his people and the colonialist a lesson in heroism, greatness and sacrifice for which he is remembered in history as one of the very rare African personalities, like Sultan Attahiru to dare colonial might and challenge the subjugation of their people.

However, colonial subjugation has not been without its attendant sociopolitical tribulation, as witnessed in northern Nigeria and the entire country to date. In the first instance, the history of the distrust between the North and South, as well as the East, which was the background factor that stimulated the crisis

---

8 See Achebe, Chinua, *Arrow of God*, AWS, Heinemann, 1964.

and violence that led to the Nigerian Civil War, has been traced by some scholars to the bitterness the North had against the other regions. Such scholars attribute the bitterness of the North against them for providing the troops needed by the colonial authorities in suppressing the Northern resistance.[9]

Furthermore, the rise of religious conflicts had its antecedent in the colonial presence, which caused division and conflict between the two major Sufi brotherhoods in the North at the time: the Qadiriyya, which had established its presence as the official and dominant order of the caliphate since the fifteenth century, and the Tijaniyya, with its strong base derived from the newly-rich traders and the bureaucratic class, who together now constituted its membership. The allegations of collaboration with the British colonial authority often levied against the former by the latter group gradually degenerated into brutal clashes in the 1940s and had direct and catastrophic effects on the political situation, especially those involving the two major political parties in the region of that era, the Northern Elements Progressive Union (NEPU) and the Northern People's Congress (NPC).[10] The resistance posed by the Mahdi group, which had the reputation of being feared by the colonial authority, was also remarkably relevant in understanding the colonial involvement in instituting the religious conflicts that became established in the northern Region.[11]

Conclusion

Certainly, these crises, including several others, such as the emergence of the El-Zakzaky-led Muslim brotherhood of the 1980s, the Maitatsine of the 2000s and the more recent Boko Haram, can be linked to the gradual, calculated and treacherous

---

9   Ibid, International Crisis Group.
10 See Loimeier, Roman (1997), *Islamic Reform and Political Change in Nigeria*. Evanston; Paden, John N. (1973), *Religion and Political Culture in Kano*. Berkeley: University of California Press.
11 See Lovejoy, Paul E & Hogendorn (1990), J.S "Revolutionary Mahdism and Resistance to Colonial Rule in the Sokoto Caliphate, 1905-1906", in *Journal of African History*, Vol.31, no.2, pp 217-224.

undermining of the Shari'ah law by the British colonial authorities in Northern Nigeria. For centuries, the region had been governed in line with the Shari'ah, thereby respecting the religious sensibilities of the people, but overnight the British replaced it with the penal code, a code that was alien and less than respectful to their Islamic beliefs. This act itself speaks volumes about the domineering power of imperialism, which had little, if any respect, for the right to worship of any conquered territory and its people. Indeed, this ambiguity, as well as the inadequacy of the new laws to fully establish the desired accord between the different social groups who were forcefully amalgamated, continue to serve as the source of the conflict involving the people, as they strive to live together in an arrangement that was lopsided from the very beginning.

References

- Cabral, Amilcar (1982), "Weapon of Theory", in *Unity and Struggle*. London: Heinemann.
- Cesaire, Aime, Pinkham, John trans. (1972), *Discourse on Colonialism*, New York and London: Monthly Review Press.
- Fanon, Frantz (1983), *The Wretched of the Earth*, London: Pelican Books.
- Ilyin, S and Motylev (1986), A. Sdobnikora, Galina trans. *What is Political Economy?* Moscow: Progress Publishers.
- Isichei, Elizabeth (1973), *The Ibo People and the Europeans*, New York: St. Martin's Press.
- Olorunleke, Ojo. "Images of the Colonial State in African Literature: A Prolegomenon", in Olorunleke, Ojo and Ladele, Lola (eds) *New Perspectives in Linguistics and Literature*, Lagos: Ilu Project Associates, 1999.
- Shagari, Shehu. "Foreword", in Yerima, Ahmed. *Attahiru*, Ibadan: Kraft Books Limited, 1998.
- Yerima, Ahmed (2005), *Ameh Oboni: The Great*. Ibadan: Kraft Books Limited.
- _____ (1998), *Attahiru*. Ibadan: Kraft Books Limited.
- _____ (2009), *Discourse on Tragedy*. Minna: Gurara Publishing.

Chapter Five

Literature and History: Celebrating the Heroism of Attahiru in Ahmed Yerima's Attahiru

Jeremiah Methuselah

Introduction

"History belongs to the people; it emanates from the people. Historical events are specific significant happenings from which a given society or a people would want to learn. The job of a playwright…is therefore to arrange these significant happenings into a structure, a sense, an episodic structure of exploration of the materials gathered." (Yerima 59).

The above quote from Yerima sets the tone for this chapter, which basically sets out to discuss the heroism of Sultan Attahiru, the last sultan of the Sokoto Caliphate. The idea is to compare between the historical Attahiru and the artistic Attahiru. Using the concepts of artistic truth and historical truth, it will also attempt a content analysis of the play, *Attahiru*. The objective is to highlight the two concepts and explore which of them best explicates the heroism of Attahiru in greater detail.

Historical Truth Versus Artistic Truth

One can understand historical truth from the phenomenon of history itself, which embodies "the branch of knowledge dealing with past events... a continuous systemic narrative of past events as relating to a particular people, country, period, person and so on." (Webster's *Encyclopedic Unabridged Dictionary of the English Language,* 1989:674). It should be noted that this history, whether of an individual, a people, or a group, spans over a wide expanse of time. In this wise, the narratives concerning gigantic empires that had existed in time past are compressed in a few cryptic sentences or paragraphs. Depending on the particular issue the historian sets out to highlight in this narration, he may not delve into the nitty-gritty of the issues, but as he makes a sweep of the period, he "tends to emphasise the movements, the 'big moments', the crucial decisions and the 'personalities' rather than everyday events." (Etherton, 1982:143). This is so because "History is but a fraction of the past, presented as a coherent story. No one wants to tell the story of the whole past, and no one could. Evidence exists for no more than a small splinter of what has gone on in the past. It is impossible to recover the whole past." (Kimball, 2012: 6).

Based on the above understanding of history, historical truth is conceived as the received idea of what has been projected in history from the point of view of the narrator/historian of something that has happened in time past. The narrator/historian may choose to remain faithful to the events that have happened. On the other hand, he/she may choose to be lopsided in his documentation of the situation so reported. The truth is, therefore, understood from the prism of his or her narration because of his or her "bias", which makes for varied interpretations of the events. (Etherton, 1982: 143)

However, artistic truth is conceived as the freedom available to the writer. In this sense, the playwright, in re-constructing, deconstructing and re-configuring historical events in such a way as to present his understanding of a certain phenomenon. This will mean that even historical issues can be tampered with by the playwright as he attempts to foreground his opinion, correct a wrong opinion or deliberately set out to alter the historical truth, itself. No wonder that Wolf (1993:49) argues that art, and in this case drama, is a "product of specific historical practices on the part of identifiable social groups in given conditions, and therefore bears the imprint of the ideas, values and conditions of existence of these groups."

A number of Nigerian historical plays are crafted on this ethos. In *Death and the King's Horseman*, the historical play by Soyinka (1975) history is tampered with so as to present the writer's quarrel with the colonial authorities for meddling into the affairs of a people as they denigrate and downgrade their culture. To drive home his point, Soyinka projects the character of Murana, the son of the Elesin Oba as an educated and enlightened student reading in a school abroad. Olunde the fictional equivalent of Murana, vested with this paraphernalia of Western knowledge still does not flinch from carrying out an assignment that he believes is directly rooted to the well being and continued existence of his people.

A similar situation presents itself in the play *Morountodun* by Femi Osofisan (1982) where the dramatised Agbekoya uprising was reinterpreted and reinvigorated to be radically different from its historical copy. Femi Osofisan who was commissioned to write a play projecting female heroism fused the Moremi myth and the Agbekoya uprising and constructed a powerful young heroine in the name of Titubi, an uptown girl, who ended up becoming the heroine of the Farmers' Movement. In an ironic twist of events very much identifiable with the 'Stockholm syndrome', Titubi makes a turn around and aligns herself with the poor farmers after living with them and experiencing their suffering and pain.

Also, the historical plays of Irene Salami, (2001) like *Emotan: The Benin Heroine, Idia, the Warrior Queen*, rehash history, but with a slight tinkering of the facts, in this case to showcase the power and glory of women by categorically and forcefully pushing the argument that they are not just the weaklings that society has configured them to be. Therefore, Emotan is courageous enough to organise a secret army to take on Uwaifiokun, the usurper, when the men could only peep from the rear in fear. (Jeremiah, 2008:162) *In Idia, the Warrior Queen*, Salami (2001) calls Idia, the queen mother, "the queen," even though she was not the ruling monarch. As the power behind Oba Esegie, the then Oba of Benin, Salami seems to suggest that she was the proxy queen; even to the extent of elevating her in the title of the play: Idia, the Warrior Queen. Indeed, the facts as they are presented in history do not exactly project the issues as sharply as they are presented in the two plays, even if they subtly suggest that. This explains Yerima's (1999:189) assertion himself that:

> "...the use of historical materials in a work of art, is the attempt by man to further explain the significance of the historical event in a less serious story telling version or style even while still using the facts of the historical events."

The artist's use of the expression "less serious" should not by any means be construed to mean cheapening the work, but, in his own words, a way of adding "entertainment elements and aesthetic embellishment values to the facts of history." (Yerima 1999:189). Furthermore, Yerima adds that "history ...must go beyond documentation, for in the process of historicism, a form of alteration must take place for history to have a sharper meaning to the people." (Yerima 1999:103) This will certainly account for the embellishments and additions of the entertainment elements to the historical material, without which the work may just end up as a 'closet' play, incapable of coming alive on stage to achieve the level of entertainment desired by the playwright.

The various recreations of the story of Oba Ovonramwen of Benin further lend credence to this argument. In *The Trials of Oba Ovonramwen* by Yerima (1998), there is a departure with the earlier version of the Oba's story titled *Ovonramwen Nogbaisi* written by the erudite playwright, Ola Rotimi (1974). In Rotimi's version, the Oba is presented in less complimentary perspectives, probably toeing the official line of thinking as documented by the then colonial authorities. Specifically, the Oba is shown to be weak, indecisive, irascible, very vindictive and brutal. Yerima's version, however, celebrates the courage and resilience of the proud king, who stands up against the brutal machinery of the invading British colonialists that come to plunder and loot his kingdom.

Yerima signifies Ovonramwen as a victim, rather than the offender; a prey, rather than the predator. The suggestion, therefore, is that if the Oba engages the British in a fight, it is consequent to the fact that they have invaded his kingdom and threatened his stool. He could do nothing else, but fight back. In both narrations, there is a slight difference with the historically documented version.

This brings to mind the issue of truth in art. Given the multiple nature of the Ovonramwen's story, which of them is real? Indeed, is there absolute truth in art? Poetic license invests on the author the power to alter the existing situation to suit his/her ideological or philosophical perspectives. No wonder Pinter (2012:3) concludes that the truth in drama is "elusive", arguing that there is no such thing as one truth, but many truths, which are also varied. In his words, "these truths challenge each other, recoil from each other, reflect each other, ignore each other, tease each other, are blind to each other." The two versions of Ovonramwen cited above provide good evidence in this regard; the two playwrights have presented slightly different versions of the 'truth' as perceived by each artist.

The Historical Attahiru

The reign of Sultan Attahiru was brief, but tumultuous, as he ascended the throne of the caliphate at the time when the colonial authorities were exerting maximum pressure on the caliphate in their effort to subdue all resistance, having vanquished most of the emirs in Hausaland and replaced them with friendlier and pliable stooges. In spite of the fact that pockets of resistance could be found here and there, by and large, the only 'last man standing' was the Sultan in Sokoto.

Attahiru, who had just ascended the throne, consistently spurned the intimidations of Lugard to subject him under the imperialistic rule of the British. In one of the correspondences with Lugard, he had made it quite clear that he did not intend to co-habit with the colonialists. Gott (2006:3) quotes him thus:

> I do not consent that any one from you should ever dwell with us. I will never agree with you. I will have nothing ever to do with you. Between us and you, there are no dealings, except as between Moslems and unbelievers — war, as God Almighty has enjoined on us. There is no power or strength save in God on high.

The eventual collision culminated in the fight in the town of Burmi, where the Sultan had gone to with his followers, after slipping through the hands of detachments of the colonial troops sent to subdue or capture him several times. The British conquerors had feared that he might strategise and start an uprising among the Muslim faithfuls on a wide scale. The narrative of Johnston (2012:14), which describes the final battle when the imperial soldiers confronted him, explains the point:

> On 27 July 1903, a little before noon, the British force appeared under the walls of Burmi and the final battle began. It was to prove easily the toughest and bloodiest of the whole campaign. The die-hards of Burmi fought with fanatical courage and devotion against the infinitely superior weapons of their enemies. Some deliberately courted death. Others lashed themselves together so that they should not be tempted to try to escape but would die together.
>
> When the fighting began, Attahiru went to the mosque. He remained there praying until he heard that the gates had been breached and then he emerged and went down to the walls. He was on foot, unarmed, and his intention was not to fight but to go out to meet his fate… Death came to him with merciful swiftness, for when he was within a stone's throw of the southern wall, he was shot through the head.

The Artistic Attahiru

The play, *Attahiru*, begins on a light note. The setting is instantly recognisable and the dialogue by the trio of Abbas, Ahmed and Yakubu — three cheeky and mischievous characters — serves to relax the audience. This is an obvious and deliberate distraction created by the playwright to lighten the mood of the play before the tragic situation unfolds later on. The discussion of the three gives us insight to the very difficult moments in the life of the caliphate. The threat of invasion by the British is very real. This, coupled with the recent demise of the late Sultan and the resultant contest for the throne among eligible members of the royal family, has created further residual tensions.

> Abbas: We cannot waste much time my friends. The fast shooting gun of the white man spits bullets of death. It talks to soldiers from afar. The princes should not squabble over who should be caliph, there is no time. I heard the white men are matching towards Argungu and Gwandu already (p.17).

The next scene ushers in the new sultan. The display of pomp attends his entrance. It is a display of monumental proportions to indicate the importance of the office of the caliph, which has the dual role of being both political and religious. The audience gets a glimpse of the display of the Sultan's political power in the next scene through the adjudication of the case between Sarkin Zango and Sarkin Fatake. The deft and objective management of this conflictual situation exposes the Sultan as a wise and focused leader who is shrewd and understands the ways of men.

From then onwards, the audience's respect for the Sultan mounts by the minute. The heroic streak in him does not make him flinch at the enormity of the problem he has at hand.

> Caliph: I am becoming caliph at the time when the history of our lives is at a delicate balance. At a time when the white man is determined to upset the peace of our lives. (p.21)

Attahiru's inauguration speech reveals his passion for his people and faith. He is also presented as fearless. In spite of the threat of the invading colonial powers, he does not appear as a frightened man or one ready to skulk away in fear. Rather, his comments reveal a valiant and philosophical personality. He accepts his fate with understanding and determination.

Predictably, this gallantry has an infectious effect on other Muslims from the rest of Hausaland, with many of them volunteering to come to Sokoto to fight alongside him in order to protect the honour of their religion. His fearlessness has the effect of galvanising them to action, so much that many from Katsina, Kano, Gombe and thereabouts pour in to honour the Caliph. Even though many of them know that they stand little chance against the firepower of the colonialists, the sheer courage and resilience of Attahiru lift their spirits to great heights. What the emirs have failed to do to rally their subjects to repulse the colonialists, the Caliph succeeds because of his demonstrable spirit of sacrifice and doggedness in defence of his faith. His zeal for his religion is unquenchable because he believes it to be a holy cause. Even as he talks about the impending engagement in Burmi, which turns out to be his waterloo, he is cool and calm:

> Caliph: I hear he plans another battle for here in Burmi. I am not afraid. Allah is here with us. After two months of flight, I believe the hijra is over, let the battle begin. I am not afraid because Allah is with us. And even if we die today, he will take us straight to heaven, because we died for him. I am not afraid because I am ready to shed the last drop of my blood to free my people. To spread the light of Islam. Are you afraid? (p. 60)

The description of the ferocity of the battle shortly after testifies to the Caliph's heroism. He is in the thick of it all to the last moment, when he is cut down by a hail of bullets. Even at the point of death, having been shot in the stomach, Attahiru hacks down two soldiers. He dies fighting. He dies a hero.

The Artistic Celebration of Attahiru's Heroism

It is important to note that the artist is not ideologically neutral. This is quite true of Yerima in *Attahiru,* where the playwright enlivens and buttresses the existing portraiture of Attahiru. Where history is static, he lifts it to a higher level by bringing it alive in the play. He succeeds in empowering the historical Attahiru by investing the fictional Attahiru with language and other artistic tools that clearly and unambiguously celebrate the essence of his heroism. He grants the audience insights into the psychological state of the Caliph; thus, not only does it sympathise with his plight, it also empathises with him in his quest to remain steadfast in the face of the looming war that will surely result in his destruction, given the superior power of the invading enemy. Throughout this action, the audience is emotionally transported to Burmi, the Waterloo of the Sultan, but unlike the invading powers, does not appear as the illiterate, stubborn and unbending desert chief. On the contrary, he is presented as a highly organised, philosophical and intrepid religious leader who is willing to die for a cause, rather than to kowtow to an infidel; a leader who is able to inspire his people to follow him to the theatre of death, knowing fully well that they are not going to return alive.

The artistic creation and embellishments of Yerima further avail the audience of this inner configuration of Attahiru, because art gives a glimpse into the mind, while history gives a picture of the past (www.librarything.com/topic/73521). Yerima (2005:190) summarises this artistic pre-occupation that, "...using the power of his imagination, [the artist] endows history with characters, dialogue, new argument, culture of music, dance, religion, to create an environment, so that history moves...without losing its original essence."

Elsewhere, Yerima (2003:113) takes this argument to a higher level, as he relates the relationship between history and artistic recreation. He maintains that:

> The dramatist also possesses a level of poetic license, which allows him to a certain extent to take some liberties with his creative freedom during the fusing together of fact and fiction, and also expanding, but by no means distorting, the historical thoughts as presented by history.

The poetic license available to Yerima, therefore, grants him the previlege of selecting materials from the real life happenings of Attahiru in order to pass across the specific message he desires of him. Thus, while history is static, art is dynamic. It is able to open the historical scenario and stretch it beyond the very narrow historical narrative. It further possesses the elasticity of expanding to reveal smaller details that can include every day humdrum, something that has already been indicated is lacking in historical narratives because of their cryptic and constrictive nature.

Similarly, as indicated earlier, the historical account of Sultan Attahiru's battle against the British colonial conquerors did not have these details, but the artistic creations in the play give it life and strengthen the tension, intrigue and suspense, until it draws out the ire of the reader in a fundamental manner to the gross injustice of the colonial system in overrunning all the indigenous institutions and those who stood in its way. The play achieves this through the dialogue generated and the audience is clearly educated to understand why, for instance, the Sultan historically withdrew from the city of Sokoto. Clearly, it was not a survivalist move by the Sultan or a cowardly flight to escape the rampaging imperial powers. On the contrary, it was a strategy to draw the British away from the city so as to minimise civilian casualty and the destruction of the city, and in order to display his rejection of the colonialists as overlords.

> Caliph: You spoke well Sarkin Kwanni. I now decree. As with my earlier letter to the whiteman, war is our only answer to his threats. We shall meet him; however, to avoid too much danger to the wives and children, outside the city. (p 47)

It is interesting to note that this last act of bravery by the Sultan differs from the historical narrative where he is reported to have been in a mosque praying only to walk out and meet a hail of fire as he gets shot through the head. Yerima's embellishment, however, constructs this battle scene with the Sultan placed in a more active role as the audience witnesses him fighting courageously with his troops. The description of his martyrdom is even more revealing and suspenseful as reported by Yakubu in the play.

> Yakubu: The greatest moment was when the Caliph fell. As the bullet struck him, he raised up his sword and screamed Allahu-Akbar! Allahu-Akbar! He was a great man indeed. With the bullets, he still cut down two more soldiers, then his Rawani loosened and his cap fell. He twisted in pain. Holding on to nothing but his guts. Slowly, he started to fall. And as he fell, the Madawaki noticed him, he covered him with his shield, the Ubandoma, all forming a human shield. But the Caliph had fallen, and with his last breath, he screamed again. (p 63)

This vivid description, apart from eliciting pity from the audience, also engenders a sense of pride and admiration for the Sultan's heroism in one breath, while at the same time drawing out his indignation against the military adventurism of the invading colonial army.

No wonder Adeniyi (2007:97) avers that, "history, which is written in the form of drama is, on a higher plane, more intense, more universal, and more philosophical than history which is written in a chronological manner and is more particular."

Conclusion

This study explicates the heroism of Attahiru, the last Sultan of the Sokoto Caliphate, by comparing the historical narrative with Yerima's artistic remake of the Sultan's very brief rule before he was overrun by the British colonialists because he refused to compromise his faith and surrender to them.

It is pertinent to note that apart from its function as a means of entertainment, drama, like most other works of art, is highly utilitarian. It is used to project messages. These messages could be mis-information or deliberate dis-information. They could also be a mere recantation of an existing situation, which is diversely chronicled by the playwright, in this case, a homologous and mere reflection of the existing situation or some sort of 'traditional sociology.' (Gugelberger, 1985:vi).

However, Williams (1977:95) maintains that a playwright should not merely reflect the ordinary appearances of his society, but the reality behind these appearances, or what the critic describes as the "inner nature of the world." This is what Yerima has done to the artistic Attahiru. He constructs him not just a figure in history, but a living, pulsating character, with definite idiosyncrasies and mien. He further delves beyond the façade to foreground the ideological bent of the society of the Caliphate, situating it in time and space. The audience is not left in doubt as to why the historical Attahiru behaved the way he did.

The heroism of Sultan Attahiru, therefore, in our view, is better celebrated in the fictional Attahiru than the historical narrative. This is because, we are transported into the world of the Caliph and we sympathise with him as we witness the rampaging colonial powers tearing his world apart; but we also stare in awe at the courage, fortitude and sheer brinkmanship of the Sultan who faced certain death heroically, taking his destiny in his own hands and dying for his belief, instead of grovelling at the feet of the detestable colonialists.

References

- Adeniyi, Victoria (2007), "A Comparative Study of Rotimi's *Ovonramwen Nogbaisi* and Yerima's *The Trials of Oba Ovonramwen*" in *Muse and Mimesis: Critical Perspectives on Ahmed Yerima's Drama*, (ed.) Adeoti, Gbemisola. Lagos: Spectrum Books.

- Etherton, Michael (1982), *The Development of African Drama*. London: Hutchinson University Library.

- Gott, Richard (2006), "Death of a Sultan" Web. 29th November, 2012. <www.guardian.co.uk/commentisfree/2006/.../post57>

- Gugelberger, George M. (ed) (1985), *Marxism and African Literature*, London: James Currey.

- "Harold Pinter: Nobel Lecture: Art, Truth & Politics", (2012) Nobelprize.org. http://www.nobelprize.org/nobel_prizes/literature/laureates/2005/pinter-lecture-e.html (30/11/2012).

- Jeremiah, S. Methuselah (2008), "Women and 'Heroism' in Modern Nigerian Drama: An Analysis of Irene Salami's Emotan: A Benin Heroine" in *KADA: Journal of Liberal Arts*, Faculty of Arts, Kaduna State University: PYLA–MAK.

- Johnston, H. A. S. (1967). *History of the Defeat of Sultan Attahiru in Burmi-Bajoga*, London: Oxford University Web. 28th November, 2012 < http://jajuwa.com/blog/?page_id=923>.

- Kimball, Alan (2012), "Ways of Seeing History" web, http://Pages.uoregon.edu/Kimball/ways.htm. (28/11/2012)

- Osofisan, Femi (1982), *Morountodun and Other Plays*, Ibadan: Longman.

- Rotimi, Ola (1974), *Ovonramwen Nogbaisi,* Benin City: Ethiope.
- Salami, Irene Isoken (2001), *Emotan: A Benin Heroine.* Jos: Mazlink.
- Soyinka, Wole (1975), *Death and the King's Horseman,* London: Eyre Methuen.
- <www.librarything.com/topic/73521> (Retrieved 28th November, 2012) Web.
- Webster's *Encyclopedic Unabridged Dictionary of the English Language* (1989), New York: Grammercy Books.
- Williams, Raymond (1977), *Marxism and Literature.* Oxford: University Press.
- Wolf, Janet (1993), *The Social Production of Art.* London: Macmillan.
- Yerima, Ahmed (1998), *Trials of Oba Ovoramwen.* Ibadan: Kraft.
- ------- (1999), *Attahiru.* Ibadan: Kraft Books.
- ------- (2003), *Fragmented Thoughts & Specifics.* Ikeja: Bookplus.
- -------- (2005) "Sultan Attahiru, the European Conquest and Dramaturgy" in *Northern Nigeria: A Century of Transformation,* 1915-2005.
- Yakubu, Mahmud Alhaji, Ibrahim Muhammad Jumare and Asma'u Garba Saeed (eds),*One Hundred Years of British Rule in Northern Nigeria,* Zaria: Arewa House, Centre for Historical Documentation and Research, Ahmadu Bello University.

Chapter Six

Trans-Fictional Migration and Inter-Textual Re-Interpretation: The Grimm Brothers' Tales in Muslim Hausa Literature

Abdalla Uba Adamu

Introduction

Intertextuality, one of the central ideas in contemporary literary theory, is not a transparent term and so, despite its confident utilisation by many theorists and critics, cannot be evoked in an uncomplicated manner. Such a term is in danger of meaning nothing more than whatever each particular critic wishes it to mean (Allen 2000). Julia Kristeva's attempt to combine Saussurean and Bakhtinian theories of language and literature produced the first articulation of intertextual theory in the late 1960s. Her main introduction to intertextuality argues that, 'any text is constructed as a mosaic of quotations; any text is the absorption and transformation of another. The notion of *intertextuality* replaces that of inter-subjectivity, and poetic language is read as at least double' (Kristeva and Moi, 1986:37).

Texts are, therefore, conjoined with others to reflect what could be called 'textual migration'. For, as Martinez (1996: 268)) argues, 'the concept of intertextuality requires...that we understand texts not as self-contained systems but as differential and historical, as traces and tracings of otherness, since they are shaped by the repetition and transformation of other textual structures.'

This intertextual template extends to more than shifts in narrative location and its context. A very common reflection of this narrative shift is in filmic adaptions of books as remakes. As Horton and McDougal (1998: 3) note, 'in terms of intertextuality...remakes-films that to one degree or another announce to us that they embrace one or more previous movies — are clearly something of a special case, or at least a more intense one.'

This chapter approaches textual migration from the intertextual perspective. It analyses the intertextual relationship between a cultural product, the story, and its trans-migrational adaptation, as an intervention on an existing discourse formation, which includes both the original product or text and the discourses using it, originating it, deriving from it or surrounding it. This intervention amounts to both an interpretation and an appropriation of the original text. In this regard, Landa (2005: 181) notes that, like other intertextual modes (translations, critical readings), adaptations produce a 'retroactive transformation of the original rather as it is used and understood in specific contexts and instances of communicative interaction.'

To investigate this textual migration, the chapter shall analyse two stories from the Grimm Brothers' collection of fourteen stories that were adapted in northern Nigeria by Abubakar Imam in the Hausa compendium of stories, *Magana Jari Ce,* 'ability to tell stories is a valuable possession', (Bargery 1943), published by the British colonial administration in Nigeria in 1940. As Bargery further notes,

> 'although the bulk of the stories are of foreign origin, few of the listeners will realise this, far from whatever source they may have been culled, they have been thoroughly assimilated by the able Hausa author, Malam Abubakar Imam Kagara, and then retold by him in his own words. They are in fact stories by a Hausa for Hausas—individuals and places are given Hausa names, and in other ways, the stories are very successfully given a true African setting.' (Bargery 1943: 100)

The original Grimm Brothers' stories were written by Jacob Ludwig Grimm (1785-1863) and Wilhelm Carl Grimm (1786-1859) in the early 1800s; and depict life as generations of central

Europeans knew it — capricious and often cruel. The two brothers, patriots determined to preserve Germanic folktales, were only accidental entertainers.

Inspired as children by a library of old books with tales that caught their imaginations, the brothers devoted a lifetime to collecting their own stories and folktales told to them mostly by women, young and old, which they eventually compiled into a book of fairy tales. They named their collection, *Children's and Household Tales* and published the first of its seven editions in Germany in 1812. Based mainly on oral narratives, the two hundred and ten stories in the Grimm's' collection represent an anthology of fairy tales, animal fables, rustic farces, and religious allegories with an everlasting literary value.

Grimm's Fairy Tales, as the English version is usually called, pervades world culture. So far, the collection has been translated into more than one hundred and sixty languages, from Inupiat in the Arctic to Swahili in Africa. The stories and their characters provide one of the most enduring cases of intermedial transformation — shifting from the pages into virtually every media: theatre, opera, comic books, film, paintings, rock music, advertising, fashion, etc. In the United States, the Grimm's collection furnished much of the raw material that helped launch Disney as a media giant.

In his analysis of the emergence of the Grimm Brothers' tales as international intercultural icons, Dollerup (1999:289) argues that they collected the tales to preserve the German cultural heritage in the wake of threats from Napoleonic Wars, 'and not because they intended to have the tales translated. For socio-cultural, geographical, and historical reasons, the Grimm and Andersen tales fused into an international genre as a result of translation.'

However, this analysis does not focus on the textuality of the main European stories, but the elements of the stories and how these elemental structures are intertextually altered to fit into an African Muslim society of the 1930s.

British Colonial Translations Bureau in Nigeria

In 1929, the British colonial administration in Nigeria set up a translation bureau initially in Kano, but later moved it to Zaria in 1931; it became the Literature Bureau in 1935 (Hayatu (1991). The first director of the bureau was a Mr. Whiting, although he was replaced later by Dr. Rupert East. The objectives of the bureau were to:

- translate books and materials from Arabic and English;
- write books in Hausa;
- produce textbooks for schools; and
- encourage indigenous authors.

Mr. Whiting's tenure saw the Hausa Roman script versions of some Arabic texts detailing local histories, notably *Tarikh Arbab Hadha al-balad al-Musamma Kano*, translated in English as *The Kano Chronicles* by H. R. Palmer and published in the *Journal of Royal Anthropological Institute*, Vol. 38 (1908) pp. 59-98 and re-published in his *Sudanese Memoirs* (3 volumes: London, 1928), 3: 92-132. An extended Hausa translation of this manuscript was supervised by Rupert East as *Hausawa Da Makwabtansu* (Translation Bureau Zaria 1933).

The establishment of the Translation Bureau ensured, through a literary competition in 1933, that a whole new set of reading materials, and consequently literary style, was created for the Muslim Hausa in northern Nigeria. This yielded the first clutch of now Hausa *boko* (modern writing in Roman alphabet) literature written in classical Hausa *(Ruwan Bagaja, Shehu Umar, Gankoki, Idon Matambayi, Jiki Magayi)* published in 1935. Since the scholastic tradition of the Hausa has always been the preserve of the Malam (teacher, scholar) class, even in popular literature the fountainheads carved out of that class reflected their antecedent scholastic traditions. Thus, the novels were written mainly by the scholars, with some, like Abubakar Imam who wrote *Ruwan Bagaja*, being quite young at the time (he was twenty-two when he wrote the novel). They had deep Islamic roots and actually required some convincing to even agree to write in the *boko* (Romanised) scripts in the first place, considering such activity as a dilution of their Islamic scholarship.

The main focus of the Translation Bureau was just that — translation of literary works using the sparkling brand new Romanised Hausa script. It was only when Dr. Rupert East took over in 1932 that it acquired the *persona* of what Dobronravine and Philips (2004) refer to as *Istanci* and became devoted to the wholesale translation of works into Hausa from far and near (although the further, the better because nearer literary communities, both geographically and culturally, such as The Sudan and Egypt were somehow ignored). The aim was to generate reading materials; more essentially, to enable colonial officers to polish their practice of Hausa language for communication than to empower the "natives" with enriched literary heritage. It was this obsession with translation of carefully selected works, rather than fully encouraging local indigenous initiatives into literary explorations, that earned this era of Hausa literary development the epithet of *Istanci* — principally due to the forceful nature of the Rupert East, its main protagonist.

For Rupert East, the most outstanding of the five Hausa novels published in 1935, was Abubakar Imam's *Ruwan Bagaja* (The Healing Waters). However, it was clear from the plot elements and general thematic structure of the novel that it was not a Hausa tale, unlike others that had clearly identifiable Hausa settings. Abubakar Imam, in an interview with Nicholas Pwedden (1995: 12, 14) stated that he was "inspired" to write *Ruwan Bagaja* after reading *Muqamat Al Hariri*: "in that story *(Ruwan Bagaja)* there were two characters — Abu Zaidu and Harisu — with one trying to defeat the other through cunning. I also used two men, on the basis of that technique, but I used the Hausa way of life to show how one character (Abubakar) defeats the other (Malam Zurke)."

It was this "inspiration" that was to become the root of the glocalisation of the foreign media by the Hausa performing artistes, which was heavily promoted by the British. In effect, Abubakar Imam and the British had planted a Trojan Horse within the entertainment mindset of the Hausa.

The *Muqamat,* translated into English by various authors as *The Assemblies of Al-Hariri: Fifty Encounters with the Shaykh Abu Zayd of Seruj Maqamat* was written by Abu Muhammad al-Qasim Hariri (1054-1121) and was widely available among Muslim scholars and intellectuals of northern Nigeria in its original Arabic, as set reading material for the advanced course of Arabic grammar after the completion of the Qur'anic phase of a Hausa Muslim's education.

Other sources used in writing *Ruwan Bagaja* included the core plot elements from *The Grimm Brothers' Fairy Tales* (especially *The Water of Life* from where the book derived its title), *Sinbad the Sailor,* and stories from *A Thousand and One Nights.* Thus, *Ruwan Bagaja* actually marked the transition from *Istanci* — direct translations of other works into Hausa — to its adaptive variety, *Imamanci* — the "transmutation" of transnational literature into Hausa mindset. Imam revealed he was taught this art of literary transmutation by Rupert East, who also,

> ...taught me many dos and don'ts. For example, he taught me never to allow a miscreant to triumph over a good character in any fictional story, such as a cheat or a fraud, even if he appears to be winning in the beginning and he is being highly respected and praised. That it is better to make him the loser at the end... On translation, he said if someone utters something nice, either in English or in Arabic, or any other language, when translating it into Hausa, you shouldn't be enslaved to the wordings of the statement, trying to act like you're translating the Koran or the Bible. What you're supposed to do, as long as you fully understand what the man said, *is to try and show genius in your own language just as he did in his,* i.e. yours should be as nice in Hausa as his was nice in English. That way Dr. East kept teaching me various techniques of writing until I understood them all (Pwedden 1995: 87, emphasis added).

Rupert East was, thus, the originator of Imamian transmutative strategy — *genius in your own language* — while Abubakar Imam was its script reader. It is from this transmutated strategy of Abubakar that we received the term *Ofishin Talifi*, for the Translation Bureau (instead of its original translation of *Ofishin Juye-Juye*, literally, 'the office for making copies'), and later, *Majalisar Dinkin Duniya* (literally, 'the council for sewing the world together'), for the United Nations.

Imamanci, as a literary technique and emergent media technology device, worked brilliantly because of the skills of the adapter, Abubakar Imam. However, Imam was to acknowledge the Svengali in Rupert East, when the latter recruited him, albeit temporarily, to work on producing more reading materials along the mold of *Ruwan Bagaja* and using its adaptive literary technique for the newly re-named Literature Bureau. According to Imam,

> From then on, he (East) assembled for me many story books in Arabic and English, especially Iranian texts. Fortunately I knew Arabic because I had learned it right from home. That's why I could understand the Arabic books unless... the language was too advanced. I read all of these books until I understood the techniques of established writers. When Dr. East realised that I had finished, he told me what to do and I set out to write. The first book I wrote was Magana Jari Ce (Speech is an Asset). Pwedden (1995: 88).

This book, *Magana Jari Ce*, became the unalloyed classic of Hausa literature; despite the heavy dosage of foreign elements it contained from books as diverse as *Alfu Layla wa Laylatun, Kalilah wa Dimnah, Bahrul Adab, Hans Andersen Fairy Tales, Aesop Fables, The Grimm Brothers' Fairy Tales, Tales from Shakespeare,* and *Raudhul Jinan* (Abdallah 1998).

Magana Jari Ce is composed of about eighty stories — mainly narrated by a parrot, Aku (although joined in a competitive mode by another parrot, Hazik), to various audiences and settings. In an interview (Wali 1976), Abubakar Imam stated that he had taken the figure of the parrot and its technique of story-telling from a Persian book, most likely *Tuti-Name* (Book of Parrot), written by Zia ul-Din Nakhshabi (Kablukov 2004). Indeed, further analysis of *Magana Jari Ce* reveals the following as its source material:

> Eleven stories from *A Thousand and One Nights*
> Two stories from the Indian collection *Panchatantra*
> Two stories from a Persian version of the Indian collection *Sukasaptati*
> One story that is of Persian origin
> Fourteen fables from the Grimm Brothers'
> Two fables from Hans Andersen
> Seven short stories from *Decameron* by Boccaccio
> One based on a Biblical story (from Old Testament)
> One based on a Greek myth about the king of Macedona
> One based on a fable by W. Hauff
> Fourteen stories were either original or derived from unknown sources (Jez and Stanislaw, 2003: 23-28).

The narrative style adopted in *Magana Jari Ce* is closely patterned on *A Thousand and One Nights*, in that the narrator relates a series of stories to delay the departure to war of a very strong-willed prince; whereas in the original *A Thousand and One Nights*, the narrator created the stories to delay the execution of a stubborn princess.

The pattern adopted by the British in creating globalised literature for indigenous African audiences seemed to have been generic to all parts of Africa. For instance, in East Africa, the British colonial administration followed a close strategy of educational development as that of northern Nigeria. Thus, when Tanganyika became part of the British empire in 1919, the school system was modernised and the Swahili language was then standardised in 1925-30. In the following years, there was the need for Swahili reading matter and also as a medium to propagate the modern way of life in a world widely ruled by Britain.

An important medium in this respect was the monthly journal *Mambo Leo* (Today's Affairs), founded by the Education Department in Dar es Salaam in 1923. Besides essays and news of all kinds, the journal also contained entertaining texts, among them translations of foreign literature. These were usually issued in a serialised form. Issues from the initial period of 1923-32 include adaptations of literary tales, such as "*The Voyages of Sindbad the Sailor*" (1923-24), *"Aladdin and the Wonderful Lamp" (1925-26)*, *"Ali Baba and the Forty Thieves"* (1926), Longfellow's *Tale of Hia-watha* (1927) or Daniel Defoe's *Robinson Crusoe* (1928). All of these stories were published without any introduction, source reference or further comment. Further translations included Stevenson's *Kisiwa Chenye Hazima (Treasure Island;* 1929), Haggard's *Mashimo ya Mfalme Sulemani (King Solomon's Mines;* 1929), Kipling's *Hadithi za Maugli, Mtoto Aliyelelewa na Mbwa Mwitu (The Story of Mowgli, the Child Who Was Raised by a Wild Dog, The Jungle Books; 1929)*, Swift's *Safari za Gulliver (Gulliver's Travels;* 1932) among others (Geider 2004: 252).

The intertextual path, therefore, seemed to have been directly created by the British colonial administration in their African colonies as a practical alternative acceptable to them in tackling the problems caused by the dearth of indigenous literature. This was more so as both Tanganyika and northern Nigeria had a strong base of the oral tradition, which could easily be transmutated into the written text, in order to serve the same purpose as the imported story books.

Grimm Brothers' Tales in Africa

The story sources analysed in this chapter are four – two original translations into English from the German stories in the Grimm Brothers' collection; and two corresponding intertextual renderings in Hausa language by Abubakar Imam. To facilitate the analysis, each story is given a code which more easily identifies it; for example CG for Clever Gretel, and KDK for *Labarin Kalala da Kalalatu*. The listing of the sources is as follows:

- Original: 'Der gute Handel' [The Good Bargain], *Kinder- und Hausmärchen* [Children's and Household Tales, 1857] No. 07 [TGB]
- Translation: 'Kwadayi Mabudin Wahala' [Greed is the gateway to misery] (Magana Jari Ce, Vol 3, pp. 96-106 [KMW]
- Original: *'Das kluge Gretel'* [Clever Gretel], *Kinder- und Hausmärchen* [Children's and Household Tales, 1857] No. 77 [CG]
- Translation: '*Labarin Kalala da Kalatu*' [The Story of Kalala and Kalalatu], *Magana Jari Ce*, Vol 1, pp. 14-18. [KAK]

Case Study #1: 'Clever Gretel': The Original German Version Translated into English

KHM 77 [English] - Clever Gretel (Vol 1, Nr. 77)

The story is about an extremely vain cook, Gretel, who not only seemed to like dressing in red, and twirling around the kitchen, but also had a penchant for wine and the food she cooked for her master. One day, he asked her to prepare a meal of two fowls for himself and a guest who will be joining them later. She scalded the chickens, plucked them, put them on the spit, and towards evening set them before the fire, that they might roast. With the chickens roasting over the fire, Gretel kept taking a swig of her favourite wine, all the time muttering about the lateness of the master and his guest.

When the chickens were all done, the aroma became too much to bear for Gretel, and helped along by a continuous supply of wine, she began to eat the chickens bit by bit until nothing was left. Just at about that time, the master returned with the guest and instructed Gretel to bring the meal to the table, while he sharpened a knife.

Gretel, knowing there was nothing for them to eat, ran to the guest and informed him that he should disappear because her master was sharpening a knife to cut off the guest's ears. The guest ran away on hearing this. Gretel then went to the master and scolded him for bringing in a greedy guest who had taken off with the two chickens. The master ran out after the guest, with the knife still in his hand, asking the guest to stop so that he could take only one. The guest, thinking the master meant only one ear, kept running away.

Labarin Kalala da Kalalatu: Clever Gretel in Hausa

KHM 77 [Hausa] – 'Labarin Kalala da Kalalatu' [The Story of Kalala and Kalalatu], Magana Jari Ce, Vol 1, pp. 14-18.

Once upon a time there was a man, Kalala, who lived with his wife, Kalalatu. Kalala was a very generous man, who always invited guests to have dinner with him. He used to have the dinner with his neighbour, but had to stop it because the neighbour kept complaining about Kalalatu's cooking. When it got too much, he stopped and, instead, went out in the highway and invited complete strangers. Kalatu, his wife, did not like having guests to dinner because she always got a tiny portion; whereas she would get more when there were just the two of them. She got her own back at the husband by simply splitting any meal into two and eating one-half. If Kalala complained, she replied that she was able to salvage only the little he could now see, as the rest had been burnt. He never complained about this because he was a patient man.

One day, he went to the market and bought two hefty chickens, which he instructed her to cook. She obliged, but while she was cooking, the aroma kindled her craving. She started lamenting that, despite her craving for these chickens, she would probably only end up with a tiny thigh. She continued cooking the chickens, but eventually the craving overcame her and she started eating bits and pieces, until eventually she ate away half of a chicken. Kalala had earlier told her to take the thigh as her share.

She now ran to the door to see if Kalala had returned with the expected guest and when she did not see them, she sat down, looking at the whole chicken and a half, lamenting to herself that they would get cold before Kalala and the guest arrived. Since she had no reasonable explanation for how half of the chicken disappeared, she decided to eat the other half too, leaving only one chicken. When Kalala and guest still did not show up, she ate the other chicken as well.

Soon after, Kalala and the guest arrived and he called out to her to prepare the dinner for the two of them. Kalala in the meantime fetched a knife and started sharpening it. While Kalalatu was thinking about what to do, she heard the noise of a guest greeting at the doorway. When she answered the door, the guest informed her he had been invited to a dinner with Kalala, praying for the couple, *"Allah Ya saka mu ku da alhairi"* [May Allah reward you abundantly with His grace]. Kalalatu glared at him, berating at his foolishness to expect a dinner invitation from a total stranger. She explained to the guest that Kalala was actually mentally deranged; he usually would invite a guest to his house on the pretext of eating dinner, only to cut off his ears. Indeed, right now he could be heard sharpening a knife to cut off the guest's ears, so advised the guest to run away, which he did.

She then went to Kalala and berated him on his manner of randomly extending invitation to unknown people to dinner, because the latest guest he invited had stolen the two chickens and run off with them. Kalala then ran out of the house with a knife in hand, calling after the guest to give him at least one – meaning one of the chickens. The guest thought Kalala meant his ear, so kept running. Kalala was unable to keep up with him and eventually gave up and returned home. Kalalatu asked if he had retrieved the chickens and he replied in the negative. He vowed never to invite unknown guests to his dinner table again. [Personal translation.]

Intertextual Interpretation of CG and KDK

While *Clever Gretel* (CG) and *Kalala da Kalalatu* (KDK) share the same plot elements, the transfictional migration of CG created a different setting and characterisations in KDK. In CG, a landed master apparently in a big farm house, typical of

European estates has a cook, while in the KDK the two had to be married. This is because it would not be feasible to explain to Muslim Hausa children of the 1930s how a man and a woman could cohabit in the same house, without being married, and without being related in any way. Imam, therefore, brings in marriage as the moral and religious element to explain the cohabitation of the Master and the Cook.

The psychological state of Gretel is revealed in CG - fondness for wine, and probably getting drunk; indeed, her errant behaviour is explained on the basis of her intoxication and consumption of copious amount of wine. However, Imam could not bring the Muslim Kalalatu to drink; he, therefore, makes her into a whining housewife – forever complaining about her husband's generosity in inviting total strangers to dinner, while virtually denying her a full taste of what she cooks, despite her toils and labour. Thus, in both two cases, the women are reflected as weak and susceptible to their inner desires; although more so with Gretel, who, in addition to whining, has vanity and wine added to her mental portfolio.

A common frame to both CG and KDK is the feature of inviting guests to dinner. While this might be a European tradition, it is firmly entrenched in Islam, as indicated in *Surat Al-Insan*, which says of Muslim believers:

> They [are those who] fulfill [their] vows and fear a Day whose evil will be widespread. And they give food in spite of love for it to the needy, the orphan, and the captive. Surat Al-'Insan (The Man) 76:7-8.

Imam, therefore, domesticated the story within the framework of the Islamic injunction concerning generosity to strangers. Consequently, by using Islamic motifs within the context of the original story of non-family feeding, Imam domesticated the Grimm Brothers' tale to Muslim Hausa community.

While in CG, the story did not exactly end — a final scene is missing to indicate the consequences of the Master's invitation — Imam finished his own rendering by closing the tale neatly in the form of a pledge by Kalala not to invite guests to his dinner table again. While this might have provided the creative Imam the justification he needed to close the story — and provide a punch line with the premise of a stolen dinner — it also injected a lot of humour into the rendition (e.g. by suggesting that the guest is mentally deranged).

Illustrations and Visual Iconography of KDK

In order to strengthen the storylines in *Magana Jari Ce,* the editor (Rupert East) utilised copious illustrations that bring out the main plots of the stories — adapting some from the original illustration in the Grimm Brothers' tales. The illustrations were made by the Belgian artist, Jacqueline De Naeyer, who was employed by Rupert East after World War II to work at the Gaskiya Corporation. East eventually ended up marrying De Naeyer and moved back to the UK with her (Furniss 2011). Her illustrations of the various Gaskiya Corporation publications were quite illuminating for their reflection of the Hausa society in the 1930s. The sketch of the domesticated Clever Gretel story in *Kalala da Kalatu* in particular is a good example, as shown in Fig. 1:

Fig. 1. Kalala da Kalalatu [Clever Gretel]

The figure very well communicates the last scene of both the CG and KDK stories, when the Master/Kalala runs out of the house with a knife in hand, asking the guest to stop and give him 'one'; the flowing gowns ('babbar riga') of the men; furthermore, the picture of the feet of the guest running shoeless visibly demonstrates his desperation and the haste in which he leaves the house — a typical depiction in Hausa comic scripts of someone running away from danger. Kalalatu is shown in the background with an impressionistic glee on her face, while the dog (not mentioned anywhere in both the CG and KDK narratives) adds colour to the situation by shown to be yelping at the guest as well.

What seems to be communicated most effectively, however, is the look of terror on the guest's face. Altogether, the illustration provides enough evidence of the character of the *dramatis personae* in the story, as well as its farmland setting – for it is clearly not depicting a highly densely populated cluster of villages. This interplay between the visual elements in Fig. 1 communicates the comical nature of the story, helped along by the inscrutable face of knife-wielding Kalala and the terror-stricken guest.

Case Study 2: 'The Good Bargain': The Original German Version Translated into English

KHM 7 [English] - The Good Bargain (Vol 1, Nr. 7)

A peasant sold his cow for seven silver coins (talers). On the way home, he heard frogs in a pond calling 'aik', 'aik', 'aik'. Thinking they were referring to his money, he berated them for saying it was eight ('aik'), insisting that the correct amount was seven. When they continued, he threw the seven coins into the pond for them to verify. When they continued with their 'aik' song, he left, frustrated at their stupidity and inability to count properly.

Next, he slaughtered another cow hoping to sell the meat. On the way to the market he met a pack of dogs, led by a greyhound, which kept yelping at the meat. He then decided to give the meat to the dog with the intention that should the dog eat it, he, the peasant, would then collect the payment from the dog's master. He then went to the master after three days to collect the money. The master became annoyed at this request and kicked the peasant out, who now went to the king to complain first about his money being seized by frogs in the pond, then the butcher refusing to give him his money for the meat, which his greyhound had eaten.

The king and his daughter were amused at this narrative, which made the king so happy that he decided to give his daughter to the peasant in marriage. The peasant declined, stating that he already had a wife, and had no wish to see wives in every corner of his house. The king became annoyed, but remained calm as he ordered the peasant to return in three days for a special reward of five hundred. On the way out, he met a palace sentry who had witnessed everything. The sentry and a Jew thought the King meant to give the peasant five hundred gold pieces, so they tricked him immediately into promising to give them two hundred and three hundred, respectively, in exchange for smaller coins that had less value.

On the appointed day, the peasant returned to the palace. When he was ordered to remove his shirt, the peasant realised that the king meant to give him five hundred strokes of the cane, whereupon he shouted that under the agreement they had two hundred should really go to the sentry, while three hundred should be given to the Jew. The King then ordered the blows to be delivered to the sentry and the Jew. The King was so amused by this turn of events that he opened his treasury to the peasant to take any amount he wanted. The peasant filled his pockets with a lot of coins. However, he was heard complaining later at an inn that he was cheated by the king – since he did not know how much he had in his pocket, whereas he was certain if he had been given the five hundred the king mentioned at first that would have been more substantive.

The Jew, who followed him to the inn, overheard this and reported to the King, who in turn and in rage, asked the Jew to bring back the peasant. The Jew was happy, certain now that the peasant would also be punished. When the Jew returned to inform the peasant about the summons, he felt he needed a new coat befitting his new moneyed status, in order to appear more presentable before the king,. However, he could not get any around; the Jew, therefore, offered to lend him his own coat so as to hasten the return to the palace. The peasant was satisfied with this, put on the Jew's coat, and the two went off to the palace.

When the king confronted the peasant with what the Jew had reported about him, he denied it and explained that the Jew was an incurable liar – so much that he could even claim ownership of the coat he, the peasant, was wearing. The Jew jumped up and explained that the coat truly belonged to him, which merely increased the ire of the king, who subjected him to another bout of punishment for slandering the peasant. Eventually, the peasant went home wearing the good coat and with some good money in his pockets, saying to himself, "This time, I made it."

'Kwadayi Mabudin Wahala' [Greed Leads to Hardship]: The Good Bargain in Hausa

KHM 07 [Hausa] Kwadayi Mabudin Wahala (Magana Jari Ce, Vol 3, pp. 96-106)

There was once a man called Dandamau who was so foolish that people considered him a simpleton. He was so doltish that he was exempted from paying the community tax. One day, however, he had a quarrel with the ward head, who vowed to put him on the list of those who must pay the tax, arguing that if Dandamau was really such a dolt, how could he have maintained his family?

Thus, Dandamau was forced to find job as an apprentice for a woodcarver where, after working for some time, he was able to earn nine coins, which was enough to pay his tax. On the way home, he passed by a pond and heard frogs singing, 'kwas', 'kwas', 'kwas,' [Takwas in Hausa]. He stopped and started arguing with them, insisting that he had nine, not eight coins. When they continued, he threw the nine coins in the pond and asked them to count themselves. When they did not return the coins, he left, muttering about this incident of highway robbery in the pond.

Shortly after he arrived home, the ward head sent for the tax payment and Dandamau requested to be given more time. His wife also informed him that their pantry was empty. He then took one of his lambs with the intention of selling it in the market; but later changed his mind and decided to slaughter it instead and sell the meat to the head of butchers. On his way, he was accosted by a pack of dogs, led by a spotted dog, which was owned by the head of butchers. Dandamau now decided to give the meat to the dog with the understanding that it would help him to collect the money from its owner.

Later, he met the head butcher and asked for his money after recounting that the butcher's dog had taken the meat on his behalf. The head butcher pointed the dog to Dandamau and asked him to request the money directly from it — which Dandamau did, to the annoyance of the butcher. When the dog ignored Dandamau, he lamented that after their last encounter the dog must have become mute and, therefore, insisted that the butcher should pay for the meat which the dog ate. The butcher became so annoyed that he threw Dandamau out of the shop.

Dandamau then reported the case to the chief of the village, whom he met sitting in the audience chamber together with his daughter. He narrated all that happened between himself and the dog and the butcher's response. This made the princess laugh so much; she had earlier been downcast because of her mother's death. As a reward for making the princess laugh, the chief gave the hand of the princess in marriage to Dandamau. He declined, saying he already had a wife. The chief became angry and asked him to return the following day to receive 100 on his body. Dandamau left with expecting that he would be given a cash reward of one hundred coins. On his way out of the palace, he was accosted by the chief's butler, who tricked him into promising to exchange his anticipated reward of one hundred coins with other coins of lesser denomination, but of the same quantity.

However, when Dandamau returned to the palace the next day, there were no coins; instead, the chief instructed that he should be given one hundred strokes of the cane on his body for being very foolish. Weighing his new fortune before the punishment was effected, Dandamau shouted out to the chief that it should go to the butler instead, because they had agreed earlier that he should hand over "the one hundred" he was to collect from the palace. When the chief enquired about this arrangement, the butler answered in the affirmative, but explained that it was in respect of coins, not lashes. Nonetheless, the butler was made to take off his clothes and receive the one hundred lashes, as per their bargain. The chief, amazed at Dandamau's luck, then gave him the chance to go to the treasury and take as much fortune in gold coins as he could. Dandamau did just that, filling his garments with as many coins as he could carry.

However, as he walked away he began to wonder if the gold pieces he had in his pocket were equivalent to the one hundred coins he would have received the first time, complaining to himself loudly about the amount and insisting that he should have been given the one hundred coins instead of the few that he had now collected in the folds of his garment. The butler, still smarting from the lashes, overheard this, and ran to inform the chief about Dandamau's ingratitude. The chief initially wanted to dismiss this, but then decided to investigate. Unknown to them, Dandamau's brother had overheard the butler's report to the chief, and quickly scripted to his brother what to say when summoned by the chief.

When the butler summoned Dandamau to the chief's presence, Dandamau suggested that he needed to change his gown as the one he had on him was dirty due to the large number of coins he carried in its folds. The butler, eager to see that Dandamau got punished, quickly offered him the use of his own and together they returned to the chief's audience chamber. The chief started berating Dandamau about what he was alleged to have said, but Dandamau insisted that the butler was such a compulsive liar that he might even claim ownership of the gown that he was wearing. The butler quickly asserted his ownership of the gown, which the chief ignored and ordered him to pay the cost of the one hundred strokes of the cane he was earlier given, or face another round of similar punishment. The butler paid swiftly and a portion of the money was given to Dandamau, whose brother now took charge and managed it all, making them quite wealthy in a short time.

Intertextual Interpretation of TGB and KMW

While in TGB the peasant has no name, in KMW he is referred to as Dandamau, a conjured nickname that is coined (perhaps purposely for this story, as the name is not common in Hausaland) to mean 'the muddler' or one who muddles things up, either due to forgetfulness, or due to sheer doltishness. The central theme — greed does not pay — of *The Good Bargain* (TGB) is maintained in *Kwadayi Mabudin Wahala* (KMW), but with significant inter-cultural changes.

The original German word for eight, 'acht', became an onomatopoeic referent by the frogs in both Hausa, English and German. Whereas the German 'acht' and English 'eight'/'aik' share tonal antecedents, however, the Hausa word for 'eight' is 'takwas'—which has different tonal properties from the European versions. Imam's use of 'kwas', a root-derivative of 'takwas' or eight, pays homage to the original frog song lyric of 'aik'/'acht'. In this, however, Imam expects the reader to link 'kwas' with 'takwas' or eight. Further, instead of seven coins in the original, Imam changed it to nine coins — a higher value amount considering the amount of labour done to earn it.

One significant departure, though, which Imam could not transmutate effectively is the issue of rejecting the princes as a bride. In both TGB and KMW, the protagonist rejects the princess given to him as a wife. It is doubtful this could happen in Hausaland of the 1930s, when marrying such a wife would have opened the gateway for Dandamau to become a member of the gentry. Furthermore, no one dares refuse the offer of a wife by the king; especially if the bride is the king's own daughter. Nonetheless, Imam's retention of this scene in his translation perhaps has a deliberate creative strategy to further emphasise Dandamau's foolhardiness.

A plot twist inserted in KMW, which is totally absent from the original TBG, is the brother who suggests a change of shirt for Dandamau before the latter is taken to the chief's presence. In the original TGB, it is the Jew who lends the shirt. However, since the Jew has been excised out of KMW, the dastardly acts of the Jew are transferred to the greedy wily palace butler. The Jew's greed then becomes easily seen in palace butlers, most of who are of slave origin and use every means necessary to survive – including subterfuge. The presence of a brother for Dandamau presents the latter with a credible narrative presence in the story in the absence of the stereotyped greed of the Jew in TGB.

Thus, TGB ends up as an anti-Semitic narrative with the Jew portrayed as greedy and receiving the short end of the stick. Imam avoids this racial profiling by inwardly turning to the intrigues of a chief's palace and finding a villain in the butler. This is necessary in order to remove the Jew from the narrative. The possible reason for this was that Imam was given the task of translating the stories by British colonial officers. It could be possible that not wishing to cause offence, he decided to censor his writing to remove the anti-Semitism in the story. Even closer to the Germans, the Danish translators of the Grimm Brother's Tales dropped two stories that were considered anti-Semitic, including *The Good Bargain* (Dollerup 1999: 246).

Illustrations and Visual Iconography of KMW

KMW was also illustrated to further draw attention of the reader to the comic turns and events in the narrative. Even the original story has an illustration that depicts the protagonist as a wild-eyed moron.

Fig. 2: Peasant and Dandamau at the pond

The line drawings in Fig 2 employ different motifs to relate the scene at the pond. While the peasant on the left is drawn in a highly impressionistic manner typical of European art illustration, the Hausa version on the right again reflects a typical Hausa landscape, with sparse vegetation (despite being close to a body of water). The Dandamau illustration, however, conveys the scene more effectively, as it is a dynamic drawing which communicates action. This artistic dynamism is further reflected in Fig. 3 below:

Fig. 3: The Chief, his daughter and Dandamau

The illustration in Fig. 3 captures the scene where Dandamau relates his story to the chief, with his daughter laughing at the narrative. Despite their merriment, however, Dandamau is quite sober-faced, to indicate that to him, the incidence about the butcher's dog not paying him for the meat it ate is not funny. The artist also maintains consistency in Dandamau's dress, for we can see that he is wearing the same long gown as at the pond scene.

Thus, in the three illustrations that accompany the two stories, subtexts were created that have added value to the main narrative. This is because the interplay among the visual elements of the illustrations helps to emphasise the specific and non-specific aspects of the narratives and lend a cinematic perspective to the stories.

Conclusion

Both *The Good Bargain* and *The Clever Gretel* are comedic narratives. Abubakar Imam's rendering of the two stories took the comedic narrative a notch higher by inserting interpretative dialogue structures absent from the originals. In *"Kalala da Kalalatu"*, the first comedic point was the made-up names of the characters — such names do not exist in Hausa naming conventions, but created in sound-alike manner to give a domestic synergy between a husband and his wife.

In her attempt to frighten off the guest, Kalalatu informs him that only a deranged person would invite someone totally strange to his home for dinner, a statement that contradicts Kalala's sincere public-spiritedness (and perhaps his sense of Islamicity). Kalalatu is not against such invitations, but against the small portions she gets after her toils, whenever a guest comes to dinner. For both European and African audiences, therefore, Kalalatu/Gretel's actions might have signaled a blow for women's rights in the domestic sphere.

Kalala da Kalatu Islamises *Clever Gretel* by marrying Gretel to a husband, rather than co-habiting a large farmhouse with a male master — a situation that is culturally not acceptable to Muslim African audiences, even if acceptable to the non-African audiences.

Further identities were brought in to make the adapted Hausa narrative of *The Good Bargain* more acceptable and interesting. In giving the peasant a specific name in Imam's rendering of the story as *Kwadayi Mabudin Wahala,* Imam, therefore, re-orients the narrative to make it more distinctly African. This is because almost all African folktales are rooted in specific naming conventions of characters. KMW gave the peasant two names

— his actual name, Dandamau, and his community referent, Dolo. Dandamau is a play on 'damawa', to muddle things, thus Dandamau can mean 'muddled one', while Dolo means simpleton — all combined to paint the picture of an apparently unintelligent person. It would have been difficult for Imam to use peasant — *dan kauye*, country bumpkin – in his translation, as that would not have been considered politically correct. By giving the original German peasant an African name, Imam, therefore, created a metafictional character in which a secondary character is created within the narrative of a primary character.

Getting rid of the Jew character — either for aversion to anti-Semitism in Imam, or out of fear of what the European colonial overlords would think of an African portrayal of a Jew —created a narrative discontinuity for Imam. He solved this by creating another metafictional character in the form of a brother for Dandamau who leads the remaining part of the narrative, since Dandamau is too much of a simpleton to wriggle out of the situation. This poetic license, therefore, gave Imam the opportunity to reinforce the concept of one being one's 'brother's keeper' in a virtually literal sense and further brings out the African sense of community responsibility towards each other. The peasant in TGB has no brother, at least in the English translations of the tale.

While the stories of *Magana Jari Ce* analysed in this paper are treated as inter-cultural texts — since there is no cultural contiguity between the source texts and target texts — they nevertheless, provide an inter-cultural mirror of the society. They also demonstrate the Imamian strategy of creating a wholly new fictional substrate on which to affix his characters using more comedic frames, which, subsequently, became characteristic of all Abubakar Imam's fictional works. Thus, Imam's re-orientation of the original source texts has succeeded in creating a literary corpus that has become, to all intents and purposes, totally African.

References

- Abdallah, A. M. M. (1998), "Abubakar Imam: Nazarin Tushe da Ginuwar Ayukansa na Adabi" [Abubakar Imam: Analysis of the Original Sources of his Literature] (Unpublished PhD thesis) Kano: Bayero University, Kano, Nigeria.
- Allen, G. (2000), *Intertextuality*, London: Routledge.
- Bargery, G.P. (1943) '*Review of Magana Jari Ce.*' Africa, 14 (2), 99-100.
- Dobronravine, N. and Philips, J. E. (2004), "*Hausa Ajami Literature and Script: Colonial Innovations and Post-Colonial Myths in Northern Nigeria*", Sudanic Africa 15 (2004): 85-110
- Dollerup, C. (1999). *Tales and Translation: The Grimm Tales From Pan-Germanic Narratives to Shared International Fairytales.* Amsterdam: J. Benjamin.
- Furniss, G. (2011), "On Engendering Liberal Values in the Nigerian Colonial State: The Idea Behind the Gaskiya Corporation. *Journal of Imperial and Commonwealth History*, 39 (1), 95–119.
- Geider, T. (2004), "*Alfu Lela Ulela: The Thousand and One Nights* in Swahili-Speaking East Africa", *Fabula* 45 (3/4), 246-260.
- Hayatu, H. (1991) "NORLA and the Story of Publishing in Former Northern Nigeria — An Overview from the Colonial Times to the Present", in Hayatu, H. (ed), *Gaskiya Corporation Zaria: 50 Years of Truth: The Story of Gaskiya Corporation Zaria*, 1939-1991, Zaria: Gaskiya Corporation.
- Horton, A., & McDougal, S. Y. (1998), "Introduction', Horton, A., & McDougal, S. Y. (eds.), *Play It Again, Sam: Retakes on Remakes,* pp. 1-12. Berkeley: University of California Press.

References

- Imam, A. A. (1940), *Magana Jari Ce, Zaria:* Literature Bureau. 3 vols. Illus.

- Jez, B., & Pilaszewicz, S. (January 01, 2003), "Foreign Influences and Their Adaptation to the Hausa Culture in *Magana Jari Ce* by Abubakar Imam," *Studies of the Department of African Languages and Cultures,* 33, 5-28.

- Kablukov, E. (2004). "India and Central Asia: Cultural Relations in the Middle Ages". *Dialogue (A Quarterly Journal of Astha Bharati) 6 (2).* Retrieved from http://www.asthabharati.org/Dia_Oct04/Kablukov.htm.

- Kristeva, J., & Moi, T. (1986), *The Kristeva Reader,* New York: Columbia University Press.

- Landa, J. A. G. (2005), "Adaptation, Appropriation, Retroaction: Symbolic interaction with Henry V. In M. Aragay (ed.), *Books in Motion: Adaptation, Intertextuality, Authorship* (pp. 81-200). Amsterdam: Rodopi.

- Martínez, M. J. (1996), "Intertextuality: Origins and Development of the Concept," *Atlantis,* XVIII (1-2), pp. 268-285.

- Pwedden, N. (1995), "The Abubakar Imam Interview", *Harsunan Nijeriya,* XVII, 86-110.

- Translation Bureau, Zaria, Northern Nigeria, (1933), *Labarun Hausawa da Makwabtansu: Littafi na Biyu.* Lagos: C.M.S. Bookshop.

- Wali, Z. N. (1976), *"Nazari a Kan Magana Jari Ce",* [Analysis of Magana Jari Ce]. (Unpublished B.A. dissertation), Bayero University, Kano.

Chapter Seven

The Influence of Arabic on Nigerian Literature: A Study of Some Selected Works of Abubakar Imam

Jamiu Muhammad Yunusa

Introduction

Arabic writing and literature are the leading components of northern Nigerian literary heritage. Writing in Arabic was so widespread that even the local language of Hausa and other minority languages were written in *Ajami*,[12] the non-Arabic system of writing that was based on an adaptation of the Arabic orthography. Until now, no serious enquiry into the cultural history of the north is possible without some degree of knowledge in the Arabic language, which was why the early British colonial masters equipped themselves reasonably well with the language[13] before successfully penetrating the region. In fact, Arabic is so entrenched in the northern history that today it has become practically impossible to divest the northern Nigeria identity from its Arabic heritage.

Literacy had been established in the north long before the coming of the colonial system of Western education. This was the more reason why the colonial masters felt compelled to use the existing heritage as a tool in introducing their own language and methods of education. Thus, it was no coincidence that the leading personnel used in grounding the Western education in the region were those who were already learned in the Arabic tradition. This was done successfully through encouraging the writing of Hausa

---

12 Hans Wehr (1961), *A Dictionary of Modern Written Arabic*, Lebanon: Maktabatul Lubnan, p. 801
13 Hans Wehr (1961), *A Dictionary of Modern Written Arabic*, Lebanon: Maktabatul Lubnan, p. 801

stories using the Roman letters. At a point, a competition was introduced with good prizes attached to the winners, among whom the most successful was Alhaji Abubakar Imam.

This chapter intends to study how Arabic had a particular impact on the selection and crafting of Imam's stories, whose environment of writing was the predominantly Hausa speaking northern region of Nigeria. It is quite apparent that, although he wrote the stories in Hausa using the Roman alphabets, the corpus of his sources and styles had been influenced by those of other writers in the Arabic language and literature tradition. This shall be considered with specific reference to the stories in the two books: *Ruwan Bagaja* and *Magana Jari Ce*.

Alhaji Abubakar Imam (1911 – 1981 A.D)

"Imam was a man of many roots; his earliest ancestry could be traced to Dikwa in the former Borno Empire (now in the present Borno State). His great grandparents found themselves in the present Niger State, after a migration many centuries before the Sokoto Jihad in 1804.[14]" He was born in 1911 A.D. in Kagara, which was then a division of Kwantagora Province.

Alhaji Imam trained as a teacher at the old Katsina Training Centre, after which he took up a teaching appointment at the Katsina Middle School in 1932. He wrote his first creative story book, *Ruwan Bagaja*, when he was just twenty-two years old. His talent and commitment to creative writing was recognised and appreciated by Dr. Rupert M. East, who invited him to Gaskiya Corporation, Zaria where he was exposed more to the techniques of writing. On his return to Katsina, he was charged with writing more books. It was then he wrote *Karamin Sani Kukumi Ne* in 1937. Imam was appointed pioneer editor of the popular Hausa newspaper, *Gaskiya Ta fi Kwabo*, that first came into circulation in 1939. He was at the helm of affairs in this newspaper for twelve years.

---

14   Ahmad al-Askandary et al, *al-Mufassal fi Tarikhil Adabil Arabiyyi* (n. d.), p. 80

He made his first trip to England in company of some West African commonwealth journalists in 1943. He was appointed the first chairman of Public Complaints Commission by the North Central State in 1974. Apart from the mentioned works, he later added others that are equally very popular like *Yakin Duniya Na Biyu, Tafiya Mabudin Ilmi, Tarihin Annabi da Halifofi.*

Alhaji Dr. Abubakar Imam died on Friday 19th June, 1981 at the age of seventy.[15] He had received many honours, such as O.B.E. (Order of the British Empire); C.O.N. (Commander of the Order of the Niger), N.N.M.C., and Hon. LLD. from the University of Ibadan.

Sources of His Stories

It is quite apparent that at the root of Imam's stories was the orature and written literature readily available in his traditional environment. He sourced his stories largely from the large volumes of narratives that were available to pupils in Arabic Islamiyah Schools in the precolonial education system of northern Nigeria. This system was practiced in almost every part of the region. A group of pupils was gathered by their teacher in a spacious area where lessons on many topics were taught in the local languages. This practice was not peculiar to the region, as it cut across all the Muslim West Africa and beyond. The difference, however, was that while some of the tales and lores narrated to the children in order to teach them about literature in other parts, the stories told to the young children in the Hausa–speaking areas were mostly Arabic stories translated and adapted to the culture in order to suit the understanding of the children.

Imam was not only a product of this foundation, he had as well acquired quality advanced knowledge in Arabic and Islamic disciplines before he was introduced to Western Education. This massive literacy background, to a very large extent, inspired his creativity, thereby making his works a true picture of his society.

---

15   A clear description of the genre can be found in Dr. Dayfi Shawqi (2005), *al-Fannu wa Madhahibuhu fin Nathril Arabiy*, Darul Ma'arif, 6th edition, p. 247.

The Mode of His Stories

The mode chosen by Alhaji Imam in writing his stories strongly suggests the influence of the Arabic literary genre known as *Maqamah*. This genre of Arabic rhythmic prose, became popular in the Abbasyd Dynasty when Arabic literature blossomed tremendously, thereby accommodating many new genres. The first person who popularised the genre was Abul-Fadhl Ahmad bin Al-Hussayn Al-Hamadhani, popularly called Badeeuz-Zamani. He was born in the middle of the fourth Hejrah century. He wrote his *maqamat* in Naysabur and died in 398 A.H.[16]

Maqamah is a literary narrative meant to be read to the audience in a short period in just one sitting. The audience contains, largely, of educated people. The plot of a *maqamah* is weaved around a particular protagonist, with the narrator reporting on the activities of this main character. In every *maqamah* the protagonist finds himself in a precarious situation, but always manipulates his way to get out of the problem. Similarly, the protagonist in most cases disguises his identity in order to conquer his victims; but as the story comes to the end, the narrator gradually uncovers his tricks, although he continues to keep it away from the audience.

In writing the stories in *Ruwan Bagaja*, Imam adopted this mode, where Alhaji is the protagonist and Malam Zurke the supporting character. The similarity with the Arabic sources is that the Hausa stories revolve around the two main characters; but, in contrast to the usual style in *maqamah*, the protagonist is also the narrator in the Hausa story. Also, in *Ruwan Bagaja* the stories are not rhythmic, but scenic in nature; and Malam Zurke, not the audience, is the victim of Alhaji's manipulation. However, like in the traditional *maqamah*, they reconcile at the end of every scene. This is just like the scenario we see in *maqamatul-Hareery* and *maqamatu Badeez-Zamani al-Hamzany* and several other *maqamat*.

---

16   *Al-Qur'an al-Kareem:* Chapter 72.

Pedagogical Traits

The direct and deep-rooted influence of the Arabic literary structures on the works of Alhaji Imam is also quite apparent; his stories are seldom narrated just for entertainment, but are didactic, meant to teach some moral lessons to the readers. *Ruwan Bagaja* is a case in point, where Alhaji meets with Malam Zurke in the proverbial kingdom of the lost.

Alhaji, a stark illiterate, finds himself in the midst of more illiterate people. Owing to his ability to recite the *Suratul-Fatihah* well, however, he is made the Imam of the villagers. His cause is further helped by the fact that the recitation of the Surah is done quietly during some prayers. He is respected in the village and held in great awe. Such is the status until Malam Zurke comes to the village. After observing a congregational prayer in the mosque behind the Imam, Zurke is appalled that such an illiterate should be made to lead the prayers. He bares his mind to the people who become shocked at his observations. When they bring this to his notice, however, Alhaji, the Imam, demonstrates rare courage by challenging Zurke to a competition between the two of them in front of all the villagers. Zurke accepts the challenge, firmly aware that Alhaji knows very little.

Unfortunately, Zurke allows Alhaji to take the initiative of starting the questioning because he thinks he can answer everything from him. This arrogance costs him dearly, as Alhaji simply outsmarts him by exploiting his popularity among the villagers and their ignorance. First, he draws a bend on the sand and asks Zurke to identify it and tell the crowd what that is. Zurke falters by first calling it (ر) r, then (ن) n. Alhaji now takes maximum advantage of the audience and charges that Zurke does not know anything, as what he wrote is the crescent of a new moon. People roar in affirmation. Zurke is so ashamed and as he is chased away from the village. The episode reveals how important it is not to get too proud, even against those who are so obviously not learned, but treat them with respect due to their position. Being knowledgeable alone is not enough to attain a leadership position; the knowledge must be matched with humility. It is always safer not to underestimate anyone, most especially an opponent during a contest.

Interaction With Invisible Beings

Another demonstration of the influence of Arabic literature on the writing of *Ruwan Bagaja* is of the encounters between Alhaji and the genies, which are an established phenomenon in Arabic literature. The holy book of Islam (The Qur'an) attests to the existence of these invisible bodies, with a chapter devoted to discussing their world and ways.[17] It is, therefore, quite apparent that this had influenced Imam to give the genies a lot of prominence in his stories. The genie encounters like this are a familiar occurrence in Arabic tales, to the point that it is a common aphorism among them that every poet has his/her own spirit that fires his imagination and creativity while composing poems.

Magana Jari Ce Volume III

This is the last volume of prose work written by Alhaji Abubakar Imam. The stories in the collection and the other two volumes are narrated by the King's parrot, which has been appointed vizier on account of its learning and wisdom. The stories owe a lot to the popular Arabic book, *Alfu Laylah wa Laylah* (One Thousand Nights and One Night). The pattern of narration is also similar to that of the Arabic source book, which has only *Shari Zad* and *Shahr Yar* narrating, with *Dunya Zad* in attendance. In *Magana Jari Ce* the narrators are the father parrot and his son *Fasihi*. Another Arabic story source book for Alhaji Imam is *Kaleelah wa Dimnah*, from which he adopts the style of telling the stories through animals and birds.

Alfu Laylah tells stories of a King Shahr Yar who is betrayed by his wife. From then on, he vows to henceforth marry for only

---

[17] Alhaji Abubakar Imam (1970), *Magana Jari Ce*, Vol. 3, Zaria: Northern Nigerian Publishing Company, p. 51.

a night and kill the unfortunate lady the following morning. This continues for some time until his vizier, whom he puts in charge of sourcing the ladies for him to marry, is unable to find any in the king's domain. Meanwhile, the vizier himself has two grown up daughters, Shahr Zad and Dunya Zad, so that when he returns home looking quite distraught, the older one tries to find out what is wrong with her father. She worries him until he explains his situation, pointing out that unless he finds the king a suitable wife before nightfall, the king will kill him instead.

The daughter immediately volunteers to be the next queen and, by extension, risks being killed in the morning. At first the father disagrees, but eventually concedes after a lengthy discussion and her strong assurance to end the king's practice of killing his wives. Thus, Shahr Zad marries the king and requests her younger sister, Dunya Zad, with whom she perfects her storytelling plan, to accompany her to her new home for the night. Upon Dunya Zad's request, Shahr Zad begins to tell a nice story, to the hearing of the king, but which she is unable to complete until dawn. The king, enchanted by the story and eager to hear the end, spares her life for another day; but just as she concludes the present story in the night, Shahr Zad begins another one, which she is also unable to conclude till dawn. This goes on interminably, making up the collection of stories in *Alfu Laylah wa Laylah*.

This brief account of the book is presented in order to help to explain its influence on the writing of *Magana Jari Ce*. Alhaji Imam himself does not hide this indebtedness, as he repeatedly alludes to the book in the narratives. A typical instance is when the vizier parrot tells his son Fasih at the end of one story that:

> *Yanzu zan ba ka misali daga cikin labarum wani littafi ne na Larabawa da ake kira* **Alfu Laylah**. [18]
>
> Now, I will give you an example from the stories in an Arabic book called **Alfu Laylah**.

---

18   Michael Worton and Judith Still (1990): *Intertextuality: Theories and Practices,* Manchester University Press, U.K. p. 1.

The entire contents of *Magana Jari Ce* could be taken to be the adaptation of *Alfu Laylah* and other Arabic story books into the Hausa language. The style, contents and mode are very much similar. *Alfu Laylah* is a collection of palace stories, but so is the king's palace the setting for the narration of all the stories in *Magana Jari Ce*. Similarly, Alfu Laylah teaches many specific morals and how to conduct oneself well in the society and so does *Magana Juri Ce*. This is not a mere coincidence, but a clear case of influence and trans-mutation, as the author had traversed, extensively, the Arabic literary texts available to him at the time before writing his own book, including *Alfu Laylah wa Laylah*.

Analysis

The significance of the Hausa language in the cultural and literary identity of the old northern Nigeria cannot be over-emphasised. This also makes the region, as depicted in the works of Alhaji Imam, unique among the constituting regions that make up the federation now called Nigeria. The uniqueness was bestowed on the region by its very long literary heritage, which conditioned its ethos and ensured the sustainability of its very strong identity.

This brings to mind the current arguments concerning the different realms of intertextuality, the theory propounded by Julia Kristeva, especially the argument that: "…a text cannot exist as a hermetic or self-sufficient whole, and so does not function as a closed system.[19] This is because the writer is always a reader of texts before he/she becomes a creator of texts. The presentation above would, to a very large extent, appear to expose the influence of the Arabic literary tradition on the development of the Hausa literature.

It is true that Arabic writing is different from the Roman orthography in which the Hausa stories were written. It is equally valid to argue that two literary writers do not have to share the

---

19   Hasan Jad (1978), *al-Adabul Muqarami* 3rd Edition, Cairo: Azhar University, p. 8.

same language for one to influence the style or themes of the other. Hasan Jad is of the opinion that there could be impacts and influences between a literary language of a community and another. Hausa literature, up to the last two decades of the twentieth century, was transformational because it was undergoing transition from being written in classical Arabic or *Ajami* to English.

It is, therefore, quite apparent that the renaissance of the Hausa literature spearheaded by Dr. Rupert M. East in the early twentieth century was not a case of reviving a dead literature or creating a literature in an unlettered community. The intertextuality in the writings of the authors of the Abubakar Imam generation suggested that they mostly composed their works using the available Arabic texts as background, as reflected in their themes and modes. The understanding here is that the content and mode of the works of the Hausa writers from that generation were bequeathed to them by Islam and the Arabic language writers. The training they acquired in the colonial schools and Gaskiya Corporation notwithstanding, this heritage of Arabic literacy tremendously shaped the direction of their writings in Hausa.

The case of Alhaji, the protagonist in *Ruwan Bagaja*, serves as evidence of the influence of the style of depicting heroic attitudes and values common in many classical Arabic texts. The heritage of sacrifice in order to safeguard the family and uphold the honour of the community is what makes him leave home in search of *Ruwan Bagaja*, in order to cure the prince of his mysterious illness. He leaves home and loses all comfort for fifteen years, until he successfully brings home the curative water, a drop of which effectively cures the sick prince. Alhaji instantly becomes a hero; this feat succinctly epitomises the age-long heritage of individuals working hard for the common good of the community.

The nature of the stories in *Magana Jari Ce* clearly displays the teacher in the author. This is not only on account of the fact that the stories are told by an elderly narrator, but also because each story has discernable goals, objectives and lessons. Besides, the narration is interactive, thereby ensuring the cultivation of an atmosphere that effective promotes teaching and learning. Each of the stories is an anecdote of a sort, buttressing the main thrust of the topic and underlining the lessons to the readers.

Conclusion

Thus, it could safely be concluded that Arabic language and literature are the original source of indigenous literary writing in northern Nigeria and this heritage has helped to determine the uniqueness and identity of the region. The literary roots of the North lie deep in its Arabic language heritage, so much that the Western education brought by the imperial colonialists later did not altogether set a new pattern for the region's writers. Even the imperialists had to study Arabic for their successful administration of the territory. The torchbearers of writing in Hausa using the Roman orthography heavily relied on their Arabic literary background to guide their choice of themes and styles. The thrust and message of their work, as demonstrated in *Ruwan Bagaja* and *Magana Jari Ce,* has continued to sustain the northern Nigerian heritage and identity. The heritage is still relevant and one could only plead for more effort in this regard as follows:

- More serious effort should be made to study of the early writers in Hausa language, especially their use of language, themes and styles.
- Similarly, there should be a concerted effort to recover, document and systematically study the Arabic language heritage in Northern Nigeria.
- The works of the early Hausa language writers should be kept in circulation by the publishers and copyright holders, in order to maintain touch with the inherited values of the society; at the moment, the publications are now in short circulation.

- The current Hausa writers should be more conversant with the Arabic language and literature, in order to expose them to additional sources and enrich their creativity.
- Writers in the northern part of Nigeria should note that an advanced study of Arabic literature will promote their understanding of the norms and values of the region.
- Contemporary literary writers in northern Nigeria and the country in general should promote good morals in their writing, in order to preserve the true identity of the North.

Chapter Eight

Sa'adu Zungur: A Literary Historian's Glimpse

Ibrahim A.M. Malumfashi

Introduction

Many, among the greatest men and women in the annals of societies, who work hard for the advancement of humanity, toiling with their sweat and blood and sometimes even losing their lives in the process, often end up as 'nonentities', on the 'off beam' side of history, without ever being adequately celebrated or acknowledged. Only the names of a few lucky ones among such men and women are captured in appendices at the end of long tales, usually re-told by those who were physically and historically far removed from the site of the events. This, however, does not matter to the actual heroes, who are normally content to strive to establish a good cause in the society, without bothering whether they personally benefit from it or leave it behind for their inheritors.

One may, thus, read the biographies of the famous Nigerian nationalists, especially the leaders who struggled against the colonial government for independence, or read the autobiographies or memoirs of the few of them who cared to write, without ever coming across the name of Malam Sa'adu Zungur. In most accounts, he is often omitted, except, perhaps, in some historical fragments on colonial-era materials, anti-colonial reports or university researches and theses. Yet, many of the more familiar names in the Nigerian anti-colonial history and the early post-colonial leaders owe much to Malam Zungur.

It is, therefore, a welcome tribute to have Mukhtar Yakubu's seminal work, *Sa'adu Zungur: An Anthology of the Social and Political Writings of a Nigerian Nationalist* (1999), which has done what scholars had previously failed to do: documenting the life and struggles of one of the foremost African nationalists who was cut short by death as the anti-colonial battle was warming up to begin on the continent. The book explains Malam Sa'adu Zungur and his profound contributions in the struggle for the nation's independence and development.

Sa'adu Zungur never aspired to hold any office or achieve popularity, but worked quietly as a true servant of the people. A poet, social critic, ideologue, organiser, philosopher, religious advocate and nationalist, he deliberately led an ascetic life, so that others might live better. Born and educated in Bauchi, Zaria, Lagos and other places, Zungur travelled widely in the North and organised the people to wake up and free themselves from colonial bondage, ignorance and poverty, at the time when few cared or had the opportunity to do so. Indeed, the best testimony to the passion, foresight and organisational ability of Malam Zungur could be deduced from Malam Aminu Kano's response, following the comments made by the famous Emir of Zazzau, the late Alhaji Jafaru, that, "the greatest damage done by Malam Aminu Kano is that he let the masses know they could say no." Malam Aminu Kano was reported to have quickly attributed their effort and achievement to Malam Sa'adu Zungur, openly declaring that "the greatest contribution made by Sa'adu Zungur to our political re-awakening is by encouraging us to confront the 'colonial dog' headlong...never to let the sleeping dog lie, wake it up and damn all the consequences" (Kano,1973).

Yakubu (1999) reports that Sa'adu Zungur was born on Tuesday 24 November 1914 and explains Zungur's family background, early educational life and career and the political awareness he developed between 1920-1932 while he was a student at the Yaba

College of Technology, Lagos. It was also at Yaba College that he picked up the stigma the colonial government later attached to him, which followed him all his life, even as he stepped up his political activities. The government had identified him as a radical and great mobiliser; hence, marked his movements at every point in order to ensure that he was never posted to work in a large urban centre, where he could influence others or have access to a big crowd, especially the educated civil servants.

Yakubu's book provides further details about Sa'adu Zungur's Yaba College experience that should be particularly interesting to literary historians. For instance, for the first time, the book publishes the unabridged copy of Zungur's famous revolutionary poem 'Addakari' that encapsulates his political philosophy and ideals. Viewed from another perspective, the story about the poem provides a significant clue to understanding how the colonialists really worked to intervene in not just the politics, but also the thinking and literary activities of the early nationalists in northern Nigeria. Until the current publication, the only copy at hand was mutilated, with some of the more critical verses deliberately edited out by those in authority, who also controlled the publishing centres in northern Nigeria.

About the Political Engineers

In order to understand the fears and actions of the colonialists, one has to go back into history and study the distinctiveness of the political situation in northern Nigeria before the British conquest of the Sokoto Caliphate in 1903. The conquest had not just imposed colonial rule, but also established a different territorial and socio-political field of power, which was distinct from the smaller elements that were fused together to constitute the new state (Kuna & Malumfashi, 1998). This needed the enactment of appropriate imperial policies whose purpose would be to establish harmony in the state as an aggregation of varied interests and nationalities, in furtherance of the colonial objectives.

However, it should be noted that the capture of the Sokoto caliphate at once marked the collapse of its precolonial political and administrative structures and the beginning of the more complicated problem of their reconstruction, in tune with the operating logic of the British colonial state. Thus, while the caliphate frontiers were somewhat amorphous, a new carved geographical and social boundary, domestically and internationally, was imposed, complete with a new superitending hierarchy of authority. The consolidation of this colonial state, as such, involved the political re-configuration of the precolonial geographical and social spaces in order to enable the retention, in a modified form, of the centralised bureaucratic organisation of the caliphate. At the same time, for reasons of expediency, the modified structure of the caliphate had to be imposed on the other areas that were never within its territory before, but which were now part of northern Nigeria.

Consequently, the new establishment faced challenges from sources that had resisted the consolidation of the new caliphate into a state, with the first deriving from the defeated and modified precolonial power structure. This included the *Ulama,* their students and the wider public who had been led to question whether the actions of the new state or, indeed, its functionaries had any foundations in the centuries-old traditions of the Shari'a. Such expression of resistance was mostly through intellectual activities, which included the writing of challenging poems and the migration of many scholars to the eastern parts of the old caliphate and beyond; although the opposition rarely resulted into open revolts, much as some of the early manifestations had hinted at that too as a possibility.

The grounds for opposing the state actions and functionaries became even sharper due to the tensions that emerged from the loss of legitimacy by the leadership of the old caliphate, following its decision to accept to subordinate itself under 'white' or 'infidel' rule. 'White' rule was not just alien, but also worked contrary to Islam; and for a significant part of the

Ulama and the general society that must be resisted in whatever form was possible. Furthermore, the precolonial resistance to the caliphate state itself that was often organised along religious lines also began to be defined by the British as 'militant Islam', which they considered a serious threat to the whole colonial state structure. This dual categorisation of 'official' and 'militant' Islam enabled the authorities to deal with the sources of the opposition in those terms. The 'militant' opposition, especially, was addressed through the deposition or murder of those that either resisted or did not support the British policy openly, or those that were considered sympathetic to the 'militant' brand of Islam. Equally noteworthy, was the fact that, in the few cases where such resistance reached open revolts, it was dealt with severely, using the scorched-earth policy.

However, as pointed out earlier, this was not the only form of resistance against the colonial state apparatus. From the late 1930s to the early 1940s it became influenced a great deal by the burgeoning agitation for independence. The *Ulama*, the emergent educated class and the peasantry all opposed the colonialists and the emirs that now ruled in collaboration with them. Here too, the reaction of the colonial government was to classify the opposition in terms of its traditional distinction between 'official' and 'militant' or 'fundamentalist' Islam. That was how the entire colonial state structure was mobilised towards dealing with the threat of the 'militant' Islam, as represented by some sects, like the *Tijaniyya*. The sect in particular was well rooted in certain cities and, thus, the 'fundamentalism' found base in these cities, which soon became popular as centres of opposition to the new political arrangements introduced by colonialism.

The most outstanding opposition usually invoked the notions of fairness, equity, the rule of law and the system of justice, as well as the exclusion of the Muslim *Ulama* class, as guardians of the inheritance of the Sokoto caliphate, from all public affairs. Such issues re-emerged as powerful tools in the battle against the colonial state in northern Nigeria, which culminated into more vocal demands for independence and the rise of some radical elements in the region, like Sa'adu Zungur.

The subsequent attempt by the colonial government to resuscitate certain precolonial public institutions, particularly the emirate authority, was an indication that the agitation for the transfer of power had raised some very serious questions concerning the legitimacy of their rule and institutions of governance. Thus, the old emirate system was brought back as the Native Authority; but although each emir now headed the new authority and was put directly in charge, the people were not deceived about the presence of the British in the background. In fact, this only produced a repeat of the situation that had happened to warrant the Jihad of 1804; namely, a rift within the state apparatus, when the political leadership lost the allegiance of the public and, consequently, was attacked by the *Ulama*.

Perhaps, the added complication now was that the problem of ineffective leadership had been further compounded by that of validity, whereby the people perceived the apparatus of the new colonial state, especially the emirs, as legitimising alien and – worse – un-Islamic rule. Moreover, the organisation of the new state structure, through the reinstatement of customary laws and local administrations, had added a new source of unease among the *Ulama*. Furthermore, the native authorities took their orders directly from the emirs, often deferring to descent and social standing, rather than education and merit, for appointments into public offices, thereby leading to serious conflict with the emergent modern educated elite who were not always from the royal houses.

These tensions, situated as they were within the colonial unitary conception of the state, began to shape the organisation of the opposition along two main patterns and justificatory ideologies: the 'conservative Islamic tendency' espoused by the groups who supported the existing NA establishment, as represented by the emirs and chiefs at the top, and the 'Islamic revolutionary tendency' that wanted a complete change or re-organisation of the system (Birniwa, 1987). The former tendency reflected more than the attempt to maintain tradition, for account must be taken of the fact that some sections of this social force had openly embraced the gradualist approach in bringing about changes in the administrative system.

In addition, and this is where the critical difference with the latter tendency lies, the 'conservative Islamic tendency' approach had called into being the entire precolonial state apparatus, in order to justify not just its rule, but also the unitary state project. In this sense it relied on the long tradition of jihad and conquest by the founders of the caliphate, and posed its current relevance in terms of finishing the task of expanding the frontiers of the caliphate that was interrupted by the colonial conquest in 1903. The ultimate goal was to ensure a smooth transition from a colonial to a neo-colonial status, against the backdrop of the achievements of the precolonial state structure and the values it represented.

Political Parties and the Emergent Nationalism

It was against this general devide, between the groups who advocated the 'conservative Islamic tendency' and those who favoured the 'Islamic revolutionary tendency' that cultural and political associations begun to emerge from the late 1930s to the early 1940s, although some of the associations initially did not demonstrate much overt or sharp distinctions. Sa'adu Zungur founded the first of such cultural associations, the Northern General Improvement Union in 1941, and it drew membership from among those who had indeterminate tendencies, including remnants of the precolonial and the colonial state. Thus, people like Abubakar Imam, Wazirin Zazzau Sanusi, Malam Julde, Malam Jumare, R.A.B. Dikko, and John Garba, the Emir of Zazzau, the Resident, the District Officer (DO) and others based in Zaria all joined hands together to form one association. The diversity of opinion among these members, who appeared not to have a distinct common interest to protect, generated heated debate, as it was bound to, and this increased when Malam Sa'adu Zungur and some few more radical members themselves openly questioned the nature and purpose of the organisation. For instance, they could not accept a situation where women were discriminated against, or condone the unjust practices of the emirs and native authorities. They not only supported their opinions with extensive quotations from the Qur'an, but also took up their pens to write and disseminate poems and songs to explain their opinions. Subsequently, the NGIU was disbanded and the government dispatched most of the members to outpost locations within and outside the province; Zungur in particular was transferred to a rural dispensary in the remote town of Anchau, to go and fight infectious diseases (Birniwa 1987).

Although the NGIU was disbanded, this did not appear to have stopped further organisation of interests along the two major tendencies identified above. Throughout northern Nigeria, from Bauchi, Kano, Kaduna, Sokoto, Katsina to Zaria, and through the pages of newspapers, such as the *Gaskiya Ta Fi Kwabo, Sodangi, Comet* and Azikiwe's *West African Pilot,* the elite frequently raised and debated important issues affecting the people, including the rules and operation of the native authorities, the position and role of the emirs in tax affairs, the relative 'backwardness' of the north and the future of the emergent post-colonial state.

The concerns were many, but three subjects stood out in these debates: the forced conscription of northerners into the military to go and fight at the war front on the side of the British during World War II; the diversion of food meant for the people to the war front; and use of forced labour at the tin mines in Jos and the Plateau. Using different media across the Northern Provinces, these and other similar issues were regularly raised and opinions strongly expressed using the literary and poetic forms. As expected, most of the criticism was against the colonial government and the native authorities, at the head of which were the emirs. The discussions were justified mainly on religious grounds, although for the 'conservative Islamic tendency' group reform was the watchword, while for those in the 'radical Islamic tendency' camp securing a more fundamental change in the system was the main goal (Birniwa, 1987).

Subsequently, associations with more defined ideological positions began to emerge that organised such debates more frequently and voicing out their grievances against the native authorities and the emirs. Thus, Sa'adu Zungur and a few friends formed the Bauchi Discussion Circle (later the Bauchi General Improvement Union) in 1943; others that appeared within a couple of years included the Zaria Zumunta Association, Sokoto Youth Social Circle, and Citizens Association of Kano. As the 1940s drew to a close, some of these organisations began to merge into political parties. This was how the Northern People's Congress (NPC) got formed from a fusion of various cultural associations, amongst which were the *Jam'iyyar Mutanen Arewa, Jam'iyyar Jama'ar Arewa,* the Sokoto Youth Social Circle, and the Citizens Association of Kano.

However, by 1951 the NPC had shed off its radical members and clearly begun to transform into a party of the establishment, whose general goal was to defend the existing power structure. Due to its composition and membership in these formative years, the NPC had attempted to openly criticise the traditional establishment and advance some drastic reformist ideas, which seriously alarmed the colonial state and the emirs in particular. The tension had triggered the challenge to the early radicalism and led to the emplacement of mechanisms for accommodating reforms aimed at improving, rather than changing, the colonial establishment. These reforms were effected through preventing NA and government officials from participating in politics and coercing the 'old guard' emirs into accepting the inevitability of peaceful reforms, if violent changes were to be prevented. It was actually the action of ridding the NPC of its radicalism and radical elements that brought about the rift between the conservatives and radicals at the party's convention in Jos in 1950, during which several of the revolutionary members were expelled.

The 'Islamic revolutionary tendency', is itself historically grounded, for it derived from the long tradition of protest activity and resistance by the *Ulama* and the peasantry. The critical issues it exploited to demonstrate relevance in the struggle against the colonial state were the Islamic notions of justice, fairness, legitimacy and piety. In this sense, it also traced its origins back to the jihad; for it had often claimed that there was a fundamental distinction between the ideals and practices of the original jihadists and their heirs under the command of the white government.

They were quick to point out that while the former had emphasised fairness, justice, piety, learning, contemplation and the principle of non-hereditary succession, the latter generation acted in open demonstration of unfairness and injustice, citing such examples as their selection based on a system of hereditary succession and the un-Islamic practices of the emirs, including confiscation of peasant property. The defiance was, therefore, a religious duty whose objective should not stop at sweeping away the injustices perpetrated by the whole state structure, but also against colonialism itself and its divisiveness.

The Northern Elements Progressive Union (NEPU) in the main championed the objectives of the 'radical Islamic tendency'. Initially launched in 1946 under the name of the Northern Elements Progressive Association, NEPA, as it became popularly known, had resolved to foster "mutual understanding and cooperation" between the peoples of the North, as well as to clear away the belief that "the northerner is silent because he is satisfied" (Birniwa, 1987). NEPA's objectives, right from the beginning, were radically political, expressed in pungent criticism, both of the colonial establishment and the emirs who cooperated with them. The demobilisation of NEPA in 1949 led to the formation of NEPU in 1950.

NEPU's objectives were radically different from NPC's; as demonstrated in its commitment to the "total emancipation of the *talakawa* from the domination of a privileged few, through the reform of the existing autocratic political institutions" (Birniwa, 1987). Its articulation of the anti-colonial struggle in anti-imperialist and pan-Nigerian nationalist terms also meant that it was against regionalism, as well as the colonial state. By, thus, declaring itself against regionalism and the exercise of autocratic power, NEPU was seen as posing a serious threat to the whole colonial project. This threat became even more serious in view of NEPU's efforts to build alliances within and between the country's three major regions.

The distinctiveness of the NPC and NEPU was, therefore, historically embedded in the kind of issues both came to represent. Beyond the parties were two social forces locked in conflict over the matter of domination: the nature of such domination, the relationship between those dominating and the dominated, as well as the configuration of the emergent state. These conflicts had been greatly influenced by religion, which also provided the language and tool of mobilisation. The presentations were mainly in literary discourses, with poetry in particular proving the most popular. Malam Sa'adu Zungur was the principal in this regard, churning out lines that sank the message home quickly and mobilised the people to stand up and not give in to the intimidation of the authorities.

The Quintessential Sa'adu Zungur

Against this backdrop, one could easily perceive Sa'adu Zungur in conflicting divides: being a scion of the 'Imamates', he had in him the 'radical Islamic tendencies' of protest and revolt against bad rulers and injustice, which at various stages of his life made a profound effect on his thoughts, beliefs and ideas. At the same time, the avalanche of materials he came into contact with while swimming in the turbulent waters of western education, also contributed greatly in re-shaping his world-view and philosophy of life. Right form the very beginning, Zungur's political and social struggles had prepared him for the turbulent world of fighting for a just cause. For instance, he saw no reason why women should be discriminated against in the pursuit of education. In particular, he queried the rationale of the attitude that was common in the North at the time of shunning western education, which had since become established in the other parts of the country. His concern was how the two systems of education (Islamic and Western) could be merged for the benefit of the northern societies. In terms of its quest for a better future, he advocated that the North should not go it alone, but explore the cooperation of the other regions for a pan-Nigerian solution.

Yakubu (1999) observes that Sa'adu Zungur's exchanges in newspapers, poems and letters from 1941 to 1956, were 'united by interrelated themes,' the most visible being 'justice' and the final overthrow of British colonialism and its cohorts. However, he could not fully achieve his objectives within his life time largely because he appeared to have spread himself too thinly across the country; and was often too consumed in his cause to examine the sincerity of those with whom he associated. For instance, analysts point out that while he was consumed with the desire to organise the people around Zaria and Bauchi for their development, he employed the 'wrong' set of people, with whom he was politically incongruent. Nonetheless, even though his activities have not been adequately documented or assessed, many today consider Sa'adu Zungur the father of political agitation in northern Nigeria. For instance, his NGIU in Zaria had metamorphosed into NPC; his BGUI in Bauchi had given rise to the NEPA and, subsequently, NEPU; and his association with the NCNC in Lagos had paved the way for the emergence of the UPGA. All the associations were to later develop into formidable national ideological and philosophical springboards, from which more profound political developments took off in the later years.

Unfortunately, lack of details concerning Malam Sa'adu Zungur's life had left him unacknowledged as a nationalist of note and often reduced him to a mere footnote in the anti-colonial fight in Nigeria. This image was further confounded by his insatiable desire to achieve so much all at once, which drove him to quickly move from one position to another, without waiting for it to mature. In the years between 1941 and 1948, for instance, while trying to establish viable political organisations in Zaria and Bauchi, he was attracted to explore the platform of journalism, without finding his bearing or fully establishing his authority in northern politics. Once he made name in various newspapers as a reporter of note at the time, he abandoned journalism and left the north for Lagos, where he became the Secretary General of the NCNC. This at once discounted his political image in the North and slackened his hold on his supporters and admirers. Thus, while he was busy promoting the 'national' image of the NCNC in the secretariat, other political activists, like Aminu Kano, Tafawa Balewa and Ahmadu Bello, were building strong holds, bridges and alliances within the north that saw them emerge as the giants of the region's leadership.

Thus, even if ill health had contributed in preventing Sa'adu Zungur from participating in full-time political activities from 1952, one can still infer that he could not have made more inroad in the north, because he lacked sufficient base. His relative 'juniors,' like Ahmadu Bello and Aminu Kano, had by that time engraved themselves into the hearts of the 'conservatives' and 'radicals' of northern Nigerian politics, respectively. Consequently, by the time he retired finally to Bauchi, he had "set himself up as an unofficial ombudsman, interceding in advisory capacity on behalf of NEPU" (Yakubu, 1999). From then on, he had reached an unpleasant turning point in his career and was already on course for descent into political oblivion, as a result of his miscalculated adventures.

This would appear to confer particular significance on the recent effort to research into the life and activities of Malam Sa'adu Zungur, as represented by Yakubu's (1999) work, which, however, only provides us with an anthology of Zungur's publications. There is, certainly, still the need to fully dig out the actual Malam Sa'adu Zungur from the vast collection of resources on the history of the birth of the Nigerian state, in order to fully appreciate the life and times of this genius and restless anti-colonial hero.

References

- Birniwa, H.A. (1987), 'Conservatism and Dissent: A Comparative Study on N.P.C./N.P.N. and N.E.P.U./P.R.P., Hausa Political Verse Circa 1946 – 1984,' PhD thesis, University of Sokoto.
- Dambazau L. (2001), *Politics and Religion in Nigeria*, Kaduna: Vanguard Printers and Publishers Limited.
- Dambazau, L. (1981), *Tarihin Gwagwarmaya N.E.P.U. da P.R.P. 1950 – 1981*, Zaria: Gaskiya Corporation.
- Kano Aminu, (1973), *Rayuwar Ahmad Mahmud Sa'adu Zungur*, Zaria: Gaskiya Corporation.
- Kuna, M. J. and I. Malumfashi (1996), 'The Politics of Abuse and the Poetics of Violence in Northern Nigeria, 1946-1966', Seminar paper presented at the 15th Year Anniversary of the death of Malam Aminu Kano, African Centre for Political and Social Research, Ahmadu Bello University, Zaria.
- Kuna, M. J. (2000), 'Violence and State Formation: The Case of Northern Nigeria 1900-1966,' unpublished PhD thesis Usmanu Danfodiyo University, Sokoto.
- Kuna, M.J. (1998) "The Nation-State and Violence: Incorporation, Exclusion and State Formation in Nigeria, the Case of Northern Nigeria, 1930-1966", seminar paper presented at the Political Science Department, Usmanu Danfodiyo University, Sokoto.
- Yakubu, A.M. (1999): *Sa'adu Zungur: An Anthology of the Social and Political Writings of a Nigerian Nationalist.* Kaduna: Nigerian Defence Academy Press.

Chapter Nine

From The Written to the Oral: A Survey of Hausa Prose Fiction on Radio

Sabi'u Alhaji Garba

Introduction

The Past in the Present

The art of storytelling is a well known pastime to the people of West Africa since immemorial times (East 1991:2). This explains why the written traditions in many societies in the region have developed a close relationship with the oral sources, which have tended to influence their themes and even styles, especially among the Hausa. For example, scholars have pointed out how the early Hausa published prose fiction writings in particular were rooted in the society's folkloric genres drawing many of their themes and even styles from the folktales and stories (Malumfashi, 2009). Among the prose narratives produced in 1933 and printed in 1934 and 1935, some had their sources drawn directly from Hausa history, but many were outrightly folkloric, exploiting established oral sources, such as tales and fables, which the authors now selected and rendered into the written form. *Ruwan Bagaja*, for instance, was adapted from sources that were much influenced by some popular folktales; *Gandoki* was inspired by stories about the coming of the Europeans into Hausa land; and *Shaihu Umar* was based on the history of the slave trade in Hausa land (Malumfashi, 2009: xviii). This chapter contends that the background of the early books in the Hausa oral tradition, as well as the later prose writing fashioned after them, is responsible for their popularity in many current Hausa radio programmes.

Radio listening among the people in Africa has been a popular pastime activity ever since regular broadcasts began in the continent. The Hausa society in particular, which is steeped in ancient folkloric traditions, has very much accepted the radio, which, in turn, now appears to greatly influence the re-invigoration of its story telling and listening culture. In reviewing the findings of a 1998 baseline survey by the Kano State Agricultural and Rural Development Agency (KNARDA) involving farmers in its operational area that established "over 97% of the respondents listen to radio daily, out of which over 60% had their own radios", Adekunle et al (2004) conclude that listening to the radio is, indeed, now a usual activity among many members of the rural communities in northern Nigeria. Certainly, the ordinary man in the north is attached to the radio, keeping a set wherever he is: in the house, shop and even on the farm or while rearing cattle in the bush.

The effect of this listening culture can easily be measured by the volume of correspondence the radio stations receive as feedback from their listeners (Tilde, 2010). Their devotion could be attributed to many reasons, including the following:

i. The people to whom the programmes are directed already have an established listening culture.
ii. The idea of receiving organised broadcasts in the local language from a radio station is 'novel' and the programmes are often quite stimulating.
iii. Even foreign radio stations connect with the local people easily, because they report on their anxieties, concerns and fears with some measure of objectivity.
iv. In fact, the listeners access news stories and other useful information from foreign stations that are sometimes not available to them on their national radio stations (Garba, 2011:14).

An Overview of the Emergence of Hausa Prose Fiction

Literacy and written literature began in Hausa culture with the arrival of Islam into the society in the twelfth century, when the literati began to write in their own language, using the adapted Arabic script known as *Ajami*. With the coming of the Europeans at the end of the nineteenth century, those educated in the Western-style schools now acquired another system of writing using the Roman script, known as *Boko* (see Yahaya, 1988).

Oral literature, which includes proverbs, epithets, poems, tales etc., is an indegenous culture of antiquity whose history cannot easily be determined. In refuting East's (1936:350) claim that prior to the 1930s there was no written literature by the Hausa people in the popular genres, such as poetry, prose and drama, Malumfashi (2009:xvii) maintains that East did not really research into the correct state of Hausa literature prior to the period. Indeed, he argues, the Europeans had found some written literary works in *Ajami* that included stories, tales, almara, fables, proverbs and other Hausa folkloric genres (Skinner, 1968:viii & ix). They only Romanised them and changed their style and form; and later established the Translation and Literature Bureau between 1929 and 1937, while introducing new forms of prose and drama for use in the newly established *boko* schools and the pleasure of those who could read the *boko* script.

Thus, in 1933, in an attempt to bring about a new collection of Hausa written literature, a scheme was inaugurated by the Director of Education, Nigeria, to produce Hausa books of the non-educational type, which would provide significant matter for pleasurable reading (East, 1991:1). Subsequently, the bureau organised a competition and the following books were adjudged as the best: *Ruwan Bagaja* by Abubakar Kagara; *Gandoki* by Bello Kagara; *Shaihu Umar* by Abubakar Bauchi; *Idon Matambayi* by Muhammadu Gwarzo and *Jiki Magayi* by Mr John Tafida Umaru (Malumfashi, 2009).

The Europeans and, subsequently, the indigenous government further established agencies, such as Gaskiya Corporation, Northern Literature Agency and Northern Nigerian Publishing

Company, under whose auspices several Hausa prose books were published (Yahaya, 1988). More recently, the Federal Department of Culture organised a Hausa book writing competition in 1982 and later published the entries (Mukhtar, 2004). In 1984, another set of Hausa prose publications tagged 'Kano Market Literature' began to appear (Malumfashi, 2003). These books have continued to attract attention, especially among the youths, although it is reported that their popularity is gradually dying (Malumfashi, 2011).

An Overview of the History of Radio Broadcasting in Hausaland

The history of the radio in Hausaland cannot be complete without reference to the other parts of Africa as a whole. Indeed, there were three distinct phases in the development of radio broadcasts in Africa, the first phase being the colonial or settler period, when the radio was primarily a medium brought in to serve the settlers and the interests of the colonial powers. Later (and in many cases not until towards the end of colonial rule) the local authorities gradually introduced radio services by and for the indigenous people. After the Second World War, it became official British policy to expand broadcasting to cover most of its African colonies (Mytton, 2000:5).

Broadcasting began at different times in the British West Africa: Sierra Leone in 1934, Gold Coast (now Ghana) in 1935, and Nigeria in 1936 via wired services, in which subscribers had loudspeakers (linked by wire to the radio station) installed in their homes to receive the service. Then in 1936 the British colonial administration decided to develop radio broadcasting throughout its African colonies as a public service for the indigenous people (Mytton 2000).

Broadcasting in the Hausa language began in 1939 in Ghana, along with two Ghanaian languages, Ewe and Twi, when the British administrators realised that they needed to use the local languages in order to reach out to the indigenous population (Blankson, 2005:6). The distinguished Hausa broadcaster (later Northern politician),

Isa Kaita, was based in Accra, where he became a radio announcer in 1941 in Zoy radio station at the Radio House (Hunziker, 2005 and http://en.wikipedia.org/wiki/Isa_Kaita).

Between 1935 and 1947, eighteen Radio Distribution Centres were established in the provincial headquarters in Nigeria, including Kano, Sokoto, Katsina, Zaria, Oweri and Onitsha, etc, (Moemeka, 1981:3). The colonial administration converted the Radio Distribution Service (RDS) into the Nigerian Broadcasting Service (NBS) in June 1953, with many programmes originating from within the country. This development marked the beginning of the 'indigenisation' of the broadcasting services. Bulletins were copied and translated into the national languages, such as Hausa, Igbo, Yoruba, Fulfulde, Kanuri, Edo, Ibibio and Efik (Mohammed 2004:7-8). Incorporated in 1957 as the Nigerian Broadcasting Corporation, the service monopolised radio broadcasting till 1959, when the Broadcasting Law permitting the establishment of regional broadcasting houses was passed.

Consequently, between 1959 and 1962, every one of the three regions had established a broadcast station: the Western Region in 1959; Eastern Region in 1960 and Northern Region in 1962. The number of regional radio stations witnessed an upswing with the coming of the military governments, which successively increased the number of the regions or states in the country (Ojebode et al. 2007) and every state established its own radio station. In fact, some of the states established two stations: for instance, Kano State had Kano AM and FM; and Sokoto State had Rima Radio AM and FM, etc. Brann (1995) observes that there were over one hundred broadcast languages used during the Second Republic in Nigeria.

Among all these languages, Hausa was the only language used in broadcasting news and feature programmes in more than fifteen states; the number later increased to twenty, including the new stations that opened in the Federal Capital Territory, Abuja. Indeed, full scale radio programmes in Hausa were introduced when Radio and Television Kaduna, (now the

Federal Radio Corporation of Nigeria, Kaduna) was established in 1962 (Funtua, 1997). This was an indication that the Hausa listeners were numerous and more widely spread, particularly in the northern states. Today, more than one hundred radio stations air programmes in Hausa in Nigeria, with some of them actually broadcasting 90% or more of their programmes in the language. At the international level, the British Broadcasting Corporation was the first to employ the Hausa language to reach multiple audiences across the globe, when it established the Hausa Service to cater for its listeners in West Africa in 1957 (Ibrahim, 1994; Garba, 2010 and Abubakar, 2011). Today, nearly twenty international radio stations based in different countries use Hausa for regular broadcasts (Garba, 2011).

The Hausa Novels and Radio Programmes

A common feature among all the radio stations is how they make use of Hausa written sources and the authors, in one form or another, for their regular programmes, which in many instances includes the direct reading of published Hausa prose narratives or plays on the air. The use of written materials in Hausa radio programmes had been a normal affair since the early days of radio broadcast in Africa. Yahaya (1989) in Ahmad (2006:106) quotes the late Wazirin Katsina, Alhaji Isa Kaita, recalling how he would read *Gaskiya Ta Fi Kwabo*, a Hausa newspaper, from cover to cover in his newscast in Accra, for the benefit of the Nigerian soldiers in the Gold Coast (Ghana) during the World War II.

However, Radio Nigeria Kaduna, being the first major Hausa language radio in Nigeria and Africa (Funtua, 1997), started the programme known as 'Shafa Labari Shuni' in its early days of operation, where Hausa fictional books were read to the listeners (Malumfashi, 2003). In fact, Malumfashi (2009:xiii) recalls how he once came across the translated version of *Alfu Laila* ready to be read on the Kaduna State Radio by Malam Mamman Kano, about forty (40) years ago.

Consequently, virtually all the radio stations in northern Nigeria have programmes in which Hausa prose books are read. For instance, Rima Radio Sokoto started its own programme called 'Hikaya' in the late 1970s. Voice of Nigeria, Lagos, also began its 'Katibanmu' in the 1970s, with Idris Isah Abbas, a Ghanaian, the then head of the Hausa Service, as the producer, until he was summarily sacked and asked to return to Ghana in 1984. Subsequently, Ahmad Isah Koko was asked to continue with the programme, which he has maintained until now.[20]

In 1987 Musa Muhammad Kankara started 'Kukan Kurciya', on Radio Nigeria 3, Lagos, which was also known as Bond FM, before the programme was later in the year given to Ahmad Isah Koko, who still produces it. Owing to the long experience Koko acquired in this regard, he later developed a commercial Hausa prose book reading programme called 'Rai Dangin Goro'[21], which was sponsored by the Lagos State Government from 2007-2011, before MTN Nigeria took it over, spreading it to many other radio stations in the Hausa-speaking areas of the country, including Radio Kano, Rima Radio Sokoto, Borno State Radio, Radio Nigeria Kaduna, Freedom Radio Kano, and Rahama Radio Kano.

Similarly, Radio Kano AM began the programme called 'Kunnenka Nawa' in the early 1980s; its sister station, Radio Kano FM, began its own 'Taura Biyu' in 2009. Zamfara Radio also introduced a similar programme in 1997 when the station was established. In 2008 Freedom Radio Kano started another programme called 'Ku Karkade Kunnuwanku' and Pyramid Radio arrived with its 'Ku Matso Ku Ji' in 2004. The format of all these programmes is largely the same, with virtually all of the radio stations reading the various Hausa prose books as part of their regular literary programmes. In addition, some stations partially read the books in some programmes, such as 'Zare da Abawa' of the Pyramid Radio, Kano, and 'In da Ranka' Sunday magazine.

---

20 Interview with Ahmad Isa Koko, producer and presenter of "Katibanmu", "Kukan Kurciya" and "Rai Dangin Goro" on 26/11/2012.
21 Ibid. 1

The prose reading programme usually features a single book, which is read episode by episode to the end. There follows then a special session, during which the history of the author is presented together with a brief commentary about the book, its themes and the circumstance that inspired its writing. Each episode of the programme normally lasts between 15 and 30 minutes and is repeated at a later date on most of the radio stations. Radio Kano AM airs its 'Kunnenka Nawa' on Sunday from 12:30p.m to 1p.m and repeats the programme on Monday between 11:30a.m and 12:00p.m Radio Kano FM's 'Ku Tara Biyu' (add two) comes to the listeners on Wednesdays at 9 p.m and is repeated on Wednesdays at 6 p.m Rima Radio Sokoto's 'Hikaya' comes to the listeners on Saturday between 08:30 and 09:00 in the evening. Freedom Radio's 'Ku Karkade Kunnuwanku' comes to the listeners on Wednesday between 5:30p.m and 6:00 p.m. The Pyramid Radio's "Ku Matso Ku Ji" comes to the listeners on Thursday between 10:45 a.m and 11:00 a.m and is repeated on Fridays between 6:15 p.m and 6:30 p.m Bond FM Lagos's Kukan Kurciya is broadcast every day of the week from 5 p.m to 5:30 p.m except on Saturday, when it is replaced with a phone in session, during which the listeners call to say their views on the current book being read in the programme.

It is quite instructive to note that the practice of reading published Hausa books of prose fiction in a dedicated programme has gone beyond northern Nigeria now. Koko (2012) reports that Muhammad Salisu Hamisu, a Nigerian journalist working with the Hausa Service of Radio France International and Marwan Abbas, a Ghanaian journalist, have both confirmed to him in private discussions that there is virtually no radio station broadcasting in Hausa in Niger Republic and Ghana that does not have such a programme.

The Current Context of Novels on the Radio

A recent survey has also identified some books as being particularly popular in the reading programmes of the various radio stations. For instance, the Kano Radio AM has so far read more than 100 books on the air,[22] among which were the five classical Hausa fiction texts, which featured quite early at the commencement of the programme, as follows:

S/No.	Name of Book	Author	Year of Publication
1.	Ruwan Bagaja	Abubakar Kagara	1935
2.	Gandoki	Bello Kagara	1934
3.	Shaihu Umar	Abubakar Bauchi	1934
4.	Idon Matambayi	Muhammadu Gwarzo	1934
5.	Jiki Magayi	Tafida Umaru and R.M East	1935
6.	Magana Jari Ce 1-3	Abubakar Imam	1939-1940
7.	Bala Da Babiya	Nuhu Bamalli	1950
8.	Motsi Ya Fi Zama	Aminu Kano	1953
9.	Nagari Na Kowa	Jabiru Abdullahi	1966
10.	Tauraruwa Mai Wutsiya	Umaru Dembo	1966
11.	Dare Daya	Abdullahi Ka'oje	1973
12.	Kitsen Rogo	Abdulkadir Dangambo	1978
13.	So Aljannar Duniya	Hafsat Abdulwaheed	1980
14.	Amadi Na Malam Amah	Magaji Danbatta	1980
15.	Mallakin Zuciyata	Sulaiman Ibrahim Katsina	1980
16.	Turmin Danya	Sulaiman Ibrahim Katsina	1982

---

22   Ibid. 1

17.	*Tsumagiyar Kan Hanya*	Musa Muhammad Bello	1982
18.	*Karshen Alewa Kasa*	Bature Gagare	1982
19.	*Zabi Naka*	Munir Mamman	1982
20.	*Rabin Raina*	Talatu Wada Ahmed	1985
21.	*Soyayya Gamon Jini*	Ibrahim Hamza Abdullahi	1986
22.	*In Da Rai*	Idris Imam	1987
23.	*Budurwar Zuciya*	Balaraba Ramat Yakubu	1987
24.	*Kogin Soyayya*	AM Zahraddeen	1988
25.	*Idan So Cuta Ne*	Yusuf M. Adamu	1989
26.	*Allura Cikin Ruwa*	Bilkisu S.A.F	1995
27.	*Alamomin So*	Abba Bature Kawu	1993
28.	*Allah Ya Hada Kowa Da Rabonsa*	Dan'azumi Baba	1993
29.	*Amintacciyar Soyayya Na 1*	Dan'azumi Baba	1991
30.	*Amintacciyar Soyayya Na 2*	Dan'azumi Baba	1992
31.	*Budurwar Zuciya*	Balaraba Ramat Yakubu.	1989
31.	*Dan Tasha*	Ahmed T Aminu Gagare	1990
32.	*Direban Hajiya 1*	Ahmed Musa Anka	ND
33.	*Ganjarma 1-2*	Dan'azumi Baba	1995
34.	*Garin Masoyi*	Ahed Mahmood	B.S
35.	*Hattara Dai Masoyi1-2*	Ado Ahmed	1992
36	*Hannunka Mai Sanda*	Yahaya B. Mahmud	1996
37.	*Idan Bera Da Sata 1-2*	Dan'azumi Baba	1994/1995

38.	Idan Ka Yi Da Kyau 1	Abubakar G.S Shinkafi	2000
39.	Kaico!	Ado Ahmed	1996
40.	In Da Rai...	Idris S. Imam	1987
41.	Kogin Soyayya	Ahmed Mahmood	1988
42.	Rabon Kwado	Sadiya T.U Daneji	1989
43.	Wa Ya Fi Kishi?	Rahma Abdulmajeed	N.D
44.	Kwadayi Mabudin Wahala	Alhaji Ali Haidar Aliyu	1992
45.	Makircin So...	Badamasi S. Burji	1993
46.	Me Rabon Shan Duka	Al-Hamees D.Bature	1996
47.	Me Ya Fi Kudi?	Nazir Adamu Salih	1996
48.	Na San A Rina...	Dan'azumi Babab	N.D
49.	Sai Bango Ya Tsage	Ashiru Bala Bichi	1999
50.	Turmi Sha Daka Yakasai	Kabiru Ibrahim	2000

On its part, the Freedom Radio, Kano, has so far read the following books on the air:[23]

S/No.	Book	Author	Year of Publication
1.	Ruwan Bagaja	Abubakar Kagara	1934
2.	Magana Jari Ce 1-3	Abubakar Imam	1939/1940
3.	Nagari Na Kowa	Jabiru Abdullahi	1966
4.	Duniya Sai Sannu	Ado Ahmed Gidan Dabino	1997
5.	Ayashe	Umma Suleman Shu'aibu 'Yan'awaki	ND
6.	Fitsarin Fako 1-3	Fauziyya D. Suleman	2010
7.	So Aljannar Duniya	Hafsat Abdulwaheed	1980
8.	Mata'ul Hayyat	Zahra'u Baba Yakasai	2012

---

23 Interview with Muhammad Umar Kaigama, producer and presenter of 'Kunnenka Nawa' of Radio Kano on 7/11/2012

Although no radio station has carried out a detailed listener survey to determine the actual size of the audience that listens to the Hausa book reading sessions on the air, the presenters believe that their programmes have wide listenership, judging by the volume of correspondences they receive on regular basis as feedback. For instance, Radio Kano's "Kunnenka Nawa" was a 15-minute programme, but had to later be changed to 30 minutes due to persistent requests from the listeners to extend the time[24]. A mark of the delight the listeners derive from the programme, is that they actually demanded the station to record the programme on Compact Disks for them to purchase and play back at their pleasure. At the last enquiry, about one hundred and fifty listeners had already booked for the recorded programmes, at the cost of two hundred and fifty Naira (₦250) each. The books to be recorded were: *Mazan Jiya*, *Bakuwar Fuska* and *Kundin Tsatsuba*.[25]

Furthermore, the granting of full sponsorship for the 'Rai Dangin Goro' programme by the Lagos State Government as a platform to advertise its policies and projects, as well as its subsequent take over by the MTN Company, attests to its command of a wide audience. Aisha Bello Mahmud, the presenter of 'Ku Karkade Kunnuwanku' of the Freedom Radio explains that when the programme requested the listeners to name their books of interest to be read in the later editions of the programme, she got about five hundred responses in one batch. Furthermore, the listeners and some writers themselves sent in fifty different books voluntarily.[26] Moreover, among the numerous requests the radio house got for the recorded programmes of *Magana Jari Ce* 1-3 many came from researchers and the students of tertiary institutions in the city, like the Kano State Polytechnic, Federal College of Education, Kano, Sa'adatu Rimi College of Education, Kumbotso and Bayero University Kano.[27]

24 Interview with Aisha Bello Mahmud, the presenter of "Ku Karkade Kunnuwanku" of Freedom Radio Kano on 9/11/2012
25 Ibid 3
26 Ibid. 4
27 Ibid. 6

Radio Broadcast as Influence on the Literary Works

According to Kaigama and Koko (2012) the Hausa prose reading programme aims at promoting creativity and bringing out the talent in the young Hausa writers. It also intends to promote budding writers whose works have not yet been published, as well as promote the reading habit within its community of listeners, a tradition which is acknowledged to be generally on the decline. Kaigama (2012) explains that 'Kunnenka Nawa' has now become a popular platform for advertisement, not only to the sponsors of the programme, but also the authors, because people rush to buy copies of any book that is presented. The lucky authors feel so much indebted that they often call the producer on the phone to thank him for featuring their works. In initiating the book reading programme on the air, the pioneer producers had guessed wisely that since Hausa society was steeped in the listening culture, as illustrated by the age-old tales, riddles and songs, the reading of the prose books would be a welcome idea.

In turn, the reading programmes have inspired quite a number of people to publish in their mother tongue and popularised the works by broadcasting them. The various reading programmes have no doubt been very influential in this way, as many writers, both the seasoned and new ones, making thing their early attempts, are now known in places even where their works have not yet reached. The reading broadcasts have, no doubt, been a catalyst for the current prevalence of literary works in Hausa. Producers recall with nostalgia how, in the early 1980s, Malam Ado Ahmad Gidan Dabino used to bring his own written stories to Radio Kano for airing on the 'Kunnenka Nawa' programme. By way of boosting his morale and encouraging him to explore his talent in writing, each time Gidan Dabino brought his stories, they were accepted and presented to the public. The producers believe that this early push had greatly helped the writer to become the celebrated writer that he is now (Kaigama). Similar help has been offered to so many other young writers, for whom it is always naturally stimulating to listen to their writing read on the radio. It never fails to spur them to go on and write further, until they master the craft and attain prominence.

Kaigama's assessment is corroborated by Nasiru Zango, presenter of 'In Da Ranka' of Freedom Radio Kano, who describes the rate at which they receive correspondences from listeners as encouraging.[28] Each time they require the listeners to send their reaction to the books read on the air, they receive thousands of letters. 'In Da Ranka' also encourages the listeners to communicate in other ways. For instance, members of the audience are asked to each send a 'Letter of Regret' to be read out on air, to share the story of a mistake or incident of sadness or dismay that had happened to them. Also, each Friday the presenter devotes the programme to reading out the views of the listeners on any issues of importance relevant to the programme without restriction, thereby sharpening their literary skills. According to Zango, due to the large volume of the correspondence they receive from the listeners, they are unable to take 1% in one broadcast.[29] The programme receives the correspondences through its internet website, facebook, twitter, SMS (text message) and hand-written letters.

Conclusion

From the foregoing, it can be understood that the reading of the Hausa literary works on the radio has been an important way of generating discussions on various issues in the society, a practice that in turn influences the selection of the themes of future books. The radio, indeed, provides an avenue for the writers to communicate with their large audiences directly and with ease, including those who cannot either read or buy the books. The book reading programmes on the radio have, indeed, proved a useful avenue for the promotion of Hausa written literature that should be sustained and encouraged.

---

28   Interview with Nasiru Salisu Zango presenter of "In Da Ranka" of Freedom Radio on 8/11/2012
29   Ibid. 8

REFERENCES

- Abubakar, Abdullahi Tasi'u (2011), "Media Consumption Amid Contestation: Northern Nigerians' Engagement with the BBC World Service". UK: University of Westminster, unpublished PhD thesis.

- Adekunle, A. A. et al (2002), *Agricultural Information Dissemination: An Audience Survey in Kano State*. Ibadan: International Institute of Tropical Agriculture.

- Ahmad, Gausu (2006), *"Gakiya Ta Fi Kwabo:* From the Colonial Service to Community Beacon", in Abiodun Salawu (ed) *Indigenous Language Media in Africa*. Lagos: Centre for Black and African Arts and Civilisation.

- Blankson, Isaac Abeku (2005), "Negotiating the Use of Native Languages in Emerging Pluralistic and Independent Broadcast System in Africa", in *Africa Media Review*. Volume, 13, Council for the Development of Social Science Research in Africa.

- Brann, C.M.B. (1995), "Language Choice and Allocation in Nigerian Broadcasting Services", *Africa und Ubersee* 72/2 pp. 261-281.

- East, R. M. (1936), "A First Essay in Imaginative African Literature", reprinted in Hayatu Hussain (ed). (1991), *50 Years of Truth: The Story of Gaskiya Corporation Zaria 1939-1991, Zaria:* Gaskiya Corporation Limited.

- Funtua, Mansur, Abdulkadir (1997), "Popular Culture and Advertising in Hausa: Cultural Appropriation and Linguistic Creativity in Radio Advertisements by Bashir Isma'ila Ahmed," unpublished Ph.D thesis submitted to the SOAS, University of London.

- Garba, Sabiu Alhaji (2010), "Hausa A Gidan Rediyon BBC", Department of Nigerian Languages. Sokoto: Usmanu Danfodiyo University, M.A Dissertation.
- Garba, Sabi'u Alhaji (2011), "Hausa in the Media", paper presented at the 24th Conference of the Linguistic Association of Nigeria, held at Bayero University, Kano.
- Garba, Sabi'u Alhaji, "A Survey of Radio Stations Broadcasting in Hausa in Nigeria" (unpublished manuscript).
- Hunziker, P. (2005), "The Story of Africa (Book and Audio CDs) African History From Dawn of Time", London: BBC http://www.bbc.co.uk/worldservice/africa/features/storyofafrica/index.html
- Ibrahim, Suleiman (1994), "BBC And The Hausas: Attempting To Influence", London: City University London. M.A. Dissertation.
- Isa Kaita *http://en.wikipedia.org/wiki/Isa_Kaita*.
- Koko, Ahmad Isa (2012) Verbal Interview
- Malumfashi, I.A. (2003). "Adabi da Bidiyon Kasuwar Kano a Bisa Faifai: Takaitaccen Tsokaci", Paper presented at the Conference on Hausa Literature organised by Centre for Hausa Studies, Usmanu Danfodiyo University Sokoto.
- Malumfashi, Ibrahim (2009), *Adabin Abubakar Imam*, Kaduna: Garkuwa Publications
- Malumfashi, I.A. (2011). "Ta'aziyar Adabin Kasuwar Kano", in Yalwa, Lawan Danladi et al (eds), *Studies in Hausa Language, Literature and Culture: Proceedings of the Sixth Hausa International Conference*, Kano: CSLN, Bayero University.
- Moemeka, Andrew, A. (1981), *Local Radio: Community Education for Development*, Zaria: Ahmadu Bello University Press

- Mohammed, U.A. (2004), "The Use of Hausa in the Electronic Media: An Evaluation of Terms and Concepts", unpublished PhD thesis, University of Maiduguri
- Mukhtar, Isa. (2004). *Jagoran Nazarin Kagaggun Labarai*. Second Edition. Kano: Benchmark publishers.
- Mytton, Graham (2000), "A Brief History of Radio Broadcasting in Africa", http://www.traculturalwriting.com/radiophonics/continents/usr/downloads/radiophonics/A-Brief-History.pdf
- Ojebode, A. and Adegbola, T. (2007), *"Engaging Development: Environment and Content of Radio Broadcasting in Nigeria"*, Lagos: Institute for Media and Society.
- Tilde, Aliyu. 2010. "Goodbye, VOA Hausa", *Discourse 108, Friday Discourse,* May 15, 2010.
- http://fridaydiscourse.blogspot.com/2010/05/discourse-108-goodbye-voa-hausa-service.html
- Yahaya, Ibrahim Yaro (1988), *Hausa A Rubuce: Tarihin Rubuce-Rubucen Cikin Hausa.* Zaria: Northern Nigerian Publishing Company.

Chapter Ten

A Historiographic Survey of Ilorin Music

Femi Abiodun

Introduction

Until recently, there was no musical genre specifically identified as the "Ilorin Music." However, scholars have since made a case for the proper classification of the Ilorin music as a brand composed of some unique musical styles, which are only played in the Ilorin Emirate of the Kwara State of Nigeria. For instance, Abiodun (2000:24) in his study of *Baluu* music concludes that it is not played anywhere else in Nigeria. In a contrastive analysis of *Baluu* and *Waka* music (an Ibadan musical type in southwestern Nigeria), he discovers that their musical structures and organisations are different. Thus, efforts have been devoted since 2001 to determine what Ilorin music history is. Moreover, Bukofier (1994) has noted that the study of the styles of non-Western music at present lacks proper historical documentation. The combined challenge of these observations constitutes the backdrop to this contribution, as the study attempts to draw from the works of the scholars in order to illuminate the history of a particular genre of music, the approach that Nketia (1994) advises ethnomusicologists and other scholars of music to adopt.

This study, while drawing from the works of professional historians and using the bibliographic and discographic methods, together with interview sessions with twenty musicians in the Ilorin emirate, investigates the historical sources of the Ilorin music. Five genres of music constitute the scope of the study: *Baluu, Senwele, Dadakuada, Agbe* and *Dundun-Sekere* music. The structural analysis of the melody, rhythm, form and texture of these musical types shows that they are different from their counterparts from southwestern Nigeria (*Waka, Apala, Fuji, Were*). These structural differences suggest a different origin, most likely in the northern Nigerian music, since they portray evidence of some northern Nigerian musical elements (falsetto voices, nasal voices, use of Arabic words, etc).

The discussion in this study is made, using four variables to determine the history, but not the story behind Ilorin music. These variables are:

a. historical accounts of cosmopolitan organisation of Ilorin;
b. cultural indices (language);
c. religion ;
d. social activities; and
e. influences of western education on these musical types.

The following questions are pertinent in the discussion on the search for historical materials of Ilorin music:

a. Can the history of Ilorin music be traced to the history of the migration of the people?
b. Can the history of Ilorin music be linked with the people's religious affiliation?
c. Can one use the present cultural indices of the Ilorin community to deduce the historical facts concerning its music?
d. Conversely, could the musical history be traced to the diverse social activities in the ancient city of Ilorin?
e. What is the impact of the western culture on the development of the ethos of Ilorin music?

The Ilorin People

Ilorin, the seat of the Ilorin Emirate and home to His Royal Highness, the Emir, is the capital of Kwara State, which was created from the former Northern Region of Nigeria in 1967. It is the principal link between Northern and Southern Nigeria. Two main rivers flow within the city – *Asa* and *Agba* rivers, on which dams have been built to provide water for the people. Usually the rainfall begins in May and ends in October. Ilorin had a population of 532,088 in the 1991 census and covers three local governments: Ilorin West with headquarters in Oja (main market in Ilorin); Ilorin East and Ilorin South with the headquarters at Oke-Oyi and Fufu, respectively.

Ilorin, like Ogbomoso further to the west, was not founded by the Yoruba, even though the two communities are on "Yoruba soil." Ogbomosho was founded by a Nupe man who was an elephant hunter and whose descendants could still be found in the Baale of Oke Elerin quarters in the town (Ogbomosho). No one remembers the real name of the hunter, but the nickname given to him by the Yoruba settlers who later joined him in the town was *Aale* (Jimoh 1994).

As for Ilorin, the first settler in the town was a Baruba hermit. He lived at a place, which till today is called "Baruba." He got to the place before Ojo Isekuse; an itinerant Yoruba hunter. Later, Emila and Afonja arrived into the same area; their descendants still live there. However, it is widely believed that Ilorin was first built as a Yoruba settlement in the 17th century by an itinerant hunter from Gambari, near Oyo-Ile. His name was Ojo, but was nicknamed Ojo-Isekuse ('Isekuse' being the nickname he acquired from the locals for his immoral sexual exploits, for which he became quite famous) and had Ayinla as his cognomen. The Yorubas called the rock on which he used to sharpen his cutlass *Ilo-irin*, meaning 'iron sharpener'. The name Ilorin, is therefore, believed to be a contraction of *Ilo-irin*, contrary to the mythical story among the people of Oko-

Erin that it was derived from Ilu-Erin, that is, 'the town of the Elephant'. The single incidence of killing an elephant on the outskirt of the town in 1824 could not have provided enough justification for the claim.

History has it that before the Fulani found their way into Ilorin, there was not a single ruler who had overall sovereignty over all the settlements. The city was host to many ethnic groups, which were scattered in hamlets headed by independent rulers. The Okesuna hamlet headed by al-Tahir, nicknamed Solagberu, was an exclusively Muslim settlement. Okelele hamlet headed by Ojo-Isekuse and Idiape hamlet headed by Afonja, were Yoruba territory. Gaa hamlet headed by Olufadi and Gambari hamlet headed by Sarki Gambari were Hausa territory (Oloru 1998:9). History also had it that Alfa Alimi, who came to Ilorin in the 18th century for missionary purposes, was invited by Afonja to become the king of Ilorin, but he declined on religious grounds, explaining that scholarship, not political office, was his main mission in Ilorin. However, he invited his son from Sokoto who, subsequently, became the first Emir of Ilorin.

The customs and traditions of the Ilorin people have predominantly been fashioned by Islam. For instance, in contrast to other Yoruba towns and villages, where various festivals are celebrated to mark one traditional myth or the other, Ilorin has no such fiestas now. The only festivals in Ilorin are Eid El-Kabir, Eid-al-Fitr and Maolud Nabiy. All these are Islamic festivals. The only other social occasions in the city are the marriage and baby naming ceremonies; even the observance of these is largely influenced by Islamic doctrines.

From the historical sketch above, it is quite apparent that Ilorin is a cosmopolitan city composed of many different ethnic groups: from northern Nigeria (Kanuri, Hausa/Fulani), Western Nigeria (Yoruba) the middle belt (Nupe and Baruba) and from ancient Mali (Okemale). It is also obvious that Islam had quite early influenced cultural activities in the city, making the dominant culture quite Islamic in its social manifestations, like in dress, customs, cultural ceremonies and other practices; only the language they speak is Yoruba. Their political structure also reflects the general principles of Islamic leadership hierarchy and values.

Every social group living in Ilorin today had migrated to the city from some other place and has its ethnic origins elsewhere else, whether Yoruba, Hausa, Fulani, Kanuri, Nupe, Baruba, Malians, Sudanese or from Agades. For instance, the Agbaji families were originally Sudanese Arabs; as well as Ile Bature at Oke Apomu, who also have Arab roots; having migrated into Ilorin from Agades, in today's Niger Republic. The Ojibara family are of Fulani descent. They initially sojourned in Bornu before migrating to Ilorin. Similarly, the Solagberu family was originally Kanuri, from Kanem Borno, while that of Magaji Kuntu was from Baruba. The Alaya family was from Nupe land; Ile Alalikinla, Ita Ogunbo and Ile Alapata are Hausas. (Jimoh: 1994)

Thus, the collapse of the Oyo Empire had originally given rise to the Ilorin Emirate and the dense population that subsequently developed was as a result of migrations from different parts of Nigeria and the West African sub-region. The migration took two distinct forms:

a. Self-migration in search of better living conditions; and
b. Slavery as a result of war (war refugees).

Self-migration is the migration process that involves individuals moving from one place to another in search of better fortunes through security, enhanced agricultural activities, trading of one commodity or another; or providing services. Whatever purposes provoke their original movements, self-migrants are people who arrive into a new environment and simply decide to settle there. Undoubtedly, such migrants come into contact with the locals in their host community and begin to interact with them immediately they arrive. This social intercourse invariably results into gradual fusion, as they adopt the local social practices through participating in cultural activities, like marriages, naming ceremonies, music, art and craft and, in some cases, religion.

However, the universal lesson of history is that military conquest was often the biggest tool of imperialism. People acquired land and property by subjugating other people who were less powerful. Isichei (1983) reiterates that:

> Powerful unified states such as Borno or the emirates of the Sokoto caliphate, became predators, prying on their neighbours which were organized in smaller units: "Nupe, Ilorin and Kontagara" established themselves as viable emirates through destruction and sale of considerable segments of their opposition.

Powerful states organised slave expeditions against weaker states in order to hunt for slaves, especially after the slave trade became quite lucrative, when the slaves were being shipped overseas from Badagry and the coastal areas. This usually brought in large migrants seeking refuge in bigger towns under the defence of powerful rulers, thereby swelling up the population of the towns rapidly. May, (in Isichei, 1983), while travelling in 1858 through Yagba land, in the present Kogi State, encountered evidence of Ilorin slave raiders in the area. This, according to him, was a popular occupation of the army of Ilorin. It is evident, thus, that Ilorin actively participated in the slave trade in the mid 19th Century. The effect was that many people who are now indigenes of Ilorin were migrants from different ethnic groups and had come into the city in order to seek cover from the slave raiders or else were brought in as a result of the slave trade expedition, making Ilorin what it is today: a confederation of people with different ethnic backgrounds who had brought in their diverse cultural practices. As Jimoh (1994) ascertains:

> That Ilorin, at a point in time was peopled almost exclusively by the Yoruba is not in dispute. However, with the passage of time the community became culturally multi-farious, following the influx of a multiplicity of other cultural and sub-cultural groups; so much that by the time civil strife

occurred between Afonja and Shehu Alimi's Jama'a about 1807, the combined population of the Jama'a in Gambari, Fulani and Okesuna areas who were mainly non-Yoruba had greatly exceeded that of the Kakanfo's compatriots who were confined to Idiape (p.9).

History as Source of Ilorin Music

Thus, Ilorin, being a multi-ethnic cosmopolitan city, had evolved as an ethno-cultural melting pot, with its people originally migrating from different parts of the West African sub-region. In doing so, they had brought along with them different aspects of their material culture, including musical instruments. Music, as it often is, remains one of the outstanding pieces of such cultural artifacts. Alhaji Ibrahim Adelodun claims that he still has relics of the *dundun* drums his fore-fathers brought from Oyo, which he keeps in his home in Idi-Ape as valuable historical artefacts, thereby confirming that the *dundun* drums were originally introduced into Ilorin when the Yoruba people migrated into the city. Similarly, the royal musical instruments (Algaita, Kakaki), which are used in the palace of the Emir of Ilorin to signify the royalty are evidence that historically many people living in Ilorin today had migrated from the Hausa/Fulani areas of northern Nigeria.

Indeed, in addition to establishing the emirate political structure of Northern Nigeria very early in its history, the Ilorin Emirate had also fused into it the northern royal musical instruments and regalia. The sound of aerophones (blowing musical instruments) that herald and applaud the arrival or departure of the Emir from the palace every day is significantly a northern culture. The musical instruments are, likewise, employed to sing the praises of the Emir at social occasions, especially the musical drum that is accompanied with the loud speech-melody, "She-e-e-u; She-e-e-u; She-e-eu!" (the Emir's praises), each time it is beaten. This speech melody, which is similar to what Nketia (1974) describes as "verbal phrase and musical phrase", is distinctly from the Hausa/

Fulani culture. As Nketia explains further, "a musical phrase may be conterminous with a sentence, a clause, a phrase, or even a word that functions as a complete utterance." In the case of the Emir of Ilorin above, the word is used to function as an utterance, accompanied with explosive sounds and special interjections in the praises of the emir.

Nonetheless, in Ilorin today, there are different musical genres that are traced to southern or northern Nigeria, including Arab-based citizens who migrated to Ilorin as a result of one migration process or another. In different studies, historical origins of some of these musical styles have been established.

(a) *Dundun* – Oyo origin (Olaniyan 1984)
(b) *Ogbele Music* – Ekiti origin (Abiodun 1994)
(c) *Sekere Music* – Oyo origin (Olaniyan, 1984)
(d) *Dadakuada* – (Adeola, 1997) Northern Islamic music origin
(e) *Baalu* – the female Dadakuada (Abiodun, 2000)
(f) *Sewele* – An adaptation of Baalu (Abiodun, 2000)
(g) *Pankeke* – Emerged from Jihad war songs (Jimoh, 1994)
(h) *Agbe Ensemble* – Nupe origin (Jimoh, 1994)
(i) *Were* – Music adopted for the Islamic festival of Ramadan (Ajirire and Alabi, 1991)
(j) *Waka* - An adaptation of Were (Ajirire and Alabi, 1991)

Thus, the history of these musical styles in Ilorin could be traced to the population migrations that followed the periods of war, as well as the local immigrations within the old Ilorin and Ekiti Empires (Opin, 1882). The Ilorin/Offa war (1880's), the Pamo war, the Gbodo, the Jalumi, the Esiele and Gbogun wars (Ilorin and Yoruba) were major historical wars that explain how the multi-layer migration accounts for the different musical genres that developed over the years, independent of the musical styles found in northern and south-western Nigeria, like *Baalu, Dadakuada, Senwele, Pankeke* which are of Ilorin origin. The mode of performance, style and structure of the music are different from other notable musical genres of the Yoruba, even though some of them are of Yoruba origin, like the *Sekere* and *Dundun* drums. Apart from the fact that they have retained their original Yoruba names, their shape, beat pattern, speech surrogates and performance style are also similar to those of the Yoruba.

However, the *Agbe* calabash drums are of Nupe origin, although in Ilorin they have lost their accompanying performance structure. For example, in beating the *agbe*, the Nupes turn the calabash upside down in a bowl of water, but the Ilorin musicians hold it in their hands while performing. The modes of performance and forms of music have changed with time. *Dadakuada* is of Kanuri/Ilorin origin (Adeola:1997) the reason being that the first set/pioneers of *Dadakuada* music (Odolaye Aremu, Jayegbade Alao) were of Kanuri origin; and, subsequently, most of the popular performers today are from the Sholagberu compound, who are Kanuri by lineage.

Cultural Indices (Language) as Historical Source of Ilorin Music

Historical and comparative linguistic analysis of the vocabulary, structure of song texts and musical terms of the vocabulary (terms for musical instruments, musical types and dances) have also proven to be quite helpful in helping to determine the historical sources of the Ilorin music. Linguistic enquiry as the basis for historical investigation reveals that some words accompanying the music performances are local to Ilorin, as they are not spoken in any other part of Yoruba land. Since the origin of the words is Ilorin, it is assumed that such music could not have come from other parts of the country. Such musical terms as *boto* (the song leader assistant) are peculiar to Ilorin and are not found in Hausa or Yoruba language. A lexicographic enquiry into the musical practices reveals that such words like *ni ha in* (in this place) *e n le fa* (a form of greetings), which are words spoken only by Ilorin people, prompt a historical hypothesis regarding the origin of the traditional music in which they commonly feature. Studies have shown that traditional music uses the language of its culture of origin, however modified. Its history can, therefore, be sought within the linguistic structure.

Religion as Historical Source of Ilorin Music

As pointed out above, unlike in many parts of the country, Ilorin Emirate does not observe any non-Islamic traditional festival; hence, it is not familiar with the musical practices attached to them. Such occasions include festivals that are normally entrenched among the Yoruba, like the Ogun, Sango, Osun and Eyo Festivals, which mark the beginning of new annual periods and are intended to appease the gods and goddesses; or the *Bori* possession in old Hausa land that celebrated the rites of passage or life in general. Instead, the people in Ilorin only mark the Islamic religious festivals and such other permitted social events and celebrations, including the Eid El-Kabir, Eid al-Fitr and Maulud Nabiy.

This has a strong base in the religious history of Ilorin, which started with the arrival of Shehu Alimi in Ilorin shortly before 1808 or 1817, as some other scholars claim. Among these are Jimoh (1997.3), who argues that, since the Sheikh originally came as a scholar and Islamic missionary from Sokoto, it would be doubtful that he left Sokoto and came to Ilorin by 1808, before the founding of the Sokoto Caliphate in 1809. This could be countered, though, by pointing at the historical circumstances prevalent at the time, which encouraged the movement of pious scholars across the West African sub-region, including Sheikh Uthman Donfodiyo himself, who founded the Sokoto caliphate.

However, what is relevant to this study was that Shehu Alimi had come to Ilorin on a religious mission; and his aspiration was to call the then pagan communities living in Ilorin and environs to Islam. When he was invited by Afonja to become the political head of Ilorin, therefore, he turned it down on these grounds and was, thus, able to focus his attention on his missionary work. Today, this effort could be judged to have been very successful, considering that almost everyone in Ilorin is a Muslim and the community as a whole that of fervent believers, whose commitment to Islam is quite established. They are in the forefront during the national Qur'anic competitions organised in the country every year and have represented Nigeria many times in similar competitions around the world, the last being in Cairo, Egypt, 2002.

In this way, in Ilorin, with its history of massive influx of people with assorted cultural backgrounds, Islam has remained the common denominator and most powerful unifying social factor. This accounts for the triumph of the Islamic culture in the city, including some Islamic musical genres. Prominent among these are the *Were* and *Waka*. Other forms of music that have Islamic origins include *Fuji*, which is an offshoot of *Were* (an Islamic music used to wake Muslims up for the meal at dawn during Ramadan). Today in Ilorin there are sixty-three (63) Fuji musicians officially registered with the local branch of the Performing Musicians' Association of Nigeria. In fact, Fuji is performed during all Islamic celebrations, where the participants welcome it in place of the other musical genres, like *Juju*, which have roots in non-Islamic traditional practices.

Historical evidence and the structural analysis of the song text, song form, performance mode and practice suggest that religion prompts the origin of such music as *Waka* and *Alasalatu* musical groups in Ilorin. The exponents claim that Islam prompts the formation and organisation of such musical ensembles.

Western Education as Historical Source of Ilorin Music

Another factor that has influenced the pattern and structure of the Ilorin music was the growth of the Western system of education in the wake of British colonial conquest at the close of the Nineteenth Century. The first school in Ilorin was established in 1914, followed by other educational institutions.

This had enabled many indigenes of Ilorin to travel abroad and learn about the social culture of other countries in the world, including their music. Besides, the Christian missionaries had also introduced many musical genres to the Ilorin community quite early through their mission schools, beginning with the marching songs the children were taught to sing every morning at the opening of the school, accompanied with the beating of the drums. The hymnals at the church service and the choruses were so inspiring that they were also used to preach to the people.

This was further consolidated by the western cultural practices, like the writing down of oral compositions and perfecting them ahead of the public performances. Many musicians now write down their lyrics and arrange them well to perfection and so that they will not lose them. The western influence had also introduced new devices and greatly contributed in bringing variety to the musical instruments currently in use in Ilorin. The modern musical equipment (instruments and gadgets) in particular have added further value to the indigenous musical practices through the use of the amplification system - loud speakers, amplifier engines, microphones and studio facilities for organising and recording local compositions for dissemination, like *Fuji*, *Waka* and *Dadakuada*. Many have actually graduated into using the cell phone to record their music so that they would perfect the melodies (tunes). It appears that these developments have come to stay, even as they expand further to permanently become part of the historical growth of what has now evolved as the Ilorin music. Certainly, the history of Ilorin music cannot be written without a mention of the contribution of western education and its various tools and instruments.

Conclusion

Indeed, the history of the development of the Ilorin music is closely linked with the social history of the Ilorin society, as every community of people enacts only the social institutions that serve its purpose. As Nketia (1970) reiterates, "historical studies should not only cover the development and growth of forms and styles, but also the factors that have contributed to them at different historical periods." History is an account of events over certain periods, including cultural activities, like music, a factor that confers significance on understanding the different facets of Ilorin music.

From the above discussions, it could be observed that the many different musical traditions of the city of Ilorin is as a result of the migration of the people from different cultures, including the Yoruba states, Hausa/Fulani emirates, the Kanuris, Nupes, Malians, Barubas, Sudanese and even the far away Arab and Agades kingdoms. The evolution of Ilorin as an 'ethno-cultural melting pot' suggests a unique social composition, in which religion – Islam – had played a dominant role as a unifying and common factor.

In attempting to document the historical origins of the genres of Ilorin music, this paper seeks for a fresh opening in the study of Nigerian music, through advocating for the use of evidence in the people's history as a viable means of establishing their musical history. The musical activities of every society evolve along with the trends in its development; therefore, the history of any people reflects in the history of its musical practices.

References

- Abiodun, Femi (1995), "The Performance Practice of Ogbele Music in Ekiti". Paper presented at the Second National Conference of the Association of Nigerian Musicologists. Obafemi Awolowo University, Ile-Ife
- Abiodun, Femi (2000), "The Life and Works of Yewande Agbeke, a Baalu Musician in Ilorin", Unpublished M.A. Thesis, Obafemi Awolowo University.
- Adeola, Taye (1997), "Dadakuada Music: A Socio-Musical Studies" Unpublished M.A. dissertation, Obafemi Awolowo University.
- Ajirire, Tosin and Alabi, Wale (1992), *Three Decades of Nigerian Music*, Lagos: Limelight Showbiz Publication Limited.
- Danmole, H.O. (1980), "The Frontier Emirate: A History of Islam in Ilorin". Unpublished Ph.D. thesis, University of Birmingham
- Isichei, E. (1983), *A History of Nigeria,* Ibadan: Longman Inc.
- Jimoh, L.H.K (1994), *Ilorin: The Journey So Far,* Ilorin: Atoto Press Ltd.,
- Na'Allah, AbdulRasheed, (1994), "Dadakuada as One of the Oral Art Forms in Ilorin" *Africa Notes,* Vol. 18 (122) pp. 29-51
- Nketia, J.H.K. (nd), "History and the Organization of Music in West Africa", Unpublished Manuscript, University of Ghana.
- Nketia, J.H.K. (1974), *The Music of Africa*, London: MGBO Publications Limited.

- Olaniyan, C.O. (1984), "Composition and Performance Techniques in Yoruba Dundun-Sekere Music," Unpublished Ph.D Dissertation, Queens University, Belfast, 1984.
- Oloru, A.J. (1998) *A Guide to Ilorin.* Ilorin: Nigeria Limited.
- Roberto, N. (1983), "The Social Evolution of the Afro-Cuban Drum" *The Black Perspective in Music* 11 (2) New York: City University.

PART THREE:
LITERATURE AND IDENTITY

Chapter Eleven

Literature and Identity in Northern Nigeria

Yakubu A. Nasidi

Introduction

> Maybe the target nowadays is not to discover what we are, but to refuse what we are... (Michel Foucault) [emphasis added]
> No identity is stable in today's wild, recombinant mix of culture, blood and ideas. Things fall apart; they make themselves anew. Every race carries with it the seeds of its own destruction. (Eric Liu)

Like Gizo and Koki (the protean couple in Hausa trickster tales), literature and identity go hand in hand. To talk of a people's or a nation's literature is to talk of their identity; and all talk of identity soon includes questions of literature or, more broadly, of culture. Who are we as a nation, a group, an ethnic or cultural collectivity? What are our defining characteristics, what are the cultural and linguistic affiliations? In terms of values, behaviour patterns or even physique, what is it that differentiates US from those that are 'NOT-US?'

What are the main forms of our collective identification? What is our inner essence, our quiddity? All communities, the Wazirin Sokoto, Alhaji Junaidu (1972:8) once said:

> have an inner life, a spiritual dimension which makes them what they are, gives them their autonomy and helps them to rise beyond their present to greater achievement.

Elaborating further, he explained:

> I am speaking here of the values which they have about their place in the world, about the correct relationship between men, about the proper ways to behave in conducting the affairs of men and their own views about what constitutes their identity. (Junaidu, 1972:8)

Identities, especially primordial ones, involving ethnicities and cultures, even national identities, involve attachment to a place; they involve rootedness, and Octavio Paz would probably be right in seeing in the problem of identity, "the psychic, historical and cultural reality which lies beyond our outward appearance."

All questions of identity, therefore, operate at the deepest level of the community. "The oldest problem of human society," Bill Clinton (2002) once observed," is "the fear of the other." Identities, in the last resort, are, thus, a form of refuge, intended to stave off 'the fear of the Other,' a shelter from 'crisis and alienation.' They are, therefore, irreducibly, social or collective. The realm of identity is also the realm of what Terry Eagleton (2000) calls 'social subjectivity,' uniting individuals in 'universal subjecthood' – at least in relation to a cultural, ethnic or national collectivity. Culture comes in here because it is 'the domain of social subjectivity' and, as with culture, so also with literature. Both literature and culture are linked because they are both concerned with social subjectivity – that is to say, with our identity. In fact, as Eagleton (2000) further argues, the shaping of social subjectivity, of collective cultural identity, was part of the raison dêtre of literature.

Literature is, thus, heavily implicated in questions of identity, not only in relation to the language it deploys, but as a consequence of the values it affirms. With the German Romantics, in reaction to the hegemony of French Classicism, literature was seen as an occasion for 'affirming national identity' and of getting to know 'the unique racial genius of a people.'

Literature and Identity

However, this has not always been so. With the classicals, writing/creativity was a slow process of apprenticeship, painfully learnt at the foot of a master – with clear-cut RULES and procedure, in tandem with the laws of nature. In Pope's inimitable words:

> First follow nature, and your judgement frame
> By her just standard, which is still the same:
> Unerring nature, still divinely bright
> One clear, unchanged and universal light
> Life, force, and beauty must to all impart,
> At once the source, and end, and test of Art.
> (Pope: Essay on Criticism)

Then came the Romantics and, at one fell swoop, declared the autonomy of Art and of the artist, shifting emphasis in the fashion of Roland Barthes from work to psychology. Thus, the mind of the individual writer, his inner being, became the sole criterion for judging a work of art because it was felt that he was a spokesman from a higher truth. In some even more extreme formulations, the writer was declared, as in symbolist aesthetics, to be the guardian of the chemistry.

As with the German Romantics, so it was with the first crop of African writers, at least, with the first or second generation. Here, one need not repeat Soyinka's famous dictum, but its essential thrust was obvious: Literature was burdened with the task of carrying either the community's or the nation's identity and of conveying its essential meanings through the agency of that most gifted of creatures, the African writer, who was now cast either in the role of a teacher (Achebe) or of a prophet or visionary (Soyinka).

Thus, the saddling of literature with questions of identity, of a racial or cultural essence, was, in the African context, a reproduction of the dominant tendency of literary thought in the European metropolis. The Western ideal of culture or literature was simply countered by an African ideal, rooted in an alternative humanism — to show that Africans did not hear of culture for the first time from the white man, etc., to paraphrase Achebe. The ideological upshot of all this is very much obvious: African literature is taken to be a repository of "the defining values and identity of African culture and society." It would then follow, from this, that when we say Northern Nigerian Literature or even more descriptively, 'Literature in Northern Nigeria,' we mean a species of imaginative writing that encodes some essence or unique ontology – of the cultural and geographical landscape known as northern Nigeria.

Thus, anyone interested to know the character of the North or the Northerners should read *Gandoki, Ruwan Bagaja* or *Magana Jari Ce,* if he can read Hausa; if not, the person should read *The Last Imam* or any of Zaynab Alkali's texts, as one would come into direct contact with the inner essence, the soul of the inhabitants of the North. As a tourist, a business executive or an investor from outside the area, one will then be in a better position to understand who the people are and the way they live. In more playful moments, one could always fancy oneself as playing the role of a cynical interlocutor in some poststructuralist script of one's own imagining: If there is a northern Nigerian literature, is there also a southern Nigerian literature? If not, why not? Within the North itself, if there is a Hausa literature, it also follows that there should be Kanuri literature, a Tiv literature, an Igala Literature, a Gbagyi literature and so many others, based on our several ethnic and cultural identities.

Identities unite, but they also divide. They pretend to speak to an essence, but they are never given, or natural. All identities are invented and constructed – even fabricated based upon a notion of 'we versus them,' of 'same versus the other.' There can be no concept of who or what we are as a people without a countervailing concept of what we are not. In short, no identity can be constituted without pressing a mute button somewhere, and when one day the mute button is released, what we thought was a monolithic and non-contradictory terrain suddenly becomes contested by a plurality of voices, by ancient, but repressed configurations.

On such a contested terrain we now stand. The old idea of the North as a monolithic, single identity — the 'One North phenomenon', as Kwanashie (2002), calls it — has given way to a fissiparous tendency, with different groups laying claim to their own unique identities. Whither then Northern Nigerian Literature or Literature in Northern Nigeria? If, as Obafemi phrases it, Northern Literature is 'the reflective tool' of a 'northern dream and essence', what becomes of its role when that dream is fractured?

History and Identity

Generally speaking, as we go about chasing identities and essences, we often fail to grant history the pride of place it deserves in such a discussion. History is necessary because it can help to uncover what identities, especially the larger ones, conceal or repress. Foucault (1982) refers to this as "the systematic dissociation of identity", a task which is crucial, because this rather weak identity which we attempt to support and to unify, a mask, is itself only a parody: it is plural; countless spirits dispute its possession; numerous systems intersect and compete. History, therefore, helps to pry open identities, releasing the countless spirits imprisoned by the 'hegemonic father.'

It is, therefore, salutary and intellectually beneficial that the organisers have framed the general theme as 'Literature, History and Identity in Northern Nigeria.' Without the necessary attention to history, any discussion of identity would have ended up as a contribution to ideology rather than to criticism. At this stage, a brief look at the history of literature in northern Nigeria is in order.

Literature in Northern Nigeria

Considering its antecedents, it could safely be argued that literature in northern Nigeria (in the Roman alphabet) was conceived and delivered within the context of colonial hegemony. Its beginning was an act of cultural violence involving what Adamu (2006) describes as "the forceful intrusion of the Roman alphabet." It became clear to the British imperial powers quite early after taking over the territory that the colonial project in northern Nigeria was not going to be particularly easy because there was already an enduring cultural system, a prevailing hegemony securely in place among the people, complete with its literature in the *Ajami* script.

Ajami had developed its own forms of literacy based upon the local adaptation of the Arabic writing in the northern areas since the eleventh century; especially after the Sokoto Jihad at the beginning of the 19th century. The difficulty in getting the Roman script to root it out was, understandably, quite obvious, as captured in the following recollection by an observer:

> The first reactions of Hausa readers [to the Roman script] were not altogether favourable. The Arabic script and literacy in it had the advantage of being already in use; restricted though Ajami literacy may have been at the time, it was established. The Roman script, on the other hand, was automatically associated with "foreign", "pagan" or 'unbelievers' ideas.' The common name given to this Roman-script-based-literacy – boko – might well have been associated with the English word "book" and with the Hausa original sense which means "deceit" or "fraud." (Petr Zima, quoted in A. Gerard, 1981:62)

It was, therefore, clearly going to be a case of one hegemony trying to supplant another. At the centre of this agonistic drama of cultural incorporation was Dr. Rupert M. East, "one of the most significant colonial personalities in the cultural and literary history of northern Nigeria", as Aliyu (1990) describes him. Fully aware of the difficulties he faced, East proceeded with the cunning and tenacity of the imperial officer fully dedicated to the calling of his empire.

Since a system of cultural representation already existed, he knew his task involved not only the introduction of a new script, but the supplanting of one consciousness by another. Here is how he puts it himself:

> The first difficulty was to persuade these malamai that the thing was worth doing. The influence of Islam, superimposed on the Hamitic strain in the blood of the northern Nigerian, produces an extremely serious-minded type of person. The act of writing, moreover, being intimately connected in his mind with his religion, is not to be treated lightly...To these people, therefore, the idea of writing a book which was frankly intended neither for the edification of the mind, nor for the good of the soul, a "story" book which, however, followed none of the prescribed forms of storytelling, seemed very strange. (R. M. East, quoted in A. Gerard, 1981:63)

Of greater significance, however, was the personal relationship between East and Alhaji Abubakar Imam, a graphic case of cultural tutelage, in which the latter would learn at the foot of his benefactor "the many do's and don'ts of fiction writing." (Adamu, 2006). There was a clear division of labour, for while East engaged himself in direct translation of words (mostly from Arabic and the oriental languages) into Hausa, Imam became responsible for adaptations and transpositions of published works from Arabic and other sources into a recognisably Hausa setting, so as to make them more digestible to the native Hausa reader. The two writers have since been turned into paradigms of 'creativity' by the Hausa literary critics: 'Istanci' for East's example and 'Imamanci' for Imam's.

More worthy of note is that it was in this context of hegemonic tuition between master and subaltern that *Magana Jari Ce* (strangely referred to as "the unalloyed classic of Hausa literature" by Adamu) emerged as the most outstanding Hausa literary text. Imam then became a 'trans-discursive author' of sorts, initiating a tradition in which his acolytes, rather than invent their own stories, would continue to adapt borrowed tales to a Hausa/northern setting. Garba Funtua, Ahmadu Katsina and Ahmadu Ingawa (the so-called second generation of Hausa writers) were all heavily reliant on foreign (mostly eastern) sources; as, indeed, have been all subsequent generations and their practices. Consequently, Hausa/Northern literature has been a largely reactive enterprise since it has never been able to supersede the templates imposed by East and Imam, as Adamu (2006) claims. Even more fatally, when it was introduced in the 1930's by the Lebanese and the Syrians in Kano, the cinema merely continued with "the entrapment of Hausa culture within an essentially Western European entertainment ethos." Thus, Kannywood, when it eventually arrived, could not unchain the muse of Hausa creativity; instead it represented a mere 'leap' of dependency 'from the screen to the street.' (Adamu, 2006). So much then for identity.

However, it should be noted that the coming of published literature in English or the other European languages to Nigeria or Africa did not necessarily represent a moment of cultural triumph for the colonisers; and nowhere is this more graphically illustrated than the case of Dr. East who knew that for the 'Hausa book literature' to take root, the pre-existing creative fields of the Hausas or the Tivs or the Fulanis had to be broken down and their cultural systems reconstructed. Therefore, the full significance of "Literature in Northern Nigeria" can be appreciated only in terms of a history and a particular relationship, not in terms of an identity or an essence.

Even so, the practice of literature in the Roman script is here to stay with us. Its engagement with questions of power and domination aside, literature subsists here as part of a burgeoning culture industry. Books of fiction are now available in both English and Hausa, and those thought to be academically worth it are taught as part of a canon within the context of a discipline or a new epistemology, in the literature departments or Nigerian and African languages in the universities. Those that fail to make the mark are designated as pulp fiction or 'Kano Market Literature' or *Soyayya* soft fiction, for the entertainment of housewives and cultural simpletons.

In terms of identity, therefore, a distinction is already emerging along class and professional lines. Some authors, like Ibrahim Tahir and Zaynab Alkali or Abubakar Gimba, are good enough to be taught in university departments, while others are not. As academics are driven by professional necessity to stake out a new epistemological field, postgraduate courses are being mounted and the Ph.Ds are piling up on Tahir, Gimba, Alkali and a few others.

Yet, on the whole, if we must talk of 'Northern Nigerian Literature', as opposed to a 'Southern Nigerian Literature', the picture is not a very encouraging one. A recent observer tells us why:

> ... with the exception of Abubakar Gimba's contributions in prose, which while noteworthy are hardly stratospheric, there have been no important novels in English from northern Nigerian since Yari and Sule's contributions in the mid '70s. Neither has poetry or drama been exceptional. And the question is – Why? (R. U. Ali 2012 www.gamji.co...)

In answering his own question, he suggests possible reasons for the puerility of Northern fiction in the English language: writers' unfamiliarity with the rudiments of the English language, which leads them

i. to make 'shocking grammatical errors.'
ii. a chaos of misperception (sic)

With regard to the first point, Jibril has noted long before now that:

> ... whereas literature in southern Nigeria has been flourishing at the expense of literature in local languages, literature in Hausa has flourished at the expense of literature in English. (Jibril, 1990:97)

Gerard (1981), a decade before Jibril, would have perhaps been right to have detected a peculiar strain in Hausa writing, which he characterised as 'linguistic misoneism.' Consequently, as Ali (2012) observes, even the so-called soyayya soft fiction written in Hausa has tended to be more vibrant artistically and, therefore, "far ahead of its counterpart in English." Furthermore, Gerard (1981:70-71) also thinks that with the events that occurred in Hausa writing since the end of World War II — the growth of prose fiction and drama, thematic innovations in the traditional poetic form, the use of printing and the modern media — its evolution has remained grounded in a rigid linguistic misoneism. Hausa literature has stubbornly resisted the encroachment of the coloniser's language, which has been so successfully adopted by the other two main ethnic groups of Nigeria, the Ibo and the Yoruba.

Is this then a case of cultural bifurcation, a dual heritage, or, to go back to our earlier term, a case of two identities within one practice?

The language problem is very serious and it is still a raging controversy in literary theory and criticism. Yet, much of the debate, it seems, fails to sufficiently take cognisance of the complex cultural legacy of colonialism. The cultural forms of colonialism, as we are all aware, "did not replace our indigenous forms but lie side by side with them." Consequently, as argued elsewhere in a recent write-up (Nasidi, 2010:23):

> The cultural situation in Nigeria is therefore best described as a PALIMPSEST: the old is there, residual but visible, but it is being overlain by a new and more pervasive one, whose influence derives from the fact that it is linked to technology and modern structures of power.

If one writes in English, one is instantly linked to a national and global audience (if one is good enough to write a classic, that is); one is likely to make all the money, especially dollars, but one is also instantly cut off from one's own people, the majority of whom do not speak English or French and who will always be there in their own cultural and linguistic world. As pointed out by Ofosu-Appiah (1977:31) several decades ago:

... however much we try, we shall never be able to turn our masses into English and French speakers.

As far as identity is concerned, therefore, the choice is clear for the Nigerian or African writer: write in English or French and gain recognition nationally and globally; write in a local language and what you lose in global recognition you gain in your own people's recognition and cultural solidarity.

Nonetheless, is it really as rigid and as undialectical as that? Does writing in the so-called local languages preclude international or global recognition? If one writes a classic in Hausa, Ibo or Yoruba, it can, of course, be translated into the so-called international languages. Only a few months ago, Achebe could boast that *"Things Fall Apart now exists in nearly sixty world languages,"* (*Sun Literary Review,* Sept 1, 2012:41). That could be quite correct, except of course, that it does not exist in his own Igbo language. The novel has global recognition, but lacks local identity; it is visible all over the world, but has no linguistic links to its assumed culture. Hence, the stridency of Ngugi's recent campaigns: Africans, he says,

> must learn how to write in their local languages and avoid saying the languages are too many, hence, the need not to use them...Those who speak and write in other people's languages are simply saying they are under enslavement, while those who use their languages frequently are economically empowered. (Ngugi, Sunday Trust, July 29, 2012:22)

As Ofosu-Appiah (1977:31) points out, proficiency in English should not preclude proficiency in one's mother tongue. In fact, he says, "it is more honourable and intelligent to be proficient in your mother tongue as well as in other tongues." Furthermore, proficiency here does not mean that of speech, but of writing and creativity as well. "In much of the debate so far", says Kofi Anyidoho (1977:1):

> one small but significant point is hardly ever mentioned, perhaps because it is an embarrassment: the fact that

although a majority of African writers and scholars have access to a mother tongue, only the exceptional ones are literate enough in their mother tongues to do creative, let alone scholarly writing in them. To have a mother tongue is one thing; to make it functional and creative is another *thing altogether.*

The problem exists largely with our universities, not just with the identity of the writers or even of our literature; with the way and manner in which the disciplines have been institutionalised and are being taught. The real issue is our pedagogical culture. Our old man of learning, Alhaji Junaidu, the Wazirin Sakkwato (1972), would, thus, be right to have called our universities "cultural transplants whose roots lie elsewhere." For instance, it does not seem to make much intellectual sense teaching Hausa literature and English or any other literature in rigidly compartmentalised forms, without bringing them into some kind of dialectic; without creating any sort of dialogue between them. This is where the true challenge lies, for us as scholars of literature – whether it is northern Nigerian or English.

As pointed out by some colleagues at conferences of this nature some years back, the role of translation in opening up cultures and bringing them into a fruitful embrace has for too long been ignored.

In addition, to take another cue from Ofosu-Appiah: just as Arab scholars had translated Aristotle, Euclid and other Greek authors into Arabic, so must we endeavour to translate the great works of other civilisations into northern and the rest of Nigerian languages (and vice versa) — so that we open other great traditions of thought to the masses of our people.

REFERENCES

- Adamu, A. U. (2006), "Divergent Similarities: Culture, Globalisation and Hausa Culture and Performing Arts" in Ahmad, S. B. and Bhadmus, M. O. (eds), *Writing, Performance and Literature in Northern Nigeria* (Proceedings of the 3rd Conference on Literature in Northern Nigeria), Kano: Bayero University Press.
- Ali, R. U. (2012), "On Northern Nigeria Literature and Related Issues", http://www.gamji.co.02/12/2012.
- Aliyu, S. A. (1990), "The Place of Rupert East in the Culture and Literature of Northern Nigeria" in Abdulraheem, O. (ed), *Essays of Northern Nigeria Literature,* Vol. 1., Kano: Bayero University Press.
- Anyidoho, K. (1997), "Language and the Politricks of Knowledge", An Inaugural Lecture, delivered at the University of Ghana, Legon, December 18, 1997.
- Appiah, O. (1997), "On Building an Intellectual Community in Africa", in *Colloquium on Black Civilisation and Education: Colloquium Proceedings,* Vol. 1.
- Clinton, B. (2002), "The Struggle for the Soul of the 21st Century", http://www.bbc.co.uk/arts/news.comment/dimbleby/print_clinton.shtml.
- Eagleton, T. (2000), *The Idea of Culture,* Oxford: Blackwell.
- Foucault, M. (1982), "The Subject and Power" in Critical Inquiry. Vol 8, Summer.
- Gerard, A. (1981), *African Language and Cultures: An Introduction to the Literary History of Sub-Saharan Africa,* Harlow, Essex: Longman.
- Jibril, M. (1990), "Northern Nigeria Literature and the English Language" in Abdulraheem, O. (ed), *Essays on Northern Nigeria Literature,* Vol. 1, Kano: Bayero University Press.

- Junaidu, W. (1972), *The Relevance of the University in our Society,* Zaria: Ahmadu Bello University Press.
- Kwanashie, G.M. (2002), *The Making of the North in Nigeria,* 1900 – 1965, Zaria: Ahmadu Bello University Press.
- Nasidi, Y. (2010), *The Role of Culture in Peace Building and National Integration,* National Council for Arts and Culture Annual Lecture Series, Abuja.
- Pope, A. (1994), *Essay on Man and Other Poems,* Toronto: Dover Publications.

Chapter Twelve

Decoding Collective Identity Through Literature: A Reading of the Literary Tradition in Ilorin Emirate

Hamzat I. AbdulRaheem

Introduction

The collective effect of some dominant features of Ilorin, which include its geographical location and traditional administrative status as an emirate with a northern/Islamic system, but speaking Yoruba as its lingua franca, have often brought controversy concerning its real identity in Nigeria. While political actors from the North and Southwest may accept or reject the northern status of Ilorin according to the dictates of their situations, the present study considers the polemics about the identity of the Ilorin people from the perspectives of their literary tradition. This is in recognition of the fact that literature is the mirror through which a people's identity, passions and perceptions are best seen and appreciated.

Ilorin: The Historical Formation

Historians differ on who founded Ilorin; thus, while Omo Ikokoro (2011) explains that Eyinla or Ayinla first settled down in the area, others think that it was Ojo Isekuse from the Ilota side. Yet, other writers believe that the place now known as Ilorin was mostly virgin land inhabited by a Baruba hermit family whose original settlement is still called Baruba, near Idi Ape. However, Samuel Johnson (1921) argues that the city was built by Laderin, the great grandfather of Afonja, the Aare Onakakanfo of Yorubaland. Johnson further states that Ilorin was ruled in succession by the Laderin family up to the fourth generation. This view may be one of the major causes of controversy concerning the true origins of the city. Some historians have later debunked that submission, based not on the genealogy of the Afonja, but of his fathers' rule over Ilorin. For example, Al-Ilory (Abdullahi, 1987) asserts that not much was reported about Ilorin before the advent of Afonja and Alimi; and there were practically no news about Laderin's father or grandfathers. Ilorin, therefore, must have begun to be established only some 30-40 years before the arrival of Sheikh Alimi, between 1770 to 1800 CE.

It should be pointed out that this early settlement was only in respect of the area inhabited by the aboriginal Yorubas. Even so, there were also other autonomous settlements around the area, including those of the Fulani headed by Olufadi, the Gambari group, which was made up of a mixed grill of Gobir, Hausa, Nupe and Kenberi; and the Kanike headed by the *Sarkin Gambari,* who was called Bako. There was also a Muslim settlement known as Okesuna led by Solagberu. Al-Ilory (Abdullahi, 1987) describes Okesuna as the first village where Islam stabilised in Yorubaland. In fact, the people were so committed to the Islamic tenets that the village came to be popularly known as the place or "quarter of the faithful."

Thus, from this diversity, it was inevitable that a common ruler would emerge to unify all the different segments into a single community, especially considering the general insecurity prevailing at the time arising from communal wars and the need to meet other necessities of life. It was left to history to really say whether such a leader first came from one of the aboriginal Yoruba, the Gambari, Okesuna or any other unknown group. This was particularly because by that time, virtually of the people had been assimilated into speaking the Yoruba language, although they had originally come from different ethnic groups. For, instance, Olufadi, the head of the Fulani group bore a Yoruba name; and Solagberu, the leader of Okesuna and a Kanuri man, also bore a Yoruba name. This would seem to confirm Al-Ilory's (Abdullahi, 1987) conclusion that, regardless of the present political demarcation, which puts it in the North, Ilorin is essentially a Yoruba town. The name, Ilorin itself, which is either derived from *Ilu erin* 'the town of elephant' or *Ilo irin* 'sharpening of the iron', also confirms its Yoruba status. However, it was the arrival of Sheikh Alimi that further attracted people from different ethnic groups to come and live in the city, thereby making it a melting pot and a settlement of nationalities from different backgrounds, now destined to live together as one, sharing a common faith, language and fortune.

No doubt, the significant position that Ilorin came to occupy and its role in history was as a result of the arrival of Sheikh Alimi, whose first son, Abdus-Salam, became the expected leader that unified the different segments of the city into a strong whole. It is, however, not the place of this paper to analyse the political implications of these developments in the current discourse on the history of Ilorin, but to look at the overall impact of the antecedents on the literary tradition of the Ilorin Emirate.

Ilorin: Culture and Language

Thus, Ilorin people, having come from a variety of cultural backgrounds, are unique in developing some peculiar cultural practices and a literature that is also unique in its features. This is now evident from some of the pattern of social activities observed in the city, such as birth, marriage and funeral ceremonies, as well as other religious festivals, all of which are strongly rooted in the Islamic traditions. Similarly, the original Fulani, Yoruba, Nupe and Hausa cultural practices had, under the overriding weight of the Islamic doctrine, all melted together into a unique culture that is first reflected in the language they now commonly speak. That was how, the Yoruba dialect spoken in Ilorin came to be strongly influenced by many northern languages, most especially Hausa, Fulfude and Nupe. Arabic, being the language of Islam, has also had its impact on the Ilorin Yoruba, as well as the social values of the people. Such common Ilorin Yoruba words as *Ama* (but), *Gunmasi* (conjunction), *Delili* (proof), *Laluri* (necessity),

Emide (in short), *Katu* (just), *Sakani* (near), *Sasa* (palor), *Eeba* (yes) are all a reflection of such influence.

In his research work on the subject, Katibi (2011) identifies several words and expressions that are peculiar to the Ilorin Yoruba dialect. They include the following examples, as compiled by the present writer:

1. Common Names		
Words	Meaning	Examples
Alangua	Sub-district head	*Ba mi lo si odo Alangua Wara* (Go on my behalf to the Assistant District Head)
Kau	Uncle	*Mo lo si odo Kau mi* (I went to my uncle)
Magajiya	First daughter	*Fatimoh ni magajiya Dr. Katibi* (Fatimoh is the first daughter of Dr. Katibi)
Daudu	First son	*Ahmad ni Daudu Prof. Raji* (Ahmad is the first son of Prof. Raji)
2. House and Household		
Saure	Corridor	*Baba wa ni Saure* (Baba is in the corridor)
Fada	A place where traditional title holder receives visitors	*Balogun wa ni Fada* (Balogun is at the royal hall)
Agode	Veranda	*Awon omo n'sere ni Agode* (Children are playing in the veranda)
Aganrandi	A half-door	*Pa Aganrandi de* (Shut the half-door)
Kaa	Backyard	*Omo wa ni Kaa* (The boy is at the backyard)

3.	Common expressions		
	Al Ali kua	Where as	*Ole ni omo na, Al alikua omo Alfa ni* (He is a thief whereas, he is the child of an Alfa)
	Saman sagudu	To hail somebody	*Saman sagudu omo na* (May the boy be praised)
	Giriman kai	Arrogance	*Omo na ni giriman kai* (The boy is arrogant)
	Dama	Relief	*Are okunrin na ti n dama* (The man's illness is getting better)
4.	Food		
	Masa	Local cake made from maize	*Mofe je masa* (I want to eat cake made of maize)
	Alewa	Sweet made from sugar cane	*Mo gbadun Alewa na* (I enjoyed that sweet)
5.	Religion		
	Sooro	Mineret	*Sooro mosalasi na ga* (The mosque's minaret is high)
	Kokondo	Dome	*Konkodo mosalasi na yayi* (The mosque's dome is beautiful)
	Biya	Teach to read Qur'an	*Alfa ti biya Qur'an* (The Mallam has taught him the reading of the Qur'an)
	Senteli	Kettle	*Ban gbe senteli mi* (Give me my kettle)

Literary Tradition in Ilorin

The above examples present evidence about how Arabic and some languages from the North have come to influence the Ilorin Yoruba dialect. In the same vein, the languages have cast a lasting influence on the forms and contents of literary composition from the city, considering that literature always reflects the values and intellectual perceptions of its society of origin. Altogether, the literary tradition in Ilorin can be classified into two major divisions: the oral and the written. Within the oral literature, two major genres can also be cited as examples: *Were* and *Waka*.

Waka is a Hausa word meaning poem, verse or song, which are often used synonymously. It is one of the principal genres of Hausa literature, if not the most important, and must have come to Ilorin through the Hausa people that settled in the city. *Waka* retains this important status in the social life of Ilorin as the people's verse, which is chanted at different occasions, with the same Islamic influence glaring in the words and contents employed in its composition. One of the most popular *Waka* in Ilorin, for example, is chanted when a child has completed the study of the Qur'an and goes thus:

> *Le ileka (ya Allah)*
> *Ya Muhammad*
> *Bo lowo s'ore Anabi*
> *Yio s'ore wa*
> *Opopo Maka ma roro*
> *Aljanna nile wa*
> *Eyin te ekewu*
> *E kuya*
> *Awa njaye kalamu*
> *Min al afi Nasira*
> *Wa akaru adada*

Meaning:

> There is no god but You (Allah)
> (We praise) Muhammad
> If rich people befriend Muhammad
> He will befriend us
> The streets of Mecca are very clean
> Paradise is our abode.
>
> O you people (who did not learn Arabic)
> Poor you
> We are enjoying the benefit of Kalamu (The Pen)
> Who is now weaker as a helper?
> Who is now less in numericity?

The last two lines were allusions to the glorious Qur'an, which says: *Man ad'afu nasiran wa aqallu 'adadan.* (Who is weaker as a helper; and who is now less numerically?)

Another verse from one of the most prominent *waka* proponents in the emirate, *Labaika,* eulogises Emir Aliyu as follows:

> *Lasiko Aliyu o (2x)*
> *Mase je Kwara o reyin*
> *Lasiko Aliyu Olohun*
> *J'ohun to wan yi o de (2x)*
> *Oba olola loni dakun*
> *J'ohun to wan yi o de.*

Meaning:

> During the reign of Aliyu (2x)
> Do not let Kwara go backward
> During the time of Aliyu
> Let all the expensive things become cheap (2x)

Normally, the major themes of *Waka* are eulogy of the prophets of God or Muslim scholars, preaching of good morals and narrating Islamic stories. Another important theme is asceticism, the example of which is given below, as chanted by Labaika:

> *Adun duniya niwonba kinkin (2x)*
> *Adun ti ye gere ti I bo bomiran*
> *Adun duniyan niwon ba kinkin*
> *Yoo dabi eni pe o sayee rio (2x)*
> *Bowo iku bateda lenu aro*
> *Ema to bari ko to da yila*
> *Yoo dabi eni ti o sayeri*
> *Ana n je tenikan oni n je tenikan*
> *To ba dojumo ola a jet e lomiran*
> *yi si o yiwo naa laye nje. (11)*

Meaning:

> The sweetness of life is very little
> It moves from one place to another
> The sweetness of life is little
> It will look as if one never lived
> When death catches up with one
> One faces hostilities before noon
> It will look as if one never lived
> Changing here and there is the name of life
> Yesterday was for somebody and today for another person
> By tomorrow, it will be for another person
> Changing here and there is the name of life.

The second genre of songs is the *Were*, which is chanted to wake up the faithful to take *Sahur* (the dawn meal) during Ramadan. One of the verses counsels:

O de yin onile
Ike ko ba gbogbo yin
O wada wa alejo
Ola ko ba gbogbo wa
Atike at'ola
Ola ko boni sen la
Anabi ti o sipe wa
Ko lo ba Muhammad (2x)
Anabi ti ofi be wa.

Meaning:

> To you the residents
> Let blessing be with you
> To us the visitors
> Let mercy be with us
> Both blessing and mercy be
> With the prophet who will intervene on our behalf
> Let it be with the prophet that will intervene for us (2x).

There are many other poetic genres like *Dadakuada, Senwele* and *Orin Omo Oba* (songs in praise of princesses). All these compositions, as demonstrated above, reflect not only the cultural plurality of the people of the town, but also the general behavioural patterns and societal norms and values, which have been essentially influenced by the northern/Islamic culture.

As for the written literature, compositions in Arabic appear to be the most prominent among the early Arabic scholars from Ilorin. Their writings cover almost all the major literary genres, except drama, with the Madhu (Eulogy) and Elegy being the most prominent. As for prose, there are also short stories, biographies and novels, which deserve critical attention in view of their proliferation and quality, especially the ones written by modern students of Arabic. Another literary genre that is very common among the writers of Arabic in Ilorin is travel literature, which offers a record of their experiences and new encounters.

Most of the writings on travels are about journeys to the Holy Land for pilgrimage, or visiting Arab countries, either to seek knowledge or for religious purposes. All these writings are a reflection of the prevailing values that provide the underlying guide for both the social system and the pattern of scholarship in Arabic and Islamic studies. In fact, it is in recognition of the large collection of Arabic occasional poems in Ilorin that the Kwara State University opened a forum for the poets to present their collections for free academic review and advice. This act may be the first programme of its kind in any Nigerian university.

Creative writers in English are not as many as those in the Arabic language in the Ilorin Emirate. However, the few that are available also reflect the general literary tradition of both the Yoruba and Arabic literatures. Here, Na'Allah is a good example, not only because he employs the English language, but also because he demonstrates the linguistic plurality of Ilorin by also using Yoruba and Hausa in his poems in the collection entitled *Ilorin Praise Poetry*. One of the Hausa poems says:

A Gidan Ilori

A gidan Ilori ai salla muke
Ba mu san da kai ba,
Amman gidan Ilori, kai salla mukai!

A gidan Ilori, ai ilmi mukai
Ba mu san da ku ba,
Amma gidan Ilorin, dai ilmi mukai!

A gidan Ilori biyayya mukai
Ba mu san da ku ba,
Amma gidan Ilori biyayya mukai

A gidan Ilori magana mukai
Ba mu san da ku ba
Amma gidan Ilori magana mukai!

A gidan Ilori kiraya mukai
Ba ma san da ku ba,
Amma gidan Ilori kiraya mukai!

A gidan Ilori, albarka mu ke
Ba mu san da ku ba,
Amma gidan Ilori 'dan albarika muke!

A gidan Ilori siyasa muke
Ba mu san da ku ba,
Amma gidan Ilori siyasa mukai!

In ba ka san Ilori, ba ka san allo ba
Don ka gan Ilorin,
Tilawa mukai!

Another poem is *Dan Mali Yo Mali Yo*, which is normally accompanied by music from the talking drum or from rhythmic hand clapping:

"Song: *Dan Mali yo, Mali yo!*
Chorus: *Mali yo!*

Song: *Dan Mali yo, nawa*
Chorus: *Mali yo!*

Song: *Ya je ina ne?*
Chorus: *Mali yo!*

Song: *Ya je Ilori*
Chorus: *Mali yo!*

Song: *Ba zai dawo ba*
Chorus: *Mali yo!*

Song: *Sai a watan gobe*
Chorus: *Mali yo!*

Song: *Gobe da labarai*
Chorus: *Mali yo!*

Song:	*Jibi da labarai*
Chorus:	*Mali yo!*
Song:	*Gobe da labarai*
Chorus:	*Mali yo!*
Song:	*Jibi da labarai*
Chorus:	*Mali yo!*
Song:	*Karkad'a mu gani!*
Chorus:	(Twisting buttock, dancing more actively to drumming)
Song:	*Alis, Alis Alis!"* (13)

In Yoruba, He says:
Dogo Oni suuru (The Patient Tall Man) in praise of Emir Aliyu Abdulkabir:

> *Aa tin joba ni ilu lorin,*
> *Okan ni ti Dogo,*
> *Dogo onisuuru, Oba ni nilorin.*
> *Ateereee to kan sanma to kan le*
> *Opelenge subu lawo awo o fo*
> *Opelenge subu lodo, lodo ba faya*
> *Ti tai lara ko o,*
> *Ti ka gbaawe laaro ati l'osan,*
> *Ti ka sun mo olohun-oba Alaurabi ni*
> *Obaawa fi di omi l'ara*
> *Dogo, Abdulkadiri Baba-Agba!*
>
> *Dogo onisuuru,*
> *Won ni ori ti o dade,*
> *Kokuku ni salaidade*
> *Orun ti o wewu etu*
> *Boti le wo ekisa ri*
> *Ti abere ati owu nse ore e,*
> *Kokuku ni salai wo ewu etu!*
> *Ti gbogbo aye a maa see ni*

> *Samasangudu,*
> *Onile ola, elewu etu!*
> *Dogo, Abdulkadiri Baba-Agba*

In English, he praised Aafa Adama, Al-Ilori, as follows:

> The pigeon has been a bird
> Before lekeleke knows how to wear
> its white attire
> Now, this bird should seek knowledge
> Aafa knowledge,
> Aafa imo!
> From the pigeon of knowledge, seek
> How his attire might fit,
> Aafa Adama has
> Taught
> About the roots, and the rootedness
> The soil and the soil contentness
> The water and the water tastiness
> The sky and the sky blueness
> Aafa Adama taught knowledge
> Of lineage and lining
> Adama asked:
> How would you not know,
> There is more to see under the fadama of Ilorin!

Remi Raji comments in the back blurb of Na'Allah's collection as follows:

> Rasheed Na'Allah captures the times, legends and spaces of the city in the mellifluous tone of the court raconteur; Ilorin is the rational hybrid of cultures, its praise-song steeped in the invocation and evocation of indigenous, oriental and Western traditions. Written in English, Yoruba and Hausa, the poems are carefully stringed in short spurts of epical quality.
>
> Na'Allah... has given us a truly multilingual volume of poetry, and his offering is fresh and alluring.

These slices from the Ilorin literary tradition exhibit how the artists employ Arabic, English, Hausa and Yoruba languages to unequivocally reflect the cultural plurality, Islamic sensibility and societal responsibility of the Ilorin society. Far more significantly, they offer a deep reflection of the identity of the emirate, as well as its history and culture, which, at the same time, can best be understood and appreciated by reference to the literary tradition.

Conclusion

From the foregoing discussions, it is evident that even with Yoruba language as lingua fanca, and despite its geographical location, the Ilorin emirate, has, nonetheless, evolved a culture that cannot easily be regarded as Yoruba. This is as a result of its interplay with the multiplicity of other cultures and languages of the North, occasioned by the historical and political antecedents discussed in this chapter.

While there might still be elements of controversy concerning the political status of Ilorin, the literary tradition of the people, thus, clearly expresses the rich identity of the emirate and its strong northern sensibility. Yoruba may continue to be the dominant language of the society, but the literature projects a unique people with a different identity. This is similar to what obtains in the case of African literatures expressed in the European languages, where the languages may be European, but the atmosphere, passion and perception, are, undoubtedly African.

References

- Omo Ikokoro, A. A.: *"Taliful-Quran fi Akhbari Umarai Ilorin"* (Unpublished manuscript).
- Jimoh, L. A. (1994), *The Journey So Far*, Ilorin: Atoto Press Ltd
- Johnson, S. (1921), *The History Of Yoruba*, Lagos: CSS Bookshop.
- Abdullahi, A (1987), *Nasimu-Saba fi Akhbari-I-Islam wa Ulamai Bilad Yoruba*. Cairo: Annamudhajiya Press.
- Katibi, A. (2011), "Arabic and Non-Arabic Elements in the Ilorin Dialect of Yoruba" *Ilorin Journal of Linguistics, Literature and Culture*. Ilorin: University of Ilorin Press.
- Daba, H. A. (2006), *Dan Maraya Jos in Folkanic Perspective*, Kano: Benchmark Publishers.
- Jimba, M.M. (1997). *Ilorin Waka: a Literary, Islamic and Popular Art*, Ilorin: Taofiaullah Publishing House
- Na Allah, A. (2011), *Ilorin Praise Poetry*, Ibadan: Book Craft.

Chapter Thirteen

Self-Exploration and Split Identity in Northern Nigeria Novels: A Reading of Labo Yari's Man of the Moment

Zainab Muhammad Kazaure

Introduction

Literature, as an effective medium of communication, not only enlightens, but also raises the consciousness of the people. Thus, with the emergence of the northern Nigerian writers in English, their first focus was their immediate circumstance, exploring the effects and consequences of their mixed legacies and those of their society, in an attempt to re-affirm their identity. Ahmad and Bhadmus (2006:92) assert that it is such narratives that authenticate an ethnic group or, indeed, the ethos of a nation:

> Theoretically, identity and literature are intricately related. Every group and, indeed, every nation has stories that purport to explain its origin and portray the character traits and values of its people.

As with other experiences elsewhere in the country and the rest of the African continent, the northern Nigeria literary tradition evolved from the effects of the cultural milieu on the individual writer, his society and traditional belief, and his attempt to come to terms with the conflicting values of the past, as against the realities of the present. As Ngugi (1971:4) observes while commenting on the principles of contemporary African literature in general:

> The novelist is haunted by a sense of the past. His work is often an attempt to come to terms with a thing that has been; has struggled, as it were, to sensitively register his encounter with history and the novelist at his best must feel himself heir to a continuous tradition... He feels himself alienated, a stranger in a world he has created, yet is not his own.

The ambiguity normally results into a psychological trauma in the writer, thereby also leading to personality conflict, hybridity or double identity, which is a common feature in post-colonial writings. Such engagements are a clear exhibition of the conflicting legacies of different cultures and social conditions, which produce new settings and recreate the old identities. The inevitable, but gradual changes and challenges that arise from this situation result into the individual having difficulty in balancing between the different ethoses. Maalouf (2000:5) in *On Identity* explains that,

> Every individual is a meeting ground for many different allegiances and sometimes these loyalties conflict with one another and confront the person who harbours them with difficult choices.

Unfortunately, this is further complicated by the fact that the African novel tradition came into being out of the experiences of colonialism and also remains heavily influenced by it. The novel form, especially in the European languages, was not indigenous to Africa, as Kelani in his "The Poetics of the Post-Colonial Nigeria Novel" (2000:24) points out:

> The novel, particularly the Western novel, came to Africans because it formed part of the literature syllabus of colonialist education, which was a factor in Africa's literary development.

This would explain why the African novelists have often made these identity issues and the inevitable crisis they have always led to, a favourite theme in their works.

In northern Nigeria, one of the pioneer writers in English to explore this theme is Labo Yari, whose *Man of the Moment* reflects the conflict of the social past against the realities of today's post-colonial life. Unfortunately, critics in the north have not often given much consideration to promoting works from the northern Nigeria novelists, whereas it is only through such criticism that a writer's effort can be corrected and celebrated. Ironically, Yari's works are more popular abroad than in Nigeria or even northern Nigeria; hence, the attempt in this chapter to consider the *Man of the Moment* as a contribution to the exploration of the identity problem of the northern Nigerian in the post-colonial situation.

More specifically, the chapter intends to explore split identity as an outcome of cultural hybridity in northern Nigerian literature. A hybrid is something that is mixed, and hybridity simply refers to a mixture of some sort, but has become a useful word in discourses of racial mixing, fundamentally associated with the emergence of post-colonial discourse and its critique of cultural imperialism. Hybridity is used in relation to literature and theory that focuses on the effects of mixture upon identity and culture, with Homi Bhabha's *The Location of Culture* (1994) emerging as a key text in the development of the hybridity theory.

Theoretical Framework

'Post-colonial' in the literal sense means that 'which has been preceded by colonisation.' In practice, however, the term is used more loosely to describe not only the time since the departure of the imperial powers, but also the period before independence. It is also used to signify a position against imperialism and Eurocentrism. Post-colonial studies now cover a diverse range of issues and experiences, including the writer's use of colonial language to reach a wider audience or return to the native languages more relevant to the indigenous groups in the former colony.

The post-colonial theory can be perceived as an effort at re-affirming oneself either in terms of colour, group, nationality or individual sensitivity. It is about cultural, social, regional and national differences in experience and outlook; and discounts unequal representation of the other as immoral, uncultured and uncivilised (Graffins et al 1989:2). Ashcraft and his colleagues (1995:11) summarise it while introducing their book of essays, *The Post-Colonial Reader,* as when:

> The idea of post-colonial literary theory emerges from the inability of European theory to deal adequately with the complexities of varied cultural provenance of post-colonial writing.

Labo Yari and His Works

Labo Yari was born on 14th April, 1942 in the Unguwar Yari ward in the historic city of Katsina. He had his primary and secondary education in Katsina. In 1962, he was employed as a journalist for the Katsina Native Authority Information Service. From 1966 -1967, he studied Norwegian literature at the University of Oslo, Norway. On his return to Nigeria, he worked with the Federal Ministry of Education, as an information officer during the Nigerian Civil War. After the civil war, he was posted to Stockholm as attaché in the Nigerian embassy. He left the Federal Ministry of Information in 1980 to work for the Fourth Dimension Publishers in Enugu; before leaving again for the Northern Nigerian Publishing Corporation Zaria in 1981. In 1982, he was appointed the Managing Director of the Gaskiya Corporation. He retired as the Government Printer in charge of the Government Printing Press and all official publications of the Katsina State Government. He got married at the age of thirty-six and has six children.

Malam Labo Yari, as he is fondly called, was one of the founding members of the Association of Nigerian Authors (ANA) in 1972 and has played significant roles in promoting the growth and development of the association and literature in general in Nigeria. Labo Yari as a writer is motivated by reading good books, specifically European writings. He has five publications to his credit: *Climate of Corruption* (1978), *A House in the Dark and Other Stories* (1985), *Man of The Moment* (1992), *A Day Without Cockcrow* (1999) and a biography, *Muhamman Dikko: Emir of Katsina and His Times* (2007).

Man of the Moment

Man of the Moment was first published in 1992. It is a story of Ahmadu Baduku, a jobless and starving writer, and his ordeal in Lagos in search of a job. He finds it difficult to get his collection of poems published. The book is in form of a soliloquy, as Baduku walks near Tinubu Square in the midst of the famous Lagos traffic hold-ups. The narrative gradually explains his experiences, particularly as a writer who started at his village in northern Nigeria before coming to Lagos later.

Ahmadu Baduku, a secondary school leaver, is portrayed as the best leather worker in his entire village, which brings him fame and provides him with a source of income. However, his ambition is to become a writer, an ambition which he began nursing as a primary school pupil, as a result of a visit to his school by an English writer. All efforts by his aunt, under whose custody he grows up, to encourage him to carry on with his leather work, proves abortive. He uses whatever money he realises from his leather work to purchase writing materials and stamps for posting his poems to different newspapers and magazines. Initially, his poems are published in a few magazines and some are even read on a radio station, but this does not last as the magazines soon close down. Subsequently, he loses his job as a library assistant in the village and the situation is further compounded when he loses all encouragement and support dramatically, including the death of the aunt who has always cared for him. That is when he finally decides to move to Lagos with the hope of getting his works published.

While in Lagos, he becomes more or less like a beggar, always on the move in search of publishers or a job. He becomes frustrated and a burden to his friends until life becomes unbearable. At last, he meets Anyawu who is an intellectual; a beautiful, sophisticated woman, much influenced by the western culture because she had studied abroad. She offers Ahmadu shelter in the hope that she would be able to mould him into a specific kind of writer, but their differences bring the relationship to an end soon and, once again, life becomes difficult for him. He is about to give up towards the end of the story, when he receives a letter from a publisher that one of his manuscripts has been accepted for publication.

Split Identity

In *Man of the Moment,* Labo Yari appears set out to examine the post-colonial individual in northern Nigeria through offering a calculated assessment of the inner mind of his characters, the tension between the unstable mind of the individual and the opposing societal values. The effects of such tensions are revealed through the major characters in the texts experiencing social and cultural ruptures in an era when the individual must negotiate the onslaught of his modern life.

This is portrayed particularly in the movement of the main character, Baduku, to the city, which symbolises many problems associated with modern, alien cultures. With this movement of the protagonist to Lagos, the author exposes how the complexity of living in Lagos affects the individual, both socially and psychologically. The novel is at its best exposing the complexities and realities of urban life that is presented as being so full of falsehood and deceit and the individual is constantly being forced into a condition of "subconsciously rebelling against himself." (178).

Indeed, Ahmadu Baduku exhibits this dual identity from the beginning of the story, when he finds it difficult to choose between his traditional leather work and poetry writing. Later, he settles for writing poetry, thereby abandoning his traditional craftworks, which had initially brought him both fame and fortune. The search for publishers turns out to actually be a search for survival, for shelter, for Anyawu (when she temporarily disappears) and identity. His movement to Lagos brings him early success to his poetry effort, only for him to find the literary trade and the complexity of urban life in Lagos more difficult than he had anticipated. He makes many friends, including Anyawu, the young, beautiful, educated and westernised woman who comes to his aid while he and his manuscripts are being thrown out of the house where he had been squatting. The relationship enables him to appreciate that he survives in this urban jungle only because someone is there to offer him decent accommodation and take care of his needs. However, a mild tension soon arises between them, when he discovers that her generosity is but a way of mediating her own inner tension, as she confesses that she is in love with him. He reminds her of how his friend Okafor had introduced him to her:

> I was a combination of a drop out and a rebel whose attempts to write seemed to have been a powerful stimulus for my becoming a tramp (39).

Baduku thinks he does not understand her language, especially that of love, and requires time to reconcile his own inner conditions before he can catch up with her and interpret the feelings she has for him. At any rate, the relationship with Anyawu does not prevent him from being lonely or having nostalgic feelings about his past. Thus, in spite of their closeness there are still some fundamental differences between them, which he articulates in his typical fashion:

> The sky and the sea were as close as I was to Anyawu, yet the blue and green stripes of the horizon, which separated the sea and the sky produced a quality of separation. This

made me realise that, although I was close to Anyawu, there would always be a gap like that existing between the sea and the sky... (79).

He realises that in his relationship with Anyawu, which he calls the voyage of discovery, they have left "the world of logic behind and entered the realm where the laws are as different as the language." (112). He is always conscious of his identity and does not want her to influence him. However, at a point, he compromises his stand and wears a suit she buys him for an outing with her. He feels uncomfortable in the suit though, not only because it is the first time he ever wears a suit in his life, but because it defies his personality. When he first arrived at Lagos, he had actually despised suits and hated the idea of wearing one:

> I cannot see myself wearing them in this humid heat. If you give me a brand new suit, I will go to Tinubu Square, get the dirtiest beggar and adorn him with it, so that those uppish people, who always feel they cannot breathe unless they are in suits, will have the shock of their lives... (18).

Nonetheless, when Anyawu disappears, though temporarily, Baduku feels lonely without her, just as he normally feels even when she is present also; with the loneliness intensifying whenever he sees other men in the company of their women. The search for Anyawu almost turns him insane, wandering on the streets, talking to himself, while exploring the chaotic Lagos traffic. He enters a state of mind in which material things, his books and even his writing lose their importance for him. He questions his worthiness as a writer, contemplating whether all along, his struggle to succeed as a poet is futile and regretting all the years he wasted to perfect his skills in order to get what has all the while been there close him:

> Akpan, I have wasted my time and energy fishing in the sea close to me, while there are other seas where the fish are bigger and in abundance (144)."

The crisis within him leads him to destroy his school certificate, a prerequisite for securing the white collar job he is so much obsessed to get. He has the conviction that a meaningful writer should stay with his people, yet he moves to Lagos and as accused by his friends, he never writes on the mythology of his people. They further accuse him of writing on issues that are not relevant to his immediate society and doubt his capability as a writer; calling him a fake, claiming someone else's work.

Baduku realises that he is half a man and must search for the whole man. He concludes that Anyawu is the other half for him to be complete. This statement contradicts his earlier advice to his friend Akpan to turn down the gestures of another woman, urging him to concentrate on other (better) things in his life, because to love is a woman's lot:

> To love and love alone is the lot of women. There are many things for man to do; not just love... (126).

This explains the level of the instability that he suffers as an individual who is yet to understand himself, rather like Zahra, the central character in Gimba's *Sacred Apples,* who finally traces her confusion in life to her own lack of self-realisation:

> We know even less about ourselves, about our potentials, our real worth. And that's why we are confused about where we are heading to... (299).

Though this is an observation that relates to the plight of women as perceived by Zahra in the text, it is a comment that describes the situation affecting many westernised individuals in northern Nigerian writing.

Anyawu is another major character in *Man of the Moment* that fails to identify with her society. This is manifested in her inability to work in a government organisation when she returns to Nigeria after studying abroad. She decides to quit when she could not relate with the system. Her marriage also fails within a period of six months and she becomes a loner, but finds company in reading European writings, but which are unable to fill in the emptiness in her or make her feel adequate. She finally abandons the books, saying: "You read yet you do not see" (Yari 1991:41).

She becomes attracted to music because it is in listening to Jazz that she finds what is missing in her. Her attraction to Baduku's poems reveals how unstable her mind is. She tells Baduku that although jazz fills the gap in her, it is only his poems which make her feel completely adequate, revive her interest in literature and inspire her to write. The portrayal of such ambiguous personality is a reflection of the individual in a society that is battling with conflicting beliefs. Placed in a similar situation, Kaka, a character in Zaynab Alkali's *The Stillborn*, finds it difficult to make a choice:

> In the privacy of his room, he worships his gods. Behind the Hill Station, among the hills, he sacrifices to the gods of his ancestors. Whenever there was a Christian or Muslim festival in the village, he attended both diligently (Alkali 1984:25).

Conclusion

Altogether, the *Man of the Moment* is an extended examination of the effect of the urban environment and its modern cultures on the conflicting legacies of the Nigerian, especially, northern individual. Yari presents not only the consequences in terms of the physical effects, but also offers an exploration of the internal mental stress involved. In this way, the novel dramatises the daily battle between the individual and the cultural milieu as a process for continuous negotiation, without a definite end point.

REFERENCES

- Abdu, S. (2005) "Stemming the Identity Flux in a Hausa English Novel: Auwalu Hamza's Love Path" in *Kakaki: Journal of English and French Studies,* Vol. vii, Bayero University, Kano.
- Abdu, S. and Bhadmus, M.O. (eds.) (2007), *"The Novel Tradition in Northern Nigeria"*, Kano: Bayero University Press.
- Abramas, M.H. (2005), *A Glossary of literary Terms, 8th edition,* U.S.A: Thomson Higher Education.
- Adesanmi, P. (2008), "Africa, India and the Post-Colonial: Notes Towards A Praxis of Infliction" in Aderemi (Eds) The *Post- Colonial Lamp: Essays in Honour of Dan Izevbaye,* Ibadan: Bookcraft: pp 35-58.
- Ahmad S.B. (2003), "The Northern Nigerian Novel in English", in *FAIS Journal of the Humanities* Vol. 2 No. 4.
- Ahmad, S.B. (2006) "Constructions of Identities in Hausa Tales" in Ahmad, S.B. and Bhadmus, M.O. (eds) *Writing, Performance and Literature in Northern Nigeria,* Proceedings of the 3rd Conference on Literature in Northern Nigeria, Kano: Bayero University Press.
- Albany (2007) "Hybridity in Contemporary Post-Colonial Theory" http//www.google.com.ng retrieved on 12/5/2012.
- Alkali, Z. (2007), "Literature, Culture and National Development" in Abdu and Bhadmus, (eds).
- Anda, I.M. (2010), "Acculturation in Nascent Northern Nigerian Novels and Short Stories", unpublished PhD Thesis, Department of English and French, Bayero University, Kano.
- Ashcraft, B. Griffith S.G. and Tiffin, H. (1995) (eds.), *The Post-Colonial Reader,* London: Routledge.

- Ashcroft, Bill et al (eds.) (1989), *The Empire Writes Back*, London: Routledge.
- Barry, P. (1995), *Beginning Theory: An Introduction to Literary and Cultural Theory*, New York: Manchester University Press.
- Bertens, N. (2001), *Literary Theory: The Basics*, London: Routledge.
- Carey, John (1994), *World Literature Today*, Austin, Texas: University of Texas Press.
- "Extending the Paradigm" *Journal of Afro-European Studies* Vol. 3 No. 1, http//en.wikipedia.org/Bidungsroman retrieved on17thJune, 2011.
- Fannon, F. (1961), *The Wretched of the Earth*, U.K: Penguin.
- Gimba, A. (1994), *Sacred Apples*, Ibadan: Evans.
- "Identity Crisis (Psychology)", http//wikipedia.orgl/w/widex (27th June, 2011).
- Joseph, A (2006), *"Expanding the Frontiers of the Nigerian Novel: The Northern Perspective"* in Ahmad, S.B. and Bhadmus, M.O. (eds.).
- Kerr, D.J. (2007): "Stories in Search of Writers" in Abdu and Bhadmus, M.O. (eds), *The Novel Tradition in Northern Nigeria.*
- Kilani S. (2000), "The Poetics of the Post-Colonial Nigerian Novels", unpublished PhD thesis, Department of English and French, Bayero University, Kano.
- King, B. (1971) (ed.), *Introduction to Nigerian Literature*, Ibadan: Evans.
- Liman, A.A. (2007) "Literary Tradition and the Novel in Northern Nigeria: Theoretical Challenges" in Abdu, Saleh and Bhadmus, M.O. (eds.), *The Novel Tradition in Northern Nigeria.*
- Maalouf, A. (2000) *On Identity*. London: The Hartville Press.

References

- Malumfashi, I.A. and Ahmed, A. (2007), "Colonial Legacy and Writing Competitions in the Development of the Hausa Novel", in Abdu, S. and Bhadmus, M.O. (eds.), *The Novel Tradition in Northern Nigeria.*
- Mazrui, A. (1990), *The Triple Heritage:* London: BBC Publications.
- Ngugi, J. (1971), "The African Writer and His Past" in Heywood (ed), *Perspectives on African Literature,* London: Heinemann.
- Oba, A (1990) (ed.) *Essays on Northern Nigerian Literature* Vol. 1, Zaria: Hamdan.
- Obafemi, Olu (2010) "50 Years of Nigerian Literature: Prospects and Problems", being a Keynote Address presented to the Garden City Literary Festival held at Port Harcourt, www.gardencityfestival.com (17th June, 2011).
- Obiechina, E.N. (1975), "Background to the West African Novel" in Olaniyan, T and Onukaogu, A.A. and Onyerionmu, E. (2010) (eds), *Nigerian Literature Today.* Ibadan: Kraft Books.
- Olaniyan, T. and Quaysan, A. (2007)(eds), *African Literature: An Anthology of Criticism and Theory,* U.S.A: Blackwell.
- Sage, U. (2011) "Religious Morality and Patriotism in the Novels of Abubakar Gimba", unpublished PhD thesis, Department of English and French, Bayero University, Kano.
- Sani, A.U. et al (1997), *Creative Writing, Writers and Publishing in Northern Nigeria.* Ibadan: IFRA/Africana Book Builders.
- Taiwo, O. (1976), *Culture and the Nigerian Novel,* London: Macmillan
- Taylor, C. (1989), *Sources of the Self: The Making of Modern Identity,* Harvard University Press.
- Yari, L. (1992), *Man of the Moment,* Enugu: Fourth Dimension.

Chapter Fourteen

Vocality, Voicelessness and the Woman's Identity in Kanchana Ugbabe's Soulmates

Foluke R. Aliyu-Ibrahim

Introduction

Simpson's anthology, *The Book of Exiles* (1995), provides an insight into the various reasons people leave their countries and the different types of experiences each individual undergoes in another country. For instance, if in *Treasure Island,* the sojourn of the author, Robert Louis Stevenson, to Samoa suggests that his voluntary exile was pleasurable, however, one of the consequences of migration to another country, whether it is voluntary or not, is the conflict that occurs between the immigrant's identity of him/herself in relation to other people in the 'adopted' society and what the culture of the new place makes of that individual. Saha (2009), whose article attempts to prove that there is an exilic state in all dislocated lives, asserts that "displacement, whether forced or self-imposed, is in many ways a calamity" (p. 187).

One of the implications of this is to support a broadening of the definition of Simpson's (1995) anthology of 'exile' through the documentation of the experiences of different people across history and from different parts of the world. The examples here would include the narratives of Henry James, Ernest

Hemingway, Robert Louis Stevenson and Ayatollah Khomeini. Thus, this chapter shall consider as exiles women who are married to men from different countries other than their own and who are living in their husbands' home countries. This does not, however, mean that issues of identity cannot bedevil the man or woman who resides in his or her own country; nonetheless, that is not the focus here.

Theoretical Framework

The Nigerian feminist critic, Ogundipe-Leslie (1994), appears to have set the agenda for women writers when she urges the woman writer to be committed to correcting the misconceptions of the woman in male-authored texts, by presenting a woman's point of view in her writings. She echoes earlier critics, such as Olaniyan and Quayson, who in their anthology of critical essays, *African Literature: An Anthology of Criticism and Theory* (2007), insist that for the African writer, there is an "intersection of adversarial contexts and the flowering of the creative muse." (p. 139). Consequently, the nine essays in the section, titled 'Creativity in/and Adversarial Contexts' (pp 140-191), reflect this bias. The different contributors, some of whom are also writers, had on different fora earlier on asserted that the African literary artist must be committed to seeking answers to the many socio-economic and political problems facing his continent. This attests to the link between literature and the society, in tune with Harrington's assertions (2004) that art makes references to and comments about human activities in society.

Identity, Feminism and Nigerian Literature

Feminism in Nigerian literature began from the need to correct the stereotyped images of the African woman in writings by men that had often depicted her either as a seductress/'Good time Girl' or the Mother figure. Examples of such texts include Achebe's *Things Fall Apart* (1958), *No Longer at Ease* (1960),

A Man of the People (1966); Soyinka's *The Interpreters* (1970) and *Season of Anomy* (1973); and Ekwensi's *Jagua Nana* (1961). Thus, from a modest attempt to correct these images, the writings of the Nigerian women have now grown to challenge some of the old 'myths' about the identity of the woman and explain her role in the society.

Ogundipe-Leslie (1994) argues that of her many identities, that of the woman as wife has the weakest power, adding that misconceptions of the African woman, particularly the rural woman, have led to the belief that she is voiceless. The critic posits that the concentration of the attention of past writing on the role of the woman as wife is responsible for this misconception, especially as marriage is a major site of women's subjugation in the African continent. Ogundipe-Leslie (1994) further argues that the silence of the African women is a creation of the Western feminist texts, stating that such feminists "fail to look for their (African women's) voices where we may find them, in the sites and forms in which these voices are uttered." (p. 11) There are, therefore, avenues where women do speak out and take action: at times even their silence becomes a loud speech.

It is within the context of the arguments that this paper, specifically examines Kanchana Ugbabe's *Soulmates* (2011), with a view to ascertaining the presentation of the various identities of the woman (Indian and Nigerian), as she relates with other characters in the short stories that make up the collection.

Synopsis of *Soulmates*

Soulmates (2011) is a collection of thirteen short stories, nine of which are relevant to the present study as they tell of the challenges non-Nigerian women married to Nigerians often face. The collection of the short stories reminds one of Aidoo's *The Dilemma of a Ghost* (1965), a powerful statement on the identity conflicts and other challenges that are a natural result of such unions. The author, Ugbabe, is herself an Indian married to an Idoma man from the Benue State of northern Nigeria and, thus, provides some understanding of the identity crises resulting from culture clash that challenge such women, who can be categorised as exiles who attempt to understand the cultures they find themselves in. For the analysis in this study, the major conflict has to do with the husbands' disposition to polyandry (or polygamy, as it is commonly referred to in the Nigerian culture). While some of the protagonists are able to adjust their identities to fit in, others find it difficult and remain alienated, not only from the culture itself, but from their husbands for whom they have paid the high price of exiling themselves from their own home cultures. A part of the blurb on the back cover of the book captures the situation:

> Derived from the experiences of both an insider and an outsider, the intricate stories of Soulmates chart journeys of love, friendship, despair, daily negotiations and strategies for survival while exploring the physical and spiritual aspects of being transplanted to a foreign country, of living with fluid roots. (Back Cover)

Self-Identity of the Woman in *Soulmates*

Ugbabe presents two identities of the married woman in her collection of stories. The first is the woman who is silent in the face of challenges, while the second is vocal in her protestation of the travails she is confronted with. Interestingly, the non-Nigerian women married to Nigerians in the collection make up the first group. The second group consists of both non-Nigerian and Nigerian women.

Voicelessness as Identity

The non-Nigerian woman in the world of *Soulmates* often arrives into her host country with a concept of marriage that is totally different from what she comes to meet in the husband's culture. The narrator of '*The White Rooster*' (pp 111-122), explains:

> I was made to be part of a team, conditioned for marriage and for a life which venerated the husband. My Indian heritage kept my grandmother behind the steel almirah when she spoke to my grandfather. My mother had her marriage arranged for her at seventeen, and derived her life's satisfaction from watching my father eat his meals, and caring for his needs to the minutest detail. (p. 115)

At first reading, there seems to be a similarity between the Indian and Nigerian woman's identity as a wife; like her Indian counterpart, the Nigerian woman is expected to also obey and respect her husband. However, the meaning of the word 'team' in the quotation above contradicts the succeeding description of the actions of the Indian wife, who is described as being excessively servile. One then wonders what the role of the husband is if the man, who is expected to be a member of this team, has all his needs and desires catered for with diligence and veneration, but there is no hint of his own duties and responsibilities towards the wife.

The passage also describes more vividly the overall identity of the Indian wife in the stories in the collection, as could be observed in the Indian women's interactions with their husbands and the other characters. Indeed, Ugbabe portrays the Indian women in the related stories as being unable to exist without their men, such that they silently accept any disdainful acts from the husbands without complaints. In fact, the women are portrayed as being unable to live without their soulmates, as shall be explored in some of the stories in subsequent discussions below.

In 'Testimonies' (pp 17-24), for instance, the narrator belongs to a prayer-group made up of women who meet on Friday afternoons to exchange 'testimonies' about their lives in a devotional routine. These testimonies are supposed to imply change for the better, spiritually (p.18), an aspect of her life that makes her feel younger and more peaceful about life in general. She is however, struck by one of the women, Comfort, who is an enigma to the narrator. Comfort always remains "calm and unperturbed" (p. 21) whenever she narrates her 'testimonies'. Yet, Comfort looks "perpetually doughty and pure, pastry pure, and totally incapable of being bad." (p. 19). Comfort has a seemingly happy life — a husband who is known as a philanthropic "Father Christmas" and a maid for each of her three children (p. 23). The narrator, therefore, wonders: "What was the 'sin' all about?" (p. 23). The narrator, thus, sneaks into Comfort's home and discovers Comfort's secret: her husband and children physically abusing one of the maids over "missing plastic buckets and teaspoons." (p. 23) She realises that all of Comfort's testimonies about the incidents that have befallen her, like robberies, have been mere lies. The narrator, who reveals this secret in her own testimony, however, remains silent about her secret discovery: "I remained silent as the group joined Comfort in a chorus of praise." (p. 24).

In 'Golden Opportunities' (pp 39-47), the narrator is presented as being quite naïve, when she is swindled by Kemi, the first wife of her husband's friend. The narrator of this story is at a point in her marriage where indifference has set in. She metaphorically puts it thus:

> My friend Daphne says that the sharp bit goes out of a situation if you stick out long enough, and that you arrive at a sort of benign indifference where the boat doesn't rock too badly, even if you keep wishing at the back of your mind that you were in a different boat. (p. 39).

Kemi's arrival in the narrator's house after a visit to see her son in a boarding school, gives her, the narrator, a new insight into the circumstances of her marital life, which appears not to favour her, although she seems to be the one who finances the marriage. She and her husband "operated a joint account that was perpetually in the red" (p. 45), but whereas he fills his tank every time he passes a petrol station, she only "flogged the old Toyota on reserve and grudgingly drove in for maybe a quarter-tank of gas." Similarly, she observes that while the husband's car is in top condition all the time, hers is ever in need of repairs; and while his car is always spotlessly clean, blaring out blues and jazz music as he cruises around, hers is consistently dirty and unwashed. (p. 45) However, her naïvety is such that she is still unable to even realise that her husband is, more or less, dependent on her financially and only exploits her for his own comfort. Worse, are the husband's incurable acts of infidelity (p. 46); yet, she could describe him to her friend meekly: "My husband was not a notoriously difficult man." (p. 45)

Her plan out of the situation is even more bizarre, as she describes to her friend how she intends to make money without his knowledge, in the hope that in the end, it would give her the power to control him. In fact, she explains that she has already managed to make some "meagre savings, put together erratically over a period of ten years", changing the hiding place constantly so that he does not find her out. She now pleads with Kemi to assist her to invest the money in her trading business, so that she could grow to be rich and, therefore, use the financial power to entrap the husband to herself fully. She is scared about the unconfirmed stories that Kemi tells her about her own polygamous marriage and writes off Debo (Kemi's husband) when she learns that he has two wives, wondering all the time why Debo should choose to have a second wife (Biola) who is mild-mannered, soft-spoken and shy, as against her friend, the glamourous and miniskirt-wearing Kemi (p. 40). She becomes too blinded by her hatred for the institution of polygamy to think critically as she finally brings out all her savings and naïvely hands them to Kemi, who eventually swindles her of it all.

In 'Jaded Appetites' (pp 51-62) the reader is presented with a narrator whose gushing love is not reciprocated by her husband:

> It was our tenth wedding anniversary...My gold-fringed card on the table was gushing with sentiment. His was spare. Love for him was a benign presence like allowing the dog to lie in the kitchen and not kicking it. (pp 55-56)

The narrator then continues with the story of the love affair between a distant relative and her married lover, Armstrong, a veterinary surgeon. It is a love affair that is cyclical, as it could not possibly end in marriage. Initially, the narrator's relative believes her lover will leave his wife; however, when that fails to happen, she says she is not to get married at all (p. 57). However, she claims that she wants to get rid of Armstrong (p. 59) by Christmas, but by the new year, they are still together, although she also informs the narrator of a new boyfriend, Yinka, who has a fiancé whom he is tired of. The story ends with her curled up and resting her head on Armstrong's laps.

The story reveals that the narrator has a keen sense of observation as she realises quite early that Armstrong is merely taking advantage of her relative and would never abandon his wife for her: "I felt an intense irritation that he was a fake, phoney, a conman, a hyena in club-gear." (p. 56) Later, as she comes to understand more about him, the narrator's dislike for Armstrong increases, such that she begins to feel sorry for his wife and children (p. 58). In spite of these observations, she keeps silent and continues to watch her relative use her house to entertain him. This inaction recalls the insouciance of the silent watcher, the unnamed protagonist, in Ayi Kwei Armah's *The Beautyful Ones Are not Yet Born* (1968).

There is a similarity between the love (benign indifference) between the narrator and her husband on the one hand and the binding feelings between Armstrong and the narrator's distant relative on the other. This similarity is highlighted at the end of the story when the narrator becomes personally committed as to prepare Armstrong's lunch: "I made Armstrong a cheese sandwich and packed his supper in the food flasks." (p.61) A deeper interpretation of the incident would seem to indicate that the story of the distant relative is a metaphor for the narrator's own personal life with her husband.

Interestingly, while the reader is provided with the names of the two boyfriends (i.e. Armstrong and Yinka) of the narrator's distant relative, the relative herself is not named. Ugbabe, thus, denies the relative any identity, but subsumes it under that of her men, as though to reflect the manner in which she allows the men to take control of her life.

In 'The White Rooster' (pp 111-121) the narrator tells of her suspicions about her husband falling in love with another woman, Agnes, when he goes on transfer to the south of Nigeria, leaving her behind at home. In comparing herself with Agnes, the narrator consciously searches for the reasons for the husband's infidelity, lamenting that, "she probably knew how to love more" (p. 121). It is worthy of note that while the reader knows the name of the 'other woman' (Agnes), the identity of the narrator herself is not revealed throughout the story, but is presented as another silent observer of events who bottles up her own resentments inside her strong heart. The reader would wonder why she does not take a more active role in winning back her husband, even when she contrasts the manner her other married friends accept the infidelity of their husbands against her own inability to do so from her husband.

Thus, rather than protest to him against the affair or have a show down over it all, she could only meekly confess: "With me, it was never a honeymoon when he drove in on Friday evenings. I bristled with resentment." (p. 117) This is further reflected in her other ineffectual reactions aimed at asserting her presence in her husband's life, which are limited to token actions of "…changing things around, putting his shirts on hangers, trying to leave her stamp where she (i.e. Agnes) had been."(p. 118). The narrator does nothing categorical about her suspicions of her husband's infidelity with Agnes, but chooses to "suffer within" (p. 118), creating a psychological diversion by wondering about the funeral rite of their white rooster, which "rose like a spectre in my mind." (p. 121)

Vocality as Identity of the Woman in *Soulmates*

The voicelessness of the women in some of the stories in the collection is contrasted with the vocality of some of the women facing the same challenges elsewhere. The narrator's attitude in 'The White Rooster' (pp 113-121), for instance, can be contrasted with Flora's in 'Greener Pastures' (pp 85-99). In 'Greener Pastures', the narrator leaves her university in Kano to attend an interview in Calabar and requires accommodation for the duration of her visit. One of the professors in the narrator's university suggests she stays with Flora and Steve in Calabar, stating that he and Flora were once schoolmates. When the narrator gets to the house, Flora refuses to be hospitable. This is because Flora suspects that her husband and the narrator may have a soft spot for each other: "In that ill-lit room, her glance shifted from her husband to me, straining through those lenses to detect any associations, unspoken intimacies." (p.88) Flora would, however, not take any chances and in spite of her husband's protestation, suggests hotels in Calabar that the narrator could stay in. When her husband's protest persists, she simply walks out on the two of them, "her husband muttering after her." (p. 88) The narrator is forced to leave.

In the first short story of the collection, 'Soulmates' (pp 3- 13), from which the collection takes its name, Anita takes a decisive step to prevent damage to her marriage and sends her husband's friend, Uncle Wahab, away from their home. Initially, Uncle Wahab is welcomed into the house, but when she notices that he has a corrupting influence on her husband, she sends him away. The reader is not informed categorically how this happens; rather, Ugbabe makes the reader infer this from the conversation between Anita and her husband, Bayo. (p. 12-13)

The narrator in 'Blessing in Disguise' (pp 27- 35) is yet another woman who 'vocalises' her protest against her husband, Benson, taking a second wife after thirty-three years of marriage. Benson seeks the initial agreement of his foreign wife by telling her that he needs to marry Blessing, an Igbo girl from his ethnic group, to end a family feud over land and secure his heritage. It is not until during the traditional wedding that the narrator realises that her husband has "planned this a long time ago" (p. 34). She decides to leave abruptly: "It's not so much the man's betrayal , but the fact that I allowed myself to be cheated out of a life, without pulling the rug from under his feet first." (p. 35). While admitting that at fifty-two, she considers it too late to put up a fight and that the decision for a new life has suddenly been thrust upon her, she considers it somehow a new beginning, an opportunity to live for herself an independent life that is not necessarily tied to pleasing her husband. It will be a life of relevance and meaning to herself, as captured in the complaint by one of her friends, Helen, another 'expatriate wife' who has suffered similar humiliation: "I should have done this a long time ago. I sit like a Wedgewood ornament on the top shelf, gathering dust…things go on around me, but I am not consulted about anything." (p. 34)

'Survivor' (pp. 75-82) and 'Borrowed Feathers' (pp. 103-110) introduce another dimension to the role that Nigerian women play in issues of identity in Ugbabe's collection of stories. 'Survivor' tells the story of how Brenda, a non-Nigerian from the Dominican Republic married to Emeka, her Nigerian husband, survives the financial, matrimonial and traditional challenges she encounters. The narrator says that Brenda is adept at knowing where to get the best bargains for goods and services. She also offers advice to the narrator on how best to treat a man: "Be a partner, not a parent. Care for him but don't hover." (p. 78). She also generally gives ready-made responses to meet all matrimonial circumstances the foreign wife may encounter (pp 76, 77). The story of the 'Stew of the Week' (pp 77-78) shows how Brenda treats her husband when she gets tired of being given insufficient money for food. She sets the table as usual, but instead of food, she places the currency note her husband has given her on his plate. The narrator introduces the silent influence of Nigerian women in the story when she acknowledges: "I knew then that the outsider had acquired the tricks of the insider." (p. 78)

When her husband dies suddenly, Brenda successfully rebels against traditional practices that could affect her finances and the survival of family and children. She buys the coffin herself, locks and secures the house and heads to the village to bury Emeka. She insists her husband must be buried in the only house he built in his village, in order to prevent it being sold or taken over by his relatives. Much later after the burial, Brenda is described as looking charming in gold jewellery and driving her husband's car (p. 82). This is an indication that, unlike what obtains in the Igbo tradition, where the widow is at the mercy of her husband's family, Brenda has succeeded in taking control of her life and husband's property.

In 'Borrowed Feathers' (pp 103-110), Sophie, the foreign wife of a Nigerian, acts uncharacteristically, by confronting and warning her husband's girlfriend to keep away from him. It is uncharacteristic because before now, Sophie "could never find the suitable words to return an insult or an unjust abuse; most of the time, things bubbled inside her as hurt." (p.103) This time, when she decides to speak out, she wonders, "That was most uncharacteristic of me." (p. 103) As she engages in the verbal combat with the suspected girlfriend, it is as though she represents all the wronged married women, getting "carried away with the sanctity of marriage" (p. 106). She reels out the names of the "experienced-in-betrayal friends" (p.107) in her mind, including Jacintha, who would challenge her husband in a verbal war where she always takes the lead (p. 107); Charity, her sister-in-law, who is a smart talker and takes after their mother; and Sophie's mother-in-law, who speaks "pure poetry when provoked":

> She could strip you naked with her words in the middle of the street when you are fully clothed! She could cut you down to unrecognisable shreds when the timing was right. She could bowl you over with a conundrum. (p. 108)

Sophie's recall of her mother-in-law's statement that "every woman is sitting on a six-inch nail." (p. 110) universalises her experience of her husband's infidelity. This also confirms the inspiration that Sophie gets from her other married women friends, namely Jacintha and Charity. It should be pointed out here that the mother-in-law's apparent acceptance of her own husband's infidelity is not in conflict with her (the mother-in-law's) identity of vocality. The mother-in-law is hospitable to her husband's mistress whenever she (the mistress) comes to spend the night, not because the mother-in-law is powerless to react, but because she considers women like that as belonging to "the class of household trash" (p.110) and, therefore, she remains unprovoked. Thus, there is no need for the mother-in-law to feel threatened or unleash her "pure poetry" on the mistress, as such vocality is only exhibited "when provoked." (p. 108).

Sophie's vocality may be uncharacteristic of her at the beginning, but she remains inspired by the 'borrowed feathers' in her mother-in-law's aphorisms, even as they continue to reverberate in her mind; and she wishes she could use more of them in her encounter with her husband's girlfriends (p. 110). In universalising Sophie's experience and making her 'borrow feathers' from other women, Ugbabe brings all women, particularly Indian and Nigerian women, into a common bond and, thus, dissolves the dichotomy between the insider and outsider that inter-racial marriage imposes on them.

Conclusion

In this way, Kanchana Ugbabe's selected stories in *Soulmates* become significant as an examination of the various identities of married woman and the challenges they confront in their married life, especially the foreigners among them who are married to Nigerian men. These challenges reveal them as having two types of identities: in the first group are the 'expatriate' wives whose identities are tied to those of their husbands. The women in this group are voiceless, as they keep their frustrations and resentments within themselves. The second group comprises women who are vocal and readily express their feelings in various ways during their interaction with their husbands.

The study also reveals that Ugbabe presents the Nigerian women as being generally vocal, noting that this places them together with the second group of the foreign wives; thereby dissolving the dichotomy between the experiences of the two otherwise culturally-exclusive groups of women.

References

- Achebe, C. (1958), *Things Fall Apart*, London: Heinemann.
- Achebe, C. (1960), *No Longer at Ease*, London: Heinemann.
- Achebe, C. (1966), *A Man of the People*. London: Heinemann Educational Books Ltd.
- Aidoo, A.A. (1965), *The Dilemma of a Ghost*, Accra: Longman.
- Armah, A. K. (1968), *The Beautyful Ones Are Not Yet Born*, Oxford: Heinemann Educational Publishers.
- Ekwensi, C. (1961), *Jagua Nana*, London: Heinemann.
- Harrington, F. (2004), *Sociological Criticism*, Malden: Polity Press,
- Ogundipe-Leslie, M. (1994), *Re-Creating Ourselves: African Women and Critical Transformations*, Trenton, NJ: Africa World Press, Inc.
- Saha, A.S. (2009), "Exile, Literature and the Diasporic Indian Writer, *Rupkatha: Journal on Interdisciplinary Studies in Humanities* 1,(2), 187-197.
- Simpson, J. (Ed.) (1995), *The Oxford Book of Exiles*, Oxford: Oxford University Press.
- Soyinka, W. (1970), *The Interpreters*, London: Heinemann.
- Soyinka, W. (1973), *Season of Anomy*, London: Rex Collings.

Chapter Fifteen

The Changing Trends and Interface between Oral-Literary and Film Communication for Ethno-National Identity and Development: The Tiv Typology

Godwin Aondofa Ikyer

Introduction

The ethnic, regional and world communities are increasingly becoming susceptible to unprecedented levels of openness, such that all social groups are daily brought in to share a relatively common conception of popular culture. Cultural hybridisation and globalisation are, thus, becoming the norm; and today no society could really remain isolated within closed social or cultural boundaries. Ironically, globalisation also encourages recourse to linguistic and cultural sources of communication as entry values, suggesting that, to be truly global, the group or community has to also be linguistically and culturally 'local'. In this sense, globalisation becomes the localisation of the global, just as localisation transforms into a slice of globalisation.

The indigenous societies, which were known for their oral means of communication, had to at first make space for literary communication that was book-based; later, they had to embrace the combination of aural and visual images represented in the motion picture. In time, the film, which was technology-based, gradually rose to become a modern cultural process of communication acceptable to all societies, irrespective of class, level of education or race affiliations. However, the film is a re-establishment of the primacy of oral production, just as it captures the nuances of the society, providing the avenue for projecting the goals and vision of the society.

This interface, between the oral form of communication that was previously considered traditional and belonging to pre-literate societies and the more sophisticated literary compositions, reached its peak in the moving 'home' motion picture, which, subsequently, became the epicenter of an even greater interface for value dispersal and value generation. Not only has the development affected the dynamics of human thought, linguistic and cultural practices and value localisation, but it has also re-defined the erstwhile boundaries of ethnic groups and enabled societies to put their cultural sources to use in limitless possibilities. In addition, it has reinforced the growing multi-dimensionality of values and perspectives of groups or communities in their interactions within and with the outside world.

In reviewing these developments, this chapter considers the challenge of deploying the new 'art' of the commercial cinema, with specific reference to the Tiv society, to reinforce the current norms and local values and provide the youths especially with a suitable template for balanced cultural and linguistic aesthetics.

Language, Cultural Aesthetics and the Indigenous Film

The public screening of the first film in Nigeria in 1903 at the Global Hall, Lagos, threw challenges to the nation to create its own production, capable of representing its culture(s), language(s) and values. For it is through language and culture that the sensibilities of a people are always ascertained and articulated. Bayo Ogunjimi (200:96) points out in this direction that:

> Culture assists in a dialectical configuration for articulating the fluidity and dynamics in political, economic and social

relations. Also it attitudinises the positive flow sensibilities of all generations in the historical continuum. This reality poses a problem for the contemporary African artist who needs to mobilise the apparatus of culture to create and foster social dynamics.

Thus, the nation-state's various linguistic groups have to create a visual space for the evolution of healthy cultural and linguistic aesthetics, where the atmosphere will foster the growth of their local flora and fauna; and their values and cultural institutions will have a place of representation, recognition and re-enforcement.

Early Attempts at Indigenous Cinema in Nigeria

Issues of racial and national identities, misrepresentation of the black race and the in-human stereotyping of the African in the early films had actually made the indigenous film makers move away from the "monkey imitation" of the British empire and that of the American cinema, to produce the first indigenous feature film, *Kongi's Harvest* in 1971. The early Nigerian film makers must have felt ridiculous producing their films in a foreign language and, as though to contain the 'monkey imitation', therefore, Ola Balogun produced the feature film, *Amadi* (1975), in the Igbo language and that became the trail blazer in producing Nigerian films in the indigenous languages. *Amadi* was about a young man who turned his back on the town where he was living and returned to the village, in order to obtain peace, love and sincerity and not commotion, corruption and the decay that he found to be prevalent in the city life. The film, therefore, symbolically serves as a turning point from the use of a foreign language and its inherent stereotyping and caricature of Western values. Other films were soon to follow, including *Ajani Ogun* (Yoruba) and *Shaihu Umar* (Hausa).

These early attempts in the indigenous languages were succeeded by other films quickly, including *Ija Ominira* (1977), *Aiye* (1979) by Hubert Ogunde, *Kanta of Kebbi* (1979) sponsored by the Sokoto State Government; *Jaiyesimi* (1980), Ogunde, *Kadara/Destiny* (1981) in Yoruba and Hausa by Ade Love (Hyginus Ekwuazi: 16-18). This effort, however, slowed down considerably when the country's economy slowed down, taking its toll on the various sectors of the nation's activities.

The Re-Emergence of the Indigenous Nigerian Cinema

The film industry in the indigenous languages in Nigeria bounced back to life when the situation improved at the turn of the twentieth century and became established as a serious institution within the first decade of the twentieth century. "Nollywood" soon became its 'national' name, while the Yoruba language films were called 'Yollywood'; the Hausa language films came to be known as 'Kallywood' or, more popularly, 'Kannywood'; and the Edo language film became 'Edowood'. In this spirit, the Tiv-language productions have not been tagged 'Tivwood' yet, but are now simply referred to as 'Tiv Films'; sometimes, they are also called 'Bennywood', as they cover the Benue landscape.

There are many more variants of the indigenous 'home' video film productions across Nigeria yet to be brought to the fore of literary discourse. Within the last couple of decades, they have become a linguistic, socio-cultural and economic bedrock for growth and continuity, wielding the industry into a distinctive sub-category of cinema and reputable phenomenon. Thus, after a detailed review, Jibril (2004:52) concludes that, "this new media form has changed the landscape of visual entertainment" in Nigeria in particular and Africa in general.

Furthermore, the modern indigenous language films continue to be shaped by complex interfaces and trends, which arise from some exigencies of history and 'local' challenges, prospects and possibilities within the Nigerian nation. In fact, the most recent indigenous language films bear distinct ethnic or regional perspectives and manifest some cultural and/or religious consciousness and sensibilities, calculated to become attractive to their prospective audience. This appears to have made quite an impact on the 'national' film industry and the Nigerian nation-state in general in a number of ways. For instance, the aesthetics, mores and values of a particular ethnic or social group are often 'projected' to other groups within the country in such a way as to create a trend for self-definition and national consciousness and the platform for inducing growth and development. Furthermore, the institutionalisation of such indigenous films is a progressive step in filling the oral narrative space in the people's literary tradition with the technology-based visual productions. These distinct Nigerian film traditions could well be called a variant of the 'Indigenous African Languages Cinema'.

With the current institutionalisation of the indigenous languages cinema in Africa, the African governments should gear efforts towards promoting its technical, visual and artistic development, with various forms of support in production, marketing and distribution and localising its study in school curricula and academic discourses in the tertiary institutions. This will go a long way in making it reposition the culture, ethno-regional and national growth of the individual African societies.

Indigenous Languages Cinema and the Dialogue with the National Cinema

The Indigenous Languages Cinema (ILC) represents a dialogue with the national cinema in localising ethnic, regional and national phenomena and the sharing of roles and responsibilities. It also denotes an attempt at creating cinema commitment and values among the people and the promotion of the spirit of limitless exploration; as well as the articulation of the pains and gains of the Nigerian nation-state.

However, it is quite apparent that, at the moment, the national cinema is running low on general representation and in the effort to bridge the traditional ethnic and other associated divides and establish meaningful cross-cultural connectivity. At the same time, the local languages are being subverted, along with their socio-cultural aesthetics and values.

Within the Tiv language films in particular, the general tendency is to be cross-cultural, bilingual and ethno-national in their setting. Thus, films like *Igboji man Sule* (2012), *Tyowase* (2011), *Oradiguve* (2009), and *Mba ve gba ichaver kpa Ter koron Ve* (2011) are regional and project popular Tiv culture. They connect the audience within the geographical and linguistic space through the popular culture they generate; the modern values they depict also provide a bond with kindred spirits in the diaspora. This networking has the overall effect of ushering in new cultural, geographical and spiritual affinities among the viewers, leading to renewed consciousness and a sense of empowerment.

Background to Film Production in the Tiv society

The earliest Tiv films were in the form of newsreels and documentaries on Tiv cultural life, like the making of the *Anger*, the traditional black and white Tiv cloth, the *Kwagh-hir* drama performances, various dances and dance groups, methods of farming, folklore and mythology. There was no commercial touch to the productions as they were produced by the National Television Authority (NTA) Makurdi, the Benue State Government or such other cultural or research bodies. There are no detailed records available, but evidence suggests that the Tiv started their modern indigenous language cinema in the 1990s, as though in response to Osadebey's (1957:57) philosophy, when he urges:

> Don't preserve my customs
> As some fine curios
> To suit some white historian's tastes.

Thus, the Tiv film makers deployed the new media technology to promote their cultural practices, as well as socio-economic, political and religious ethics, in their attempt to provide links with the oral world and project the social life of the people in all its complexities. In this regard, the emergence of the indigenous language cinema has now created a collective platform for the native speakers of the language to interact and move towards other ethnic regional and national groups.

ILC and the Tiv Typology

That is also how the Tiv typology of the indigenous language cinema maintains a cultural and cross-cultural commitment and fashions a distinctive identity for the Tiv ethnic group, the region and country at large. For instance, the film *Igboji man Sule* (2012) is one of the few Tiv comedy of manners, in which a Tiv man and a Fulani man turn the town upside down through their recklessness in hilarious episodes of lying, fighting, womanising and drinking. The film erroneously attempts to exploit cultural stereotyping, but in the end comes out positively only in demonstrating social interaction among the Tiv and Fulani ethnic groups. The dialogue in particular, which is in Tiv, Hausa, Pidgin English, Nigerian English and standard English, the code mixing and code switching and the friendly relationships among the characters, all come together to generate an atmosphere of common understanding and create a binding national ethno-ethos and identity.

The film contrasts sharply with its predecessor, *Tyowase* (2011), which examines the knotty problems of Fulani herdsmen and Tiv farmers, who engage in endless clashes for herding and farming space. It overviews the internal challenges of betrayal and corruption among the people and presents the problem as begging for a solution, as observed by one of the community heads:

> *Fulani ka ve va heen ve na or mom nan lun a*
> *M-mem hen tar wase ne ga. Shin atev kpa kasev*
> *Mba kera yaren ve tseer ga, er Fulani ----; ka ve*
> *Na mbayev asev mba gen ve yevese, ve wa ve ikyav.*
> *Ve lu a m-mem ga!*

> Once the Fulani come around, nobody has peace
> In our land again. On the farms, the women refuse
> Going, else the Fulani ----; they make our youths
> Run away, overburden them and make them restless!

No doubt, the film makes a case for an amicable resolution to the unending conflict in the Tiv homeland and a cross-cultural consensus that will bring peace and happiness to everyone.

Another film, *Ayange a Masetyo* (Last Days) (2006), reviews internal conflicts among the Tiv communities themselves, arising from land disputes and from the involvement of militia in inter-clan fights. The war songs, unwanted killings, destructions and boastful statements, like *"Nomikyegh kera cie azembe ga"* ("The hen no longer fears the hawk"), collectively act to echo the theme song of the film, which is:

> *Shie zulum ve tar atenger sha*
> *Num anongo, ior akera soo ayol ave ga*
> *Kwagh er ve num anongo sha won, tar atenger*
> *Yesu hide ve o!*
>
> The last days are here, the world will tremble
> Wars will be fought, persons won't love each other
> It has happened, wars will be fought endlessly,
> The world will tremble
> Jesus is coming oh!

The Fifth Wife (2011), directed by Jack Samuels, is bilingual – in Tiv and English — and captures the internal complexities of jealousy, polygamy, and the Ingyor payback reparation prevalent in the traditional Tiv life. It presents an unduly confused rich young man, Sachia, and his adventurous uncle, Zaki Gbaka, who has twenty-five children, yet ambitiously seeks a fifth wife. In trying to create a Lacannian archetypal production, the film fails in Tiv philosophy and strength of intellect; its confusion results into the creation of an otherwise sound character who crumbles at every problem that comes his way. Two pieces of local and universal advice are, however, valuable in the film: 'No matter the strength of a farmer, he must rest a while to smoke a pipe before he continues'; and 'No one has the same mother with death and so no one should think that death will not catch up with him o! That is my widow's cry' (from the widow character, Wankur).

Mb ve Gbe Chaver Kpa ter Koron ve (2011), directed by Rev. Emmanuel Abanger and produced for the NKST Media Services by Rev Samuel T. Ikpilakaa, dedicates its attention to the less privileged, the seemingly helpless and vulnerable ones in the society. The film ends with the religious presentation and song: '*Ka we gba ichaver kpa ... ter wase yo ngu a koron we...*' ('When you seem tattered, yet our God will sew you up'). God is depicted as intervening always to restore and even re-position the seemingly helpless, vulnerable and tortuously hopeless in the community, especially 'Atindi' James Asanyi, Bende Shaayem, a central character deceived by local politicians to leave his lucrative work of being the Legal Adviser to the Benue Cement, Gboko, and go into politics, only to be abandoned by the very politicians that enticed him initially with their bursting promises, including his younger brother, Faasema.

The NKST Church is at the forefront of producing Tiv indigenous language films on diverse socio-economic, political and religious predicaments in its effort to re-position the Tiv culture and people for sustainable growth. For instance, *Oradiguve* (2009), directed by Rev. J.T. Aernyi and produced by the church, features Tiv, Hausa, Igbo and other ethnic groups and dwells on family jealousy and ends with sincere confessions by the characters, as they express their firm desire for oneness; thereby projecting the community's collective hopes and prospects for a better ethnic, regional and national identity in Nigeria. Other valuable films by the NKST Media Services, which create ethnic regional and national identity, include *Mbaihomov Mba Terankon, Uwegh ku Ter, Shima Nyian, Iyuhweka Mtuhwem* and *Kumashe Wam*. Many feel that the NKST Church deserves special thanks in its effort at creating the Tiv Language Cinema, and in the contents and quality of the productions.

Adan Wade Kohol Ga (2011), produced by Anjira Solomon, which is based on a Tiv classic novel by Suemo Chia, recreates the society's historical antecedents and values. It re-examines the old history and re-evaluates the modern values, especially their relevance in value assessment and ethnic-consciousness and the re-creation of a visionary society. *Organden Makeranta Ga* (2012) ('No One is Too Old to Go to School'), directed by Wizzkid Abena, presents the comic and mischievous life of the youths in exaggerated and unrealistic perspectives. However, the film scores poorly with the viewers, owing to its low grade production, overriding mischief and the lust for money and women, and for failing to merge the humorous episodes with a sense of vision. Certainly, the society needs such comic and humorous productions for their relief entertainment value, at least to enable the viewers to laugh it off, but there is the greater need to convert the pains into gains and the humour into probing thoughts that project the society's goals, dreams and visions.

Ikyese Kwaghyan (The Food Basket) (2012), produced and directed by Williams Kwa recreates the historical journey of the Tiv to the point where they have now become a gift of God as 'The Food Basket of The Nation'. In two hours and fifteen minutes, the director examines the privileged position of the Tiv people and prowls into their affairs to make the film's concerns different from the usual intra and inter ethnic relationships or regional divide.

These indigenous language films help create ancestral imprints; promote good internal and external harmony, co-operation and partnership; suggest ways of resolving local conflicts; and uphold patterns of realising individual aspirations. At the same time, they provide modes of recreation; promote cultural, ethno-regional and national consciousness; and project in the cinema a transnational flow of desires, understanding and harmonious relationships.

Conclusion

The indigenous language cinema is a new order of aural–visual production that occupies a special narrative space and addresses ethnic, regional and national challenges, re-positions popular culture and inspires fresh aesthetics. The emerging medium also offers a veritable platform for training in spoken and written language and other skills, a consciousness and identification of the group's values and aesthetics. Young as it is and its current difficulties notwithstanding, its forceful emergence is already providing the basis for the construction of a model of indigenous theorisation in film production and scholarship and creating a sense of inclusiveness. In addition, the translation of such films into other languages without barriers facilitates cross-cultural debates and gives expression to minority voices in the national dialogue.

In another positive trend, indigenous language films help to provide employment, especially among the youths and inspire a fresh sense of ethnic, regional and national pride; and a better understanding of the intrigues and complexities of the Nigerian society. It is the abiding hope that the indigenous language cinema will deploy technology to re-appraise our collective past and critical acumen and energy for positive growth and national development.

References

- Bayo, O. (2000), "Literature and National Development" *Major Themes in African Literature,* Damian Upata and Aloysius U. Ohaegbu (eds.), Nsukka-Nigeria: A P Express Publishers.

- Damas, L. (2000), Quoted in Peter I Okeh, "Negritude and the Issue of Identity in African Literature" ibid

- Ekwuazi, H. (1991), *Film in Nigeria,* Jos: Nigerian Film Corporation.

- Jibril, U. F. (2004), "Small Technologies: The Changing Trends in Hausa Home Video Production", *Hausa Home Videos: Technology, Economy and Society,* Abdalla Uba Adamu, Yusuf M. Adamu and Umar Faruk Jibril (eds).

- Osadebey D. (1957), "Young Africa's Plea", *An Anthology of West African Verse,* Olumbe Bassir (ed.), Ibadan: Ibadan University Press.

Filmography

- *Igboji Man Sule,* Dir. Sammy Willas. Marketed and Distributed by Famous Global CD Tek. Date of production: 2012.

- *Ayange a Masetyo* (Last Days) Directed and Produced by Praise Abraham. Date of production: 2006.

- *The Fifth Wife,* Directed by Jack Samuels, Produced by Aondofa Afaityo. Marketed and Distributed by Kennytex Productions. Date of production: 2011.

- *Mba Ve Gba Ichaver Kpa Ter Koron Ve,* Directed by Rev. Emmanuel Abanger. Produced by N. K. S. T Media Services, Produced 2011.

-

- *Oradiguve,* Directed by Rev. J. T Aernyi. Produced by N. K. S. T Media Services. Year of Production: 2009.

See also by the N K S T:
- *Mbaihomov Mba Terankon,* Directed by Rev. J T Aernyi. Produced by N K S T Media Services Marketed and Distributed by N K S T Media Services and Lamp Word Books, Makurdi, Year of Production: 2009.
- -------------*Uwegh Ku Ter*
- -------------*Shima Nyian*
- -------------*Iyuhwe Ka Mtuhwem*
- ------------*Kumashe Wam*
- *Tyowase,* Directed and Produced by Peter Terlumun Shimael Akimbo, Marketed and Distributed by Stevonyizine Ventures, No. 51 J S Tarka Way, Gboko, Year of Production: 2011.
- *Adan Wade Kohol Ga,* Story by Senator Suemo Chia, Produced by Anjira Solomon Nyiaekaa, Marketed and Distributed by Uncle N Video Production, No. 2 Shaahu Road, Gboko South, Gboko, Year of Production: 2011.
- *Organden Makeranta Ga,* Directed by Wizzkid Abena, Executive Producer, Williams Atambe, Marketed and Distributed by Williams World Entertainment, No. 27 Captain Downes Road Adekaa, Gboko, Benue State.
- *Ikyese Kwaghyan* (Food Basket), Produced and Directed by Williams Kwa, Marketed and Distributed by Stevonyizine Ventures, Gboko, Benue State. Year of Production: 2012.

Chapter Sixteen

Film and Identity Formation in Matrimonial Relationships: The Impact of African Magic Movies on Selected Audiences from North-Central Nigeria

Saudat Salah AbdulBaqi

Introduction

The Digital Satellite Television (DSTV) was launched in 1995 to offer direct broadcast of programmes ranging from general entertainment, movies, lifestyle and culture, sports, documentaries, news and commerce, children, religion, music and consumer channels to MultiChoice subscribers. Its bouquet initially had seventeen channels, which has now grown to over a hundred. The 'Africa Magic' channel joined the bouquet in 2003 and has become a stable companion to most families in the satisfaction of their entertainment needs. The channel features family-focused movies, series, sitcoms and documentaries with specific information on suitable viewing age. To adequately take care of its diverse audience in Nigeria, the MultiChoice service provider offers entertainment programmes in English, Igbo, Hausa and Yoruba, alongside special provisions for other subscribers from East, West and Central Africa. Consequently, various films are beamed in different languages to its teeming subscribers twenty-four hours non-stop, depending on their choice of channel. Scholars have already established the potency of film and its allies in societal reforms, rehabilitation, nation building, and in providing therapeutic elixir for its audience (Adediran & Adediran, 2008; Abubakar, 2008; Adeyemi, 2008; Osofisan, 2001), but the present literature seems to leave out the extent to which the films broadcast on the Africa Magic channel shape the matrimonial experiences of the DSTV subscribers. This study shall examine the phenomenon with specific reference to the communities in North-Central Nigeria.

Film as a Genre of the Mass Media

The significant place of films in promoting and projecting the peculiarities of nationhood has been underscored by the Nigerian National Communication Policy. The policy unequivocally states the roles of films in educating, entertaining and contributing to human thoughts and civilisation, (Anaeto & Solo-Anaeto, 2010). With these, films as a genre of mass media serve as surveillance apparatus, help in correlating and interpreting happenings in parts of the society, as well as being tools for cultural transformation and transmission of social heritage from one generation to the next (Lasswell, 1948). Media forms, such as television, film and print, as well as media contents, affect the way the receivers think and see the world (Littlejohn, 1999).

Films and Construction of Reality

Films take up the milieu of the environment to reflect reality in various communities; thus, mirroring the society (Adedina & Adedina, 2008). Like other tools of communication, they are the process by which reality is constructed (Littlejohn, 1999) out of the regular interaction among the people, either physically or virtually. The centrality of human interaction that shapes reality and reveals the communicative perspective in human existence, is expressed in the words of the philosopher Alfred Schutz (1970), as cited by Littlejohn (1999):

> The world of my daily life is by no means my private world but is from the outset an inter-subjective one, shared with many fellow men, experienced and interpreted by others: in brief, it is a world common to all of us. The unique biographical situation in which I find myself within the world at any moment of my existence is only to a very small extent of my own making.

Similarly, in an in-depth exposition on communicative perspectives, Pearce (1999) stresses the inseparable connection between communicative resources and communicative practices. By resources, the scholar implies ideas, values, stories, symbols, meanings, institutions and all other inputs in the building of reality, while practice refers to the product of the constructed reality; this manifests in forms of behaviours, actions and forms of expressions. Borrowing from Pearce's recursive loop of resources and practice, this study infers that films generate resources, which shape matrimonial harmony (practices).

Proceeds from the social construction of reality often provide material for ethogeny — the study of how people understand their actions within a predictable sequence of acts and the social construction of the self (Harre & Secord, 1972). Littlejohn (1999) explains that the theory of self is learned through a history of interaction with other people, who may be characters in films. The interaction with characters in films in particular creates two independent parts of every viewer: an 'inside' of feelings and an 'outside' of observed behaviours. In other words, an internalised film concept stimulates feelings in the viewer, which influence his/her behaviour in situations similar to the ones depicted in the film.

Films and Gratification of Matrimonial Needs

Proponents of the 'uses and gratification' approach to media studies argue that one's orientation towards a particular medium or programme is determined by one's beliefs in and the evaluation of the segment of the media (programme, content or an entire medium). Several studies have established the close link between the audience's expectancy values towards a segment of the media and how much they used the segment to gratify certain needs (Palmgreen, 1984). Invariably, the viewer plays an active role in selecting a medium or programme, based on his/her identified needs and trust in the selected medium or programme to satisfy these needs. The gratification sought is achieved through varying levels of psychological investment, emotional commitment and reflection (Storey, 2001).

Arguably, films help to unlock the emotions in its audience. Planalp (1999) suggests that considerations for emotions have often been ignored, denigrated or cut off from the rest of the regular social experience; so much so that individuals seek solace in films, in order to let off the steam of their bottled up emotions. However, critics caution the fallacy of purposeful, behaviouristic and mindful consumption of media content; arguing that not all media consumptions are traceable to individual needs, as some are informed by culture (Littlejohn, 1999).

Most movies on the African Magic channels are based on love, family, inheritance, economic conflict, political and power tussles, provision of empowerment, etc. The theme of love usually reflects in a show of treachery, betrayal of trust, jealousy, sadness, disgust, compassion, empathy, (Planalp, 1999) and such related issues. Films reveal a moral assessment of the realms of the real and the ideal, which was what informed this study to pose the following questions with a view to examining their impact on matrimonial harmony in the communities under study:

1. Do Africa Magic films increase your love towards your spouse?
2. Do Africa Magic films awaken the feelings of betrayal in you?
3. Are you inclined to trust your spouse more after watching Africa Magic films?

Marital harmony is determined by many factors, including how the two partners use their space, time and energy to express their individual feelings, exert power and share a common philosophy concerning the marriage (Kantor & Lehr, 1975). In an extensive survey on the concept of marriage, Fitzpatrick (1988) developed and administered a pool of questions on 1,500 married respondents. Subsequent exploratory factor analysis of the data revealed that the items measured three basic variables: ideology, interdependence, and conflict, which normally constitute the nucleus of matrimony. Upon further exploration of the data, Fitzpatrick discovered that married couples can be grouped into three distinct categories, namely: the traditional, the independents and the separates. She explains in reference to the earlier identified variables:

> **Traditional couples** are conventional in their view of marriage, value stability and certainty in role relations, are interdependent in nature, share much companionship, strive to minimise conflict, abhor infidelity, share much time and space, and the wife adopts her husband's name in place of her father's. Traditional couples are highly expressive and disclose both joy and frustration via both verbal and non-verbal cues and are supportive of each other. This description suits the underlying concept of matrimonial harmony in most parts of north-central Nigeria. Except for the adoption of the husband's name, which is regarded as optional in the Islamic faith, the notion of a happy family is built around mutual trust, loyalty, companionship, confidentiality, consensus rather than conflict, friendship, sharing of time and space. Based on this, the current study poses the following research questions:
>
> 4. To what extent do you feel loyal to your spouse?
> 5. To what extent do you confide in your spouse?
> 6. To what extent do you share the same room with your spouse?
>
> **The independent couples:** Couples in this type of marriage are unconventional in their views of marriage and hardly rely on each other. They enjoy a high sense of autonomy

and often share separate rooms in the same house. They may differ in interest and the friends they keep.

Marriages of this nature are characterised by conflict, re-negotiation on issues, power tussle and antagonism, although not devoid of free expressions and mutual understanding. By the marital values in north-central Nigeria, these characteristics constitute vices that can jeopardise matrimonial harmony. Hence, the study is wont to ask:

7. To what extent do you feel independent of your spouse?
8. To what extent do you compromise with your spouse?

The separate couples: Fitzpatrick describes partners in this marriage as emotionally divorced couples. This relationship is characterised by mutual suspicion, as the couples are not interdependent and obviously share very little in common; besides, their conflicts are short lived, not as a result of consensus, but due to threat cue appeal that is applied to gain compliance. Each partner is self opinionated and understands little of the other's emotions.

Arguably, a marriage that exhibits these traits in the north-central Nigeria is heading for the rocks. The existence of these characteristics in a tradition where mutual trust, understanding, and complimentary roles between couples are prime virtues, clearly portend doom for the marriage. To ting or promote these characteristics, this study asked:

9. To what extent do you care about your spouse's emotions?
10. To what extent does fear of implementation of threat force you to comply with your spouse's view?

Research Objectives

This study intends to examine the weight and direction of the influence of Africa Magic Movies on the sustenance of matrimonial in north-central Nigeria. In specific terms, it is designed to:

1. Determine whether Africa Magic films increase the love between spouses.
2. Evaluate whether Africa Magic films awaken the feelings of betrayal in its audience.
3. Assess whether the mutual trust between couples is strengthened by watching Africa Magic films.
4. Measure the amount of loyalty between couples.
5. Assess the extent to which couples confide in each other.
6. Establish whether couples share the same room.
7. Investigate whether couples feel independent of each other.
8. Ascertain the level of compromise between couples.
9. Establish the extent to which partners care about their spouse's emotions
10. Examine the role played by fear of implementation of threat force couples to comply with each other.

Methodology

Subjects

A total of 350 respondents were initially selected for inclusion in this study. The respondents were proportionately drawn from Kwara, Kogi, Niger, Nasarawa states and the Federal Capital Territory, Abuja; in order to be truly representative of the north-central states of Nigeria. Plateau State could not be captured due to financial and time constraints. The researcher confirmed the marital status of prospective respondents before administering the questionnaire on them. Consequently, all the selected respondents were married men and women who were assumed to be avid Africa Magic viewers. Respondents who disclosed that they did not often watch the Africa Magic films were eliminated from the study thereby reducing the overall sample size to 200. Among these 200 subjects, 130 were confirmed to still be living with their spouses in the same home as husbands and wives; 60 were married, but lived separately from their spouses; while ten of them were separated, but not divorced.

Survey Items

Items were generated round the three conceptual typologies of marriage that were espoused by Fitzpatrick (1988) to probe the influence of Africa Magic films on sustaining matrimonial harmony, as well as to proffer answers to the eleven research questions. These conceptual areas were: the traditional, independents and separates. The instruments were self-administered within a period of three weeks, with the assistance of some trained research assistants. A five-point Likert-type scale, which ranged from strongly agree (5) to strongly disagree (1), was used in the data collection.

Findings

The results of this study are reported in two parts: Firstly, the demography of the subjects are presented in descriptive analysis. Next, each of the examined themes of the Africa Magic films (love, betrayal and trust) are correlated with the three dimensions of marriage (tradition, independent, and separate), in order to establish the statistical relationship between the variables, as well as to assess the weight and direction of each of the Africa Magic films' themes on sustenance of matrimonial harmony. These analyses were performed using SPSS Version 16 for Windows. The result of the correlation is equally interpreted to test for multi-collinearity.

The focus of inspection in multi-collinearity is observing the degree of relationship that exists between the independent variables and the dependent variable. Multi-collinearity occurs when the correlation between the independent and the dependent variables on the one hand and the inter-relation between the independent variables on the other is 0.7 and above (Pallant, 2003.; Hair, Black, Babin, & Anderson, 2010). Hair et al., (2010) further explain that the existence of multi-collinearity between variables hampers the predictive power of the independent variables on the dependent, just as it makes determination of the unique roles of the independent variables difficult. Table 1 reveals the absence of multi-collinearity between the independent variables, as well as between the independent and the dependent variable. The correlation between love and tradition is 0.684, between love and independent is -0.394**, between love and separate is -0.194**, between trust and tradition is 0.421** between trust and independent is -0.347** and between trust and separates is -0.123* between betrayal and tradition is -0.624**, betrayal and independent is 0.568** while between betrayal and separate is 0.401** ; all of which are less than the upper ceiling of 0.7 (Hair, et al., 2010).

Table 1: Correlation Coefficient and Test for Multicollinearity

	Love	Trust	Betrayal	Traditional	Independent	Separates
Love						
Trust	.667**					
Betrayal	.607**	.575**				
Traditional	.684**	.421**	-.624**			
Independent	-.394**	-.347**	.568**	.505**		
Separates	-.194**	-.123*	.401**	.385**	.426**	

** Correlation is significant at the 0.01 level (2-tailed).
* Correlation is significant at the 0.05 level (2-tailed).

Discussions

The data collection and analysis in this study have been based on the generated themes of love, trust and betrayal, as portrayed in the Africa Magic films and the Fitzpatrick categorisation of marriage into the traditional, independent and separate. In this regard, it is established that only the traditional type of marriage can sustain peace and harmony, which are the major prerequisites for a happy married life.

The north-central states of Nigeria are deeply rooted in their culture, with traditions providing the template that stipulates the expected roles of the man and the woman in a marriage relationship. It is this template that is preserved in oral stories, drama, films and other works of art; and is passed on from one generation to the next. The concept of matrimony harmony in north-central Nigeria is, therefore, premised on the existence of unfettered love, mutual trust, absolute loyalty, companionship, interdependency between couples and the sharing of time and space together.

These expectations synchronise with what Fitzpatrick describes as the traditional marriage. The other two types of marriages — the independents and the separates — create an ambience of chaos, which can lead to the destruction of marriages.

The film, as a reservoir of culture and tradition, is expected in many communities to protect, project and transmit its cultural values, while guarding against their extinction. Thus, in assessing the performance of the Africa Magic films broadcast on the Digital Satellite Television (DSTV), this study discovers that the medium is highly active in preserving the matrimonial harmony of its viewers in north-central Nigeria. It is usually effective in shaping the thoughts and actions of its audience, even as it attempts to reflect the reality of the society.

The findings indicate a strong positive contribution of the Africa Magic films, based on their themes of love and trust, in sustaining matrimonial harmony in the conventional or traditional marriage type. The correlated analysis shows that, the more the films project the themes of love, the greater the likelihood of inducing marital harmony among the audience; as epitomised by the traditional type of marriage. This finding corroborates that of Fitzpatrick (1988), that a marriage that is conducted in mutual love between couples is most likely to weather all storms and will be less chaotic, record minimal conflicts and show greater understanding towards amicable resolution of conflicts.

Expectedly, an increase in the portrayal of love in films corresponds to a decrease in the likelihood of recording independent marriages in the area of study. This is indicated by the negative correlation between the theme of love and the independent marriage type. Impliedly, a relationship that is soared in love will operate on mutual interest, and induce the couple to share the same world view about marriage and speak in unison, while advancing plausible justification for differing views. Such couples will be glad to share time and space together, rather than separately, as it is with the independent couples. A relationship that lacks mutual respect is devoid of insufficient love between the partners.

Similarly, the findings have proved that an increase in the portrayal of love in the Africa Magic films leads to a decrease in the incidence of separate marriages in the north-central Nigeria. The life of a separate marriage is governed by mutual suspicion and sharing little in common, as the partners become self opinionated and do not mind disgracing each other in public on issues of differing interest, if only for one of the parties to prove its superiority over the other. This practice is antithetical to the doctrine of love, an assumption that is clearly supported by the findings in this study.

In the same vein, the projection of the theme of trust in Africa Magic films has been confirmed to have a positive impact on enthroning marital bliss among viewers from the north-central Nigeria. By inference, the higher the projected level of trust among couples, the more the likelihood of witnessing a happy matrimonial life, as expected by tradition. Mutual trust between couples enables them to repose confidence in each other, feel safe in the company of each other and be able to make informed decision on behalf of each other, owing to the magnitude of sharing, which constitutes the foundation of the relationship. This finding supports the views of Planalp (1999) that the existence of trust between communicating partners eases the path for emotional disclosures; and, by extension, strengthens harmony in the relationship.

Probing the weight and direction of the relationship between the projection of trust in the Africa Magic films and the independent type of marriage, the findings reveal a moderate negative impact of the theme on the likelihood of couples living independent lives. Regardless of the magnitude of the impact, the disclosure that an increase in the projection of the importance of trust results in a decrease in having independent marriages is gratifying. This serves as an impetus for recording matrimonial harmony with less conflict, focused interactions, productive and effective communication processes and, most importantly, ensuring proper upbringing of the children.

Results also indicate an inverse relationship between the projection of the theme of trust in the Africa Magic films and the separate type of marriage. This finding portends a healthy coexistence between couples in north-central Nigeria. Logically, the practice of mutual suspicion, being self-opinionated and showing little or no concern for the emotional feelings of each other in a marriage speaks volume about the level of trust that exists in such a relationship.

The theme of betrayal in the Africa Magic films is antithetical to the growth of marital harmony; hence, the observed strong inverse relationship between this theme and the traditional type of marriage. As earlier established, a marriage that is well grounded in love and trust will not thrive in the realm of betrayal. Betrayal is tantamount to deceit, hurt, disloyalty and disappointment, which can jeopardise the motive for matrimonial harmony.

Not surprisingly, however, the study reveals that the theme of betrayal strongly correlates positively with the independent type of marriage. Since this type of marriage is characterised by a high sense of autonomy, the partners do not repose total confidence in each other. Consequently, none of them refrains from stabbing each other in the back when the situation demands it.

The findings equally reveal a strong positive relationship between the projection of the theme of betrayal in the Africa

Magic films and the separate type of marriage. This also supports the ideals of the society, which make it difficult for one who betrays to live peacefully with a forthright person.

Corroborating the views of Littlejohn (1999), these findings confirm that films provide a moral assessment for the realms of the real and the realms of the ideal. The result is consistent with the submissions of the construction of the reality theorists. It has unambiguously shown that events in the outside world constitute potential raw materials for the film content, which in turn dictates and shapes images of reality and that of self for individuals in the society. It further confirms that, although individuals consume media contents to gratify their personal needs, the interpretation and application of the messages is informed by the society, which sets the rules and norms that govern human existence within every community.

Recommendations

The findings in this study have confirmed the productive status of film as a form of mass communication. Given the disclosure symmetry of interpretation between film content and practical considerations of marriage type, this study advances the following recommendations:

1. Films can be used as a veritable tool for enlisting positive social changes within the society. In addition to information dissemination on other forms of mass media and interpersonal channels, the adoption of films for the transmission of developmental messages will aid changes towards desired behaviours and attitudes.
2. Film producers should be conscious of the moral values in the society and reflect same in their products.
3. The contents of films should be sourced locally, rather than from foreign ideas that are not practicable within the Nigerian society.

4. Efforts should be made to minimise importation and transmission of foreign films on television stations, in order to reduce the incidence of cultural imperialism.
5. Given the erosion of geographical boundaries by cultural transmission occasioned by satellite broadcasting, Nigerian films should be censored to prevent creation and projection of bad image of the country to the outside world.
6. Future studies should try to examine the exact ways by which films gratify the needs of the audience.
7. Future studies should also examine the content of films in propagating developmental messages.

REFERENCES

- Abubakar, A. L., (2008). "Hausa Home Videos and Global Narrative Structure" in Mojaye, E. C., Oyewo, O. O., M'bayo, R and Sobowale, I. A. (Ed.) *Globalization and Development Communication in Africa*, Ibadan, University Press.

- Adeyemi, T. (2008), "Re-Inventing the African Family Through Film: Nollywood Paradigm," *Africa Through the Eye of the Video*, Swaziland Academic Publications.

- Alfred, S. (1970), On *Phenomenology and Social Relations*, Chicago: University of Chicago Press.

- Anaeto, S. G. & Solo-Anaeto, M. (2010), "Development Communication: Principles and Communicative Tool", in Mojaye, E. C. Oyewo, O. O. M'bayo, R. and Sobowale, I. A. (ed.), *Globalization and Development Communication in Africa*, Ibadan: University Press.

- Fitzpatrick, M. A., (1988), *Between Husbands and Wives: Communication in Marriage*, Newbury Park, CA: Sage.

- Hair, J. F., Black, W. C., Babin, B. J. Andersen, R. E., & Tatham, R. L. (2010), *Multivariate Data Analysis* (7th ed.), Upper Saddle River, NJ:: Pearson Prentice Hall.
- Harre, R. & Secord, P., (1972), *The Explanation of Social Behaviour*, Totowa, NJ: Littlefield Adam.
- Lasswell, H. (1948), "The Structure and Function of Communication in Society", in *Communication of Ideas*, ed. L. Bryson, New York: Institute of Religion and Social Studies.
- Littlejohn, S. W. (1999), *Theories of Human Communication*, USA: Wadsworth
- Osofisan, F. (2001), *Insidious Treason: Drama in a Postcolonial State* (Essays), Ibadan: Opan
- Pallant, J. (2003), *SPSS Survival Manual: A Step By Step Guide to Data Analysis Using SPSS for Windows* (Versions 10 and 11), Maidenhead, Philadelphia: Open University Press.
- Palmgreen, P. (1984), *Uses and Gratification: A Theoretical Perspective in Communication*, Yearbook 8, ed. R. N. Bostrom, Beverly Hills, CA: Sage.
- Planalp, S. (1999), *Communicating Emotion: Social, Moral and Cultural Processes*, Cambridge University Press.
- Storey, J. (2001), *Cultural Theory and Popular Culture: An Introduction* (3rd ed.), Pearson Prentice Hall.

Chapter Seventeen

Prose and Identity in Northern Nigeria: The Antecedents, Contexts and Implications for Literature in Northern Nigeria

Suleiman A. Jaji

Introduction

It is difficult to exhaust discussion on the topic, "Prose and Identity in Northern Nigeria", in view of its wide and controversial nature. "The imagined sameness of a person or a social group at all times and in all circumstances and being able to continue to be itself and not something or someone else", presents identity as a fixed phenomenon. Identity is a psycho–social, political and cultural issue that is centred on the assertion of unity, rather than diversity and pluralism. It is a continuous, but not static, state of individual or social group, which critics, such as Robins in Bennet and Morris (2005), contend is the cultivation and valuation of selfhood in a person or group, with the concern for sameness and continuity of the same individual or group over time. The purpose of this paper is to examine the concept of prose in general and identity in particular from the literary/historical perspective and to locate its literary, cultural expression in the prose fiction in Northern Nigeria. Therefore, viewed as an expression of the "inner essence or property" emanating from a "self-same and self-contained individual or collective", identity is, as rightly pointed out, "instituted through a play of differences", constituted in and through the multiple relations to other identities. Identity derives its meaning and distinction from what it is not, what it excludes, or "its position of distinction in the field of difference."

From a historical and political stand point, Northern Nigeria can be conceived as a conglomeration of various ethnic and social groups that share a sense of belonging as one community, with a common culture and history, in the process of the development of the Nigerian nation. These are considered as fundamental conditions for the self-expression and self-fulfilment of the individuals and groups and points at the achievements of the region as a unique political, cultural and economic entity within Nigeria. Although contemporary conception of identity is essentialist by definition, the paper recognises that more recent, and relatively critical discourse of identity, elicits anti-essentialist emphasises from the dynamism of social and global changes. However, from the perspective of the competitive, and sometimes atavistic character of the Nigerian political setting, which tends to promote regional, inter-ethnic and group rivalry, the essentialist perception of identity cannot be overlooked.

A dictionary definition of prose is that it is a piece of writing that is written in ordinary language, in contrast to poetry. The function of prose, according to Preminger and Brogan (1993), is the written representation and communication about events, processes and facts that obtain in the external world. Implicitly, literature makes truth claims about the external world, despite the fact that on the surface, it is 'fiction'. Otherwise, as pointed out by literary scholars, if the readers do not believe that literature, despite its 'fictitious' nature, makes truth-claims about life, they will not find it worth reading, regardless of its entertainment value. We should, however, note the cross-cutting relationship between poetry and prose in literature, particularly in the novel, because of its flexibility and expansiveness.

Historical Development of Prose

Preminger and Brogan (1993:1349) observe that since antiquity, the distinction between verse and prose is represented by the positions of the essentialist and the formalist discourses. For the essentialists, who are also sometimes referred to as the affectivists, the verse form is not so important in defining poetry; therefore, they view poets as more than versifiers. Western proponents of this view, include Plato, Aristotle, Cicero, Horace, Sidney, Wordsworth, Shelley, Arnold and Croce. In fact, Aristotle had argued that the metrical form was not a sufficient criterion for 'poetry' because the works of philosophers and historians were often in hexameters, although that did not make them poetry. Thus, ordinarily, form should not supersede function.

The formalists, however, consider verse as both necessary and, to some extent, sufficient for the achievement of the effects of heightened intensity and compression or figured speech, which are commonly considered the hallmark of poetry. Whereas in prose, the constitutive principle is syntax, the constitutive device of the sequence, as Jacobson (in Preminger and Brogan, 1993) opines, is design — manifested in sound and rhythm, which lead to sense and order, or "the organisation of readerly experience", in the text. The formalists deny any naïve distinction between forms and content because "the verse form is not supererogatory to prose." This opinion considers the verse form, prose and poetry as being mutually inclusive. Verse and prose are only modes, while drama and fiction are genres. Thus, "any of the three literary genres may be written in either of the modes *or any mixture thereof*" (original emphasis); as Preminger and Brogan (1993:1347) argue. Nevertheless, Aristotle in *Poetics* makes a case for plot structure in literature, mainly because "one may be a poet without versing and a versifier without poetry". However, like verse or "poetic composition", prose can be a representation of speech, such as dialogue or monologue, which are the elements that give the novel a huge success in its ability to represent ordinary, everyday speech more realistically than the other genres.

Many reasons may compel us to put our thoughts in 'black and white', including the need for self-actualisation and the socio–political imperatives of "group identity". It could be in prose, implying writing in ordinary, everyday style as opposed to the poetic or dramatic mode either as fiction or non–fiction, like biography/autobiography, diary, the journal or travelogues, with a view to keeping records, teaching lessons or just for entertainment. Historically, the "prose style" could be traced to the neo–classical period when a return to the classical rules in literature meant for example, the prevalence in drama of the concept of the "three unities" of time, place and action, which the modern novelistic tradition discards as an unrealistic epistemology, in view of the modern and technological developments that it adequately absorbs and utilises.

Edward (1990:173) suggests that up to the classical period, most serious literature was written in the poetic form, like the plays of Shakespeare, the extended story telling of Spencer and Milton, etc. Prose was reserved for non-fiction, history, philosophy, devotions and record–keeping. However, it appeared to be that the neo – classical emphasis on clarity and simplicity exemplified by the prose of Dryden (died 1700), combined with the Puritan emphasis on "the plain style" and easily understood preaching and the new demands of scientific discourse – all helped to turn prose into a flexible medium of communication. As a mirror of the society, literature in general and the novel in particular, are concerned with social and individual wellbeing and identity.

According to Shaffer (2006:15), the last part of the twentieth century has witnessed a paradigm shift in the character of both literary and national identity, because the "novel in English" has replaced the "English novel" in significance and cogency. He suggests that what was at one time on the margin of canonical literature — the English language, but non-British novel (the Commonwealth novel)— is at present squarely at its centre:

The English language novel is now genuinely an international affair with the post-colonial anglophone and "black British " works as widely read and critically esteemed as the English novelists of this period have been and will continue to be, it is the non -English novelists who now arguably dictate the parameters of literary debate and attract the most interest . As the novelist Emma Tennant as early as 1978 declared, the majority of the important "developments" in English language fiction "are as likely to come out of Africa, or the West Indies or India" as out of Britain....The single most important "development" in literature written in English Language over the past century has been its increasingly international — indeed global – nature. Once the language of a few million people on a small Island on the edge of Europe, English is now spoken and written on every continent and is an important language inside at least one quarter of the world's one hundred and sixty countries. As English has become an important international language, it has also become an important international literary language.

The post-colonial condition mentioned above is equally reflected in the former colonies of the Empire, especially in Nigeria, although the colonialists never gave the novel a chance to develop in Northern Nigeria despite their ostensible 'colonial projects' aimed at the development of education in general and the novel in particular. For example, Concertino in Joseph (2006) argues that, "it may be that the Hausa society will never create novelists, but will instead concern itself with other literary forms more relevant to its world view". In another context, he points out that Northern Nigeria "had yet to develop a literate and bourgeois class".

Although the growth of the novel is generally associated with the development of an educated middle class, what is evident is that exceptions, such as in India, have belied this rule. Thus, a close look at the colonial educational/literary projects, like the establishment of the *Gaskiya Ta Fi Kwabo* newspaper and the Northern Region Literacy Agency (NORLA), with its so-called literary competitions, would suggest that they were a mere smokescreen to put down the development of prose in general and the novel in particular in the region. Thus, contrary to what the official pronouncements and "historical records" suggest, that the colonial authority and colonialism had played a significant role in the emergence of the Nigerian novel, a brief perusal of the historical reality will prove the contrary in the case of Northern Nigeria. For example, Griffiths (2000:72) has observed that although *Gaskiya Ta Fi Kwabo* was established to "educate and inform", it also "published poems which had good message in them", or had "meat and meaning put into them", in the process of which they "insinuate, unobtrusively, articles of an educative nature." At the same time, the Hausa newspaper also published poems "praising Churchill and other leaders, condemning the Germans and Japanese and praising Nigerian troops in East Africa and Burma." On other occasions, the colonial press was used more for purposes of propaganda.

Similarly, Joseph (2005) thinks that, despite the official policy statements about developing modern Western education in northern Nigeria, the colonial officers actually frustrated the initial efforts, because they were "largely influenced by the belief that any expanded educational programme would make Northern Nigeria unduly difficult to govern as mass education in India had made Indians." The usual refrain that, Northerners did not like Western education because of its association with Christianity or they rejected 'boko' because it was paganistic, deceitful and fraudulent, was all a clever excuse, because it was contradicted by the fact that some Northern Nigerian leaders, like the Emir of Kano, Abbas and El-Kanemi of Borno, had indicated that Western education, even though "it was never regarded as a substitute for Koranic education" was, nonetheless, quite "essential in the Twentieth Century context for the material development of their people." (Joseph, 2005).

Nevertheless, the Hausa writing competition organised by NORLA in 1934 and the five novels that emerged as the winners, though "imperialist in motivation", marked, "the beginning of a systematic separation between God and Caesar in the literary production of Northern Nigeria." (Joseph 2005). Henceforth, one notes the increasing shift in creativity from the "secular concerns of the writer to the moral, social and political issues of the Islamic influence and the upsurge in writing," which culminated in the famous *Soyayya* novelists of the 80s and 90s. Abdallah Uba Adamu (2006) analyses the new spirit that brought in the Hausa novel and, to some extent, what he calls "the Hausanised English language novel" in northern Nigeria, pointing out this as marking the evolution of the collective identity of the region as depicted in the Soyayya novels. The authors, while portraying the evils in the society, are at the same time competing for space in the national artistic landscape and negotiating for a stake on behalf of their various communities, interests, values and cultures.

Thus, it could be concluded that the desire for national integration and the fight for a literary democratic space within the literary landscape, had forced the northern Nigerian elite to get out of their 'tiny shells' and project the 'northern Nigerian perspective', not from the political perspective, but on the literary creative platform. This involves drawing from their regional experiences and ideals, in order to negotiate a place at the national level for their own values and interests. The novel in northern Nigeria, therefore, had evolved in the context of a variety of complex situations that are best understood from the perspective of its history within the national set up; and the culture and religion of the northern Nigerians were as much significant in this regard as the colonial contact.

As at independence, the colonial heritage had left the three regions divided into distinct patterns of political, economic and social developments as Turaki (1993) and Griswold (2000) indicate. The West, or the Lagos/Ibadan axis, was the commercial, economic and political headquarters of the nation. The East was the most developed educationally and dominated the national administrative and managerial positions. Northern Nigeria was quite powerful politically because it had the largest population, although it was viewed as conservative and backward in Western education. Thus, in the early years of the development of the Nigerian novel, the "Ibo novel" dominated the African Writers Series, with Chinua Achebe as the general editor. The North was considered least active in the English language and the adoption of the Western cultural forms, as amply testified by Jibril (1992), Aliyu (1992) and Dara (1988), inspite of its centuries of literary tradition in the Arabic/Islamic and indigenous cultures.

This diversity of the Nigerian state has had tremendous influence on its post–colonial condition as a nation and influenced its cultural circumstances. Since literature in general and the novel in particular project the life of the people in their society of origin, in both its local and larger contexts, they are, inevitably, tools of fashioning "group identity". The concerns and identity of the northern Nigerian novel, have, therefore, become inseparable from the region's valuation of its collective self–hood and the personal conceptions of the individual novelists. Just as well, the novelists' representation of the northern Nigerian identity should best be understood through an evaluation of the history of the Nigerian novel, whose growth had been largely conditioned by the English novel.

Such an interpretation must proceed from the understanding that the novel is a cultural form that offers an amazingly good platform on which to examine the cultural construction of identity as a process that is local and global, as amply demonstrated by many scholars, among whom are Edward Said (1989, 1993) and Griswold (2000). The contention here is that the Northern Nigerian novel is, *ipso facto,* derivable from and is located on the continuum of the Nigerian national novel tradition (Jaji, 2011).

African English language writing was influenced by the interaction between the African writers and various patronages, which gave them access to established international publishing houses. The marginalisation of the Northern Nigerian literature in English, especially the novel, was foreshadowed by the politics of the international publishing outfits, such as the Heinemann Educational Books (HEB) and Chinua Achebe, as the general editor of the African Writers Series (AWS) in particular. The editor had played a crucial role in coordinating the establishment of the readership of early African writing outside Africa and the educational market within Africa. This had a profound effect on the development of the novel in Nigeria in all the regions, including the North, as well as the thematic and identity valuations and the forms of the English language texts that developed at the time (Griswold 2000). As editor of the AWS, Achebe was directly involved in scouting for and selecting many of the writers who were later published in those years. For instance, he personally located, and encouraged Ngugi wa Thiongo (then James Ngugi) as Griffiths (2000: 83) reports. The point being made here is that he could have equally focussed attention on his own country.

> Chinua Achebe simply selected the texts he believed had the most literary value, and if these reflected his own tastes and his own position in the various debates about African writing in the period, this is no more than can be expected. (Griffiths, 2000:84)

This explains why the heavy concentration of some texts, especially novels by Ibo writers, as a phenomenon in the early publication of the HEB and AWS, became suspect. Hence, the overblowing of the so-called conflict of cultures, which necessitated that, "significantly half of the first twenty English language novels in the African Writers Series were written by Ibos from Eastern Nigeria where the confrontation was most damaging to the local culture" Griffiths (2000: 84). Suffice it to say that the contention that the culture clash issue, with particular reference to its effect on the Ibo society, has been debunked as a literary phenomenon. The alleged disruption of the Ibo culture by the colonialists cannot, therefore, be said to have been borne out by the facts. Neither is it true, as pointed out by Griffiths (2000), that all the significant writings of the late 1950s and 1960s were concerned with the theme of culture conflict.

All these lead to the issue of why the Northern Nigerian writers could not be published in the Heinemann Series, even when their works were about the colonial disruption to the stability of their old societies, like *Baba of Karo*. Many of these works could not scale the editor's taste and, therefore, failed to be brought to fame under the AWS imprint. The editor's mindset about the North's backwardness in Western education might have contributed in making him not search for prospective contributors in this regard, but with the benefit of hindsight, one cannot rule out the possibility of a deliberate refusal on the part of the major publishers themselves to scout for, mentor and publish creative writers from the region. Their fear might not have been unconnected with the concern not to stir the hornet's nest, in view of the deliberate colonial policy in the region to keep the native elite in check.

There was a relaxation of this policy in the 1980s and 1990s, though, and the period saw the flowering of self–publications of northern writers on an unprecedented scale, as well as an increase in the activities of the publishing houses, like McMillan, Malthouse, Lantern, etc. (Joseph 2005). This had produced an assemblage of writers in unexpected numbers: Labo Yari, Aliyu Jibia, Ibrahim Tahir, Abubakar Gimba, Olu Obafemi, Mohammed Sule, Seffi Attah, Ada Uga, Zaynab Alkali, Mohammed T Garba, Hauwa Ali, Maryam Ali Ali, Abwa, Dangana, Sheme, Kamal Aliyu, Maiwada, Bilqisu, Doki, A T Giwa, Adamu Kyuka Usman, Wandara, Kankara, Dan Kano, Dul Johnson, Asabe Kabir Usman, Usara Hassan–Tom, Emman Usman Shehu, Balaraba Ramat Yakubu, Egya Sule and many others. The efforts of these writers and many more have created and sustained a "reading formation" with a discursive vent that inevitably reflects the history, culture and local colour of northern Nigeria.

Bennet's (2001) concept of the 'reading formations' and Foucault's idea of 'discursive formations' clarify better the context and literary significance of the novel in general and the Northern Nigerian novel in particular, in view of the polarised political configuration and the politics of literary representation in Nigeria. Bennett's arguments in particular allow us to understand reading as a "set of discursive and intertexual determinations which organise and animate the practice of reading", whereby "texts and readers are put in specific relations to one another"; and the reading public is perceived as constituting "readers as reading subjects of particular types of texts, as texts to be read in particular ways." In view of the past attitudes that denigrated the northern Nigerian novel as inferior or sub-standard in relation to the novels written by southern Nigerians, this concept of reading becomes both imperative and liberating and, therefore, significant. In the same vein, identity, especially the group identity of the North as a socio-cultural and historical construct of both the individual and the group, is most understood from the prism of the collective "horizon of continuity" of self- projection.

Bello–Kano (2002:41), for instance, posits in collaboration with others that identity is a "process" that "is never complete, always in progress and always constituted within, not outside representation." He argues further that,

> Such a "horizon of continuity", one such existentialist function is narrative, for it provides the (rhetorical and symbolic) conditions for self- projection and self-esteem (which usually and incidentally is equated with group project and group esteem). Thus, the subject invests (has to invest) in a narrative, as a mechanism by which the horizons for self – projection are guaranteed (p. 47).

The nation is, in Anderson's (1991) view, the proto-typical instance of group projection; hence, nation and narration, together with religion, could be conceived to have formed what Bello-Kano refers to as the "narrativisation of the transcendent," the classical model for the bildungsroman or the novel. On the other hand, "one of the most enduring facts of modernity is the interpellation of every person on this planet as the bearer of national identity." It is, therefore, proposed here that the concept of the northern Nigerian society, as portrayed in the novels written by the region's writers who use its physical, cultural, political and historical landscape to enact their experience, shares similarities with the other national novels. Individuals that are competent in the use of the English language deliberately create prose fiction narratives that are both local and globally effective, to imaginatively depict the society, within a particular horizon of continuity of similar or shared history, culture and/or religion, with all the conflicting social forces that go with it.

Bangura (2000), citing Alhaji Usman's struggles to implement a particular brand of Islam in his personal and family life and society, thinks that the conflict between Islam and the pre-Islamic Hausa-Fulani cultures of Muslim northern Nigeria constitute an important literary thematic concern of Ibrahim Tahir's *The Last Imam*. This could not be achieved due to the people's lack of readiness to do away completely with their pre–Islamic belief system; the contention being that it is this 'Islamic proclivity', which resonates variously in utterances, such as 'the Northern perspective', 'the northern ethics', etc. It is this condition that is responsible for Joseph's (2005) observation that the efforts of the northern elite or creative writers is geared towards the attempt by the North to distance itself, "to sever itself from its exclusivity and draw other experiences and values in order to negotiate a place for its own values, interests and experiences in national matters." Of course, the Islamic proclivity is, in essence, the major determinant of the values, interests and experiences of the majority of the North.

Against the background of the Islamic proclivity, which may not necessarily be "against the Christian presence" as Soyinka in Bangura (2000) insinuates, Islam is a potent rallying point for identity negotiation. Thus, "the conservative northern outlook" can be located at the centre of its identity, which is the central peg on which the themes of a substantial number of northern Nigerian novels are based. In Labo Yari's *Climate of Corruption*, for example, Sule refuses to budge when he questions his father's sudden transformation from a puritan, conservative Muslim to a virtual apostate who frequents church services and is also an alcoholic and a fornicator in one fell swing. The central character's question is, therefore, important in the total social symbolism of the novel:

> You told me that the Islamic system can be applied anywhere in the world. And I am fully convinced of that. So, I can't see myself rejecting those values and taking others. How will I feel? You want me to split myself into two? No… I am sure you can live here with these values. In fact you will be a better man (p.159).

It is this Islamic system of values that recurs again and again in the northern Nigerian novel as the central theme in varying forms and arguments, which distinctly identify the cultural, social and ethical touchstones of the northern Nigerian tradition, culture and history, as well as politics and society.

In *The Undesirable Element, Forgive Me Maryam* and *I'd Rather Die,* the writers grapple with the difficult task of maintaining the conservative northern outlook and the need to accept the changes brought about by global culture. For instance, in spite of Faruk's desire to fulfil his father's promise of upholding the wish and promise of filial marriage to Bintu, her desire for Western education, coupled with youthful exuberance, lands her into a situation of an unwanted pregnancy — something that is considered taboo in the North. The elimination of the undesirable element, the Alhaji, in the novel of the same title, and the survival of Bintu as a respectable member of society, indicates the author's inclination towards the modern. In a similar situation, Bilkisu in *Forgive Me Maryam* resists a forced marriage, but could not actualise her will until seven years after the demise of her father, who is the architect of the marriage. In *I'd Rather Die!*, the tension between modernity and conservatism is epitomised in the love triangle between Alhaji Maikudi, Mohammed and Fatima. The tragic death of Fatima and the defeat of Maikudi signify the triumph of modernity over conservatism and also serve as a pointer to the pervasive, stubborn and sticking quality of the conservative northern outlook that the Alhaji represents, although from a negative perspective, and which Sule in *Climate of Corruption* aptly signifies.

However, the most representative process of identity as a horizon for the continuity of the group identity of Northern Nigeria is, arguably, found in Kamal Aliyu's *Silence in a Smile* and *Portrait of a Patron*. These novels explore the tensions and conflicts exerted on a traditional Hausa–Fulani community. In the former work, the impact of the modern Western education on the patron's family is depicted in how he negotiates the traditional ethics of making sure each of his male children goes overseas to learn, but comes back home to marry a relation within the larger family. 'New found love' and Western education in *Silence and a Smile* defeats filial marriage in a situation that can best be described as a generational female rebellion.

Similarly, Abubakar Gimba represents an artistic effort to 'correct' the northern conservative outlook for the benefit of the society in a process of negotiating an identity that is unabashedly Islamic, but, certainly, not anti-Christian. The writer's knowledge of Islam is used to portray the educated, globalised Muslim woman in a changing time that has affected the definition of the role of women and their position in the society (Kabir, 2006). This thematic concern, vis-a-vis group identity, of the northern cultural set up are vividly depicted in both the *Sacred Apples* and *Footprints*. In both, there are echoes of Zaynab Alkali, with the redemptive concerns for the female person or what Onabueze (2006) calls "the suffocating and humiliating traditional and religious practices", in which "their acquisition of formal education" in both *The Virtuous Woman* and *The Stillborn* is redemptive. In the novels highlighted, the individual or group identity is by no means static. The short stories of Dul Johnson, *Shadows and Ashes* and *Why Women Can't Make it to Heaven,* vividly convey the tension of Islamic/ Christian mix of an aspect of northern Nigerian culture that is often overlooked in critical circles, but which are important constituent elements of the northern identity.

Conclusion

Thus, using a few representative texts within the context of the Nigerian national novel tradition, this assessment has focussed on the concept, history and literary development of prose and identity and the significance of both in the evolution and interpretation of the northern Nigerian novel. It traces in particular the development of literary prose writing through the ages and the transformation of the 'English novel' into the 'Novel in English'. The English novel, from where the African novel is derived, is the precursor of the Nigerian novel, while the Northern Nigerian novel is a continuum of the Nigerian novel tradition. The paradigmatic change of the novel in its global perspective has accorded the northern Nigerian writer the facility to participate in the discourse of literary representation, in which identity always plays an important role in shaping the social existence of the people.

References

- Aliyu, K (2005), *Silence and a Smile,* Kano: Myrrh
- .... (2006), *Portrait of a Patron,* Kano: Myrrh
- Bangure, A. S. (2000), *Islam and the West African Novel: The Politics of Representation,* London: Lynne Reiner Publishers.
- Bello – Kano, I. (2002), "The Other Question: Nation and Narration in the Discourse of Identity" *FAIS Journal of Humanities,* Bayero University Kano, Vol. 2 No. 1 April, 2002.
- Bennet, Grosberg and Meagan Morris (2001), *Keywords: A Revised Vocabulary of Culture and Society,* Oxford: Blackwell Publishing.
- Edward, G. V. (1990), *Reading Between the Lines: A Christian Guide to Literature,* Irvin California: Good News Publishers.
- Giwa, A. T. (1994), *I'd Rather Die!* Zaria: Ahmadu Bello University Press.
- Griffiths, G. (2000), *African Literature East and West,* London: Pearson Education Ltd
- Griswold, W. (2000), *Bearing Witness: Readers, Writers and the Novel in Nigeria,* New Jersey: Princeton University Press
- Jaji, A. S. (2011), "The Canon and Popular Fiction in Northern Nigeria: A Postcolonial Study of Eight Novels", unpublished PhD Thesis, Department of English and French, Bayero University.
- Joseph, A. (2005),"The Nature and Development of the Novel in English in Northern Nigeria", unpublished PhD Thesis, Department of English and Literary Studies, Ahmadu Bello University.

- Kabir, U. A. (2006), "Gender in the Novels of Abubakar Gimba: A Critical Analysis of the Representation of the Contemporary Muslim Woman in Sacred Apples", *Writing, Performance and Literature in Northern Nigeria: Proceedings of the Third Conference of Literature in Northern Nigeria*, Kano: Bayero University.
- Preminger, A. and Brogan, T V F (eds) (1993), *The New Princeton Encyclopaedia of Poetry and Poetics*, New York: Princeton University Press.
- Shaffer, B. W. (2006), *Reading the Novel in English 1950 – 2000*, Oxford: Blackwell Publishers.
- Sule, M. (1977), *The Undesirable Element*, Oxford: McMillan.

Chapter Eighteen

Language and Identity in Two Kannywood Films: Diction and Characterisation in Gumzak's **Aziza** and Saira's **Malika**

Aliyu Isa Sulaiman

Introduction

A work of art, like drama, is expressed through action and language. Besides plot, characters and thought, the next element of drama is diction. It is through diction/language and acting that aesthetic effect in drama can best be fully achieved. In analysing a work of drama and literature, one tends to revisit the earlier principles put forward by classical theoreticians, like Aristotle, who maintain that diction in drama should be appropriately formal, "The most beautiful language expressing the highest ideas." The language or diction in drama is expressed through dialogue, which is the playwright's principal means of expression. It serves different functions, among which are imparting information and revealing characters. Wilson (2002), Crow (1983), Agoro (2007) also share Aristotle's perspective, which is that the language of drama should best be studied in its literary aspect, so as to understand the full meaning of the intended text. Consequently, this chapter analyses the function of diction in Kannywood films using two Hausa films, *Aziza* and *Malika,* with the aim of considering the choice of words and the significant effect it has on the characters.

Diction in Drama

Diction/language means the selection of words in a literary work. Normally, writers use words to convey action, reveal character, imply attitudes, identify themes and suggest values. In the case of films, such words are expressed through language to create the dramatic world of the play. The relationship between this world and reality is metaphorical. The nature of the stage/film, therefore, the setting and the style of acting should be such as to assist the language in its creation of this metaphorical world (Agoro 2001:35).

As pointed out above, diction is the choice of words, phrases, sentence structure, and figurative language which combine to help create meaning. Formal diction, as explained by Aristotle, consists of dignified, impersonal and elevated use of language. It follows the use of syntax exactly and is often characterised by complex words and lofty tone. Middle diction maintains correct language usage, but is less elevated than formal diction. It reflects the ways most educated people speak. Informal diction represents the plain language of everyday use, and often includes idiomatic expressions, slang, contraction and many simple common words. Going by this assertion and many more others not covered here, one discovers that scholars and researchers, when commenting on the language of a film, tend to categorise it either as code switching, diglossia or borrowing words or phrases from other languages (Chamo, 2012a, Elliott, 2000) Abbas,2008 and Dakin Gari, 2004).

Language in drama can best be studied from the literary, rather than the linguistic, point of view. It is, therefore, clear when studying the language of drama that sometimes it is not the apparent meaning of the words that counts, but what they do within the context of particular situations. For instance, a play is a succession of situations of varying dramatic contexts and the words spoken by the characters must be understood, that is, as dramatic happening and not just the words said. A good dramatist then must think on at least two levels simultaneously as he writes the dialogue in the play. He must consider not only the "surface" meaning of the words, but also their overt, substantial meaning — what they do in terms of fashioning the characters, their relationships and the overall action in the play (Crow 1983).

Language in drama can be studied in two different ways, as verbal and non-verbal aspects of communication (costumes and gestures). The performers, whether puppets or human, whether male or female, are costumed, and these costumes (like our own clothes) convey a message. When we wear clothes, we are making a statement about who we are or who we want to be — our clothes help us to create the role of students, professors, artists, police officers etc. Gestures too are part of the language of life, as well as of drama. Every day in the course of countless conversations, we shrug, lean forward or draw back, thrust our hand into our pockets, cross our legs, nod or shake our heads, and engage in a hundred little actions that indicate the state of our minds. The same applies to characters in plays (Barnet & others 2001: 10).

Synopsis of the play

The data used for this research was collected from two Kannywood films, *Aziza* I and II (2012), directed by Ali Gumzak, and *Malika* 1 - 4 directed by Saira Aminu. The films were randomly selected by the researcher. They differ in terms of directors, production companies and year of production.

In *Aziza* I and II, the plot relates the story of a virgin, the eponymous character of the film, who lives in a village with her father and stepmother. This village is often frequented by Sadiq, a principal character who comes to purchase milk for his father's company. During one of these visits to the village, Sadiq meets Aziza and makes an attempt to buy the food she is selling. She refuses to sell the food to him because she detests his habit of smoking cigarettes. This is the opening confrontation. Subsequently, Sadiq stalks her to a secluded area and rapes her to avenge his humiliation. This act puts her in a difficult and shameful situation because she was found to be pregnant. As a result of the abomination she has committed, she is humiliated and excommunicated from the village because she has broken one of its customs. Thereafter, Aziza lived a tormented life crying day and night with her baby under the harsh elements. It is this cry of agony that is used to haunt and torment Sadiq in the opening scene of the film and in subsequent scenes. In an attempt to find solution to this problem, Sadiq goes back to the village in order to remedy the situation.

Malika 1-4 is a love story. The play/film has a modest plot. Abdul, who is married to Karima, is the principal male character in the movie. He works as a journalist in a newspaper company owned by his father-in-law, Alhaji. Malika, also a principal character in the film, is Abdul's first girlfriend. She goes on to gain Alhaji's love who, indeed, falls in love with her. Subsequently, this situation is unbearable to Alhaji's wife, Karima's mother. The mother solicits for her daughter's support to beg her husband, Abdul, to marry Malika so that she can stop her getting married to Alhaji.

The use of Language in the two films

In order to consider the use of language in Kannywood films, it is necessary to make some clarifications from the outset. Since language is used as a vehicle of characterisation, it is proper to note that every character is made to speak in a way that is appropriate to its class, status etc. When due account is taken of the social level of characters, the language that distinguishes them from one another and the various social classes they belong to becomes less difficult to perceive (Malumfashi, 1985; Sulaiman, 2007; and Agoro, 2007).

Words are not spoken in a vacuum, either in drama or in real life. They always belong within a context, a situation of some kind, which produces them and which helps to give them their full meaning (Crow, (1983). The procedure for analysis of language in the two films is based on the insight of Agoro as to the function of language in drama. Accordingly, Agoro (2007) observes that language serves the following functions in drama:

- It imparts information
- Reveals the themes and ideas of a play
- Reveals character
- Establishes tone and level of probability
- Reveals mood
- Directs attention to important plot elements.

Analysis

The film, *Aziza*, presents the way of life of a group of villagers. As pointed out earlier, it is the dialogue between the characters in a film that gives viewers the clue to some facts, ideas, ideals and emotional responses in each scene. The story unfolds itself through verbal and non-verbal utterances between the characters. Thus, in *Aziza*, the viewers are introduced to some information concerning the norms, values and customs of the Hausa people. The following lines by one of the village women are instructive in this regard.

Inna: …wannan yarinyar da ka ganta tare da ita, ai ba a san ubanta ba. Kuma ka ga a nan garin ana son kowacce `ya mace in za ta shiga dakin mijinta, ta shiga dakin mijinta ba tare da ta san wani da namiji ba. Idan kuwa ta kuskure to za ta gamu da kiyayya daga danginta har da sauran mutanen gari.

Inna: Nobody knows the father of the girl you saw her with. You see, in this village, it is expected of every girl that she will not know any man before marriage. If she should miss this, she will face hatred from her relatives and the rest of the society alike.

The village head also testifies before his people that it is an abomination for a child of that village to smoke cigarettes, let alone commit adultery or fornication. The penalty for such actions, according to the custom of that village, is very severe.

Mai gari: Kamar yadda duk ku ka sani bisa ga al`ada ta wannan gari, duk wadda ta yi laifi irin wannan a kan kai ta bayan gari ne a gicciye ta. Amma saboda zamani ya zo, kuma da abin da Turawa suka kawo shi, ba mu da ikon gicciye ki... Sakamakon wannan abu da ki ka yi, yanzu mun gaggauta cire ki daga cikin wannan zuri`a ta garin nan... Babu wanda zai kara ma`amala ko hulda da ke, daga yau kin zama abin kyama a cikin wannan al`umma.

Mai gari: As you all know, in accordance with the custom of this village, whoever commits this kind of offence is to be crucified. We do not have the power to do so now, due to modernity and the coming of the Europeans. As a result of this shameful act, you are now disowned by this village and nobody will ever interact with you again.

It could be noted that the practice of going to a girl's parents to solicit for their permission, even before a prospective suitor could meet her, is one of the cherished customs of the Hausa people. It, indeed, shows that when such permission is granted, thereafter no man will be allowed to formally approach her or ask for her hand in marriage. The opposite of this is what happens in the film Malika.

Malam: Ni Abdul ba abin da zan ce maka sai fatar alheri. Domin kai kadai ka taba neman amincewa ta gurin neman wannan yarinya.

Malam: I, Abdul, have nothing to say to you other than to wish you well, because you are the only person that has ever formally sought my permission to marry this girl.

One can easily understand the themes and ideas contained in a film through the language used in the conversations. The relationship between plot and character is always recognised through language and it is that which is also used to reveal what the main idea or theme of the film is. Of course, one can know of these ideas through other actions, like gestures or costumes, which some scholars argue are also part of language of films and drama.

> Aziza: Allah ya kiyaye idan haka birni yake koya wa mutane hali maras kyau na shan taba, Allah Ya raba mu da shi, Allah Ya sa mu mutu a kauye.

> Aziza God forbid, if this bad habit of smoking cigarette is what the city teaches; we seek refuge from Allah against it. We pray to Him that we die in the village.

Through these utterances, one can argue from an assessment of the language and dialogue, that the theme of this film is the confrontation between the cherished Hausa culture and modernity, between village life, which is often characterised by cultural norms and values, and city life, with its luxuries, vanity and corruption.

In *Malika*, the main idea appears to be the challenges journalists face in the discharge of their expected duties.

> Alhaji: Sanin kanka ne sakamakon wannan rubutun da muke yi, mun yi nasarar ceto miliyoyin 'yan kasuwa daga hannun azaluman jama`an kwastan, wanda kuma dakatar da rubutun na iya sa su koma su ci karensu babu babbaka.

> Alhaji: You know too well that, as a result of our writings we were able to rescue millions of businessmen from the hands of corrupt customs officials, and relenting in this effort could allow them to return to their past actions unchecked.

Language helps to reveal character, which has two meanings: either the person that appears in a play or film; or the intellectual, emotional and moral qualities that add up to make it into a distinct personality (Bernet et al, 2000). Similarly, when characters in a drama speak, they are performing at least two acts: either revealing themselves to the audience or saying something to other characters to evoking from them reactions connoting agreement, anger, amusement or some other sentiment. Thus, the real personality of a character in a film is established for the audience by the actors or actresses, through what they say and do; how they speak and act; and by the way other actors playing other characters respond to them (Crow, 1983). This can be illustrated by studying the following dialogue from the film *Aziza*.

Ciroma:	Dan zuba min kunun nan …
Aziza:	A mene zan zuba ma?
Ciroma:	A mene ki ke zuba wa mutane?
A ziza:	Ba zan zuba ma a roba ta ka kafa bakinka a kai ba.
Ciroma:	Saboda me?
Aziza:	Saboda taba.
Ciroma:	'Yar kauye, ki kalle ni dan birni ki rinka gaya mani irin wannan maganar.

Ciroma:	Serve me a little of this drink...
Aziza:	In which container?
Ciroma:	What do you use to serve other people?
Aziza:	I will not serve you in my bowl, so that you dip your mouth into it.
Ciroma:	Why not?
Aziza:	Because you smoke.
Ciroma:	Villager! You have the guts to look at me, a city man, and speak to me in such a manner.

One notes from this conversation immediately that, judging by his words and actions, Sadiq is a proud and not too refined person. Similarly, Malika's utterances in response to her old lover's teasing in the following conversation reveal to the audience who she really is:

Malika: Dadin abin shi ya kawo kansa kamar yadda ka kawo kanka. Idan ka ga dama ka tsaya ruwanka, in ka tafi, ta fi nono fari. Kamar yadda ya tafi kai kuma ka zo, haka kai ma idan ka tafi wasu za su zo.

Malika: The good thing about it is that, he came on his own, just like you have brought yourself now. If you wish to stay, that is your choice. If you go, it is good and fine with me. Just like you came after he had left, should you leave me, others will come.

Language use helps to determine the tone of a play. It indicates whether the play is comic or serious, farcical or tragic and suggests the degree of abstraction from reality (Agoro (2007). Similarly, language serves another function in revealing the mood of the *dramatis personae*. The way the characters relate to each other in the film verbally points to what is actually happening and how they are affected by it. Situation also plays a crucial role in determining the choice of words in drama. When the words are mixed up or at variance with the situation, it is refered to as "situational code-switching." This often occurs when the language use changes according to the situations in which the conversants find themselves; they may speak one language in one situation and another in a different one.

However, two factors are responsible for code-switching in Kannywood films: the emotional situation (love/sadness) or the showing of identity (Chamo, (2012b). To some critics, this form of shifting from one language to another in a speech is done in order to distinguish between characters that belong to various social classes. It will be proper to say that every character is made to speak in a way that is appropriate to his class. For instance, the language spoken by the wives of Major Lejoka-Brown in *Our Husband Has Gone Mad Again* says a lot about their social standing: Liza, the sophisticated medic, speaks in a manner consistent with her education and understanding of the world; Mama Rashida, the local market woman, displays an understanding of commerce with a local colour; and Sikirat is betrayed by her speech that indicates her lack of education and refinement. Other examples include the various shades of differences in language as used by the following pairs: Lejoka-Brown and Okonkwo in *Our Husband Has Gone Mad Again;* Jero and Chume in *The Trials of Brother Jero;* Macbeth and Macduff in *Macbeth;* and Creon and Antigone in *Antigone* (Agoro, (2007:36).

Apart from all these, another important factor in the film *Malika* is the use of figures of speech, especially figurative expressions. The figurative language is often characterised by the use of figures of speech, elaborate expressions, sound devices and syntactic departure from the usual order of literal language (Chamo, (2012b). Three figurative expressions stand out in the film: proverbs, praise-epithets and metaphorical words. In *Malika* 1-4, there is a recourse to proverbs every five minutes; a total of at least one hundred and five (105) times in all; praise-epithet occurs at least ten (10) times; and metaphorical expressions every fifteen to twenty minutes on the average, a total of at least eighty four (84) times. The ratios of such expressions are 5:1 in favour of female characters vis-à-vis the male characters.

Conclusion

It is, therefore, quite apparent that drama and films rely extensively on the use of language for their effect; exploiting the power of language and its performative abilities to convey message and bring about change. As evidenced in *Malika*, information is disseminated through language concerning the social and economic way of life of the people depicted, especially in matters of culture, politics and religion. Furthermore, it is through language that one is able to know the role played by each character in the film. Indeed, it does appear that language is indispensable even in the most visual action film.

REFERENCES

- Abbas, U. A. (2008), "Sassarkuwar Adabi Cikin Adabi: Nazarin Adon Harshe a Wakokin Fina-Finan Hausa", unpublished PhD thesis submitted to the Department of Nigerian Languages and Linguistics, Bayero University, Kano.

- Agoro S. N.A (2001), *Theatre & Drama in Education,* Caltop Publications Nigeria Ltd. Ibadan, Nigeria.

- Aristotle. (1952), "Poetics", transl. Ingram Bywaser, P. in Maynard, R.H. (ed), (1952) *Great Books of the Western World,* Chicago: The University of Chicago Press.

- Barnet, S. Burto, W. Ferris, L. Rabkin, G. (2001), *Types of Drama Plays and Context.* London. Eight Edition, Longman.

- Crow, B. (1983), *Studying Drama.* Lagos: Longman.

- Chamo, I.Y. (2012a). "Hausa-English Code-Switching in Kannywood Films", *International Journal of Linguistics,* Vol. 4 (2), 87-96, U.S.A. Available at htt//www.macrothink.org/journal/indexphp.

- Chamo, I. Y. (2012b), "The Changing Code of Communication in Hausa Films", PhD Thesis, Department of Oriental Studies, University of Warsaw, Poland.

- Dakin-Gari, A. A. (2004), "Bidiyon Kasuwar Kano: Tasirin Fina-Finan Hausa A Kan Al'adun Hausawa; Tsokaci A Kan Harshe, Sutura, Tarbiyya, Addini Da Kuma Zaman Aure", B.A Dissertation, Department of Nigeria Languages, Usman Danfodiyo University, Sokoto.

- Elliott, N.C. (2000), "A Sociolinguistic Study of Rhoticity in American Film Speech From the 1930 to 1970's", PhD Thesis submitted to the Department of Linguistics, Indiana University.

- Graeme, T. (1988), *Film as Social Practice,* London and New York. Roultledge Publishers.

- Malumfashi, I. A. (1985), "Asali da Bunkasar Rubutaccen Wasan Kwaikwayon Hausa", unpublished M.A thesis, Department of Nigerian and African Languages, Ahmadu Bello University, Zaria.

- Sulaiman I.A. (2007), "Raha a Wasannin Kasimu Yero: Tarken Wasannin Karambana" unpublished M.A thesis, Department of Nigerian and African Languages, Ahmadu Bello University, Zaria.

- Wilson, & Goldfar. (2002), *Theatre the Lively Art,* New York: McGraw Hill.

- Yerima, A. (2003), *Basic Techniques in Play Writing and Filmography,* Ibadan: Kraft Books Limited.

- Sobe Zango (Producer) and Ali Gumzak (Director), *Aziza,* Motion Pictures Enterprises.

- Asnanic, N. (Producer) and Saira, A. (Director), *Malika,* Saira Movies Investment Limited.

Chapter Nineteen

In Search of Identity: The Emerging Male and the Emergent Female in Zaynab Alkali's The Initiates

Audee T. Giwa

Introduction

Obviously, the journey between *The Stillborn* (1984) and *The Initiates* (2007) has been a long and tortuous one for the writer of the two novels, Zaynab Alkali. It took twenty-three years. What, however, is important though is not the length of time or the difficulty of the journey, but the destination arrived at. Those who think Alkali's *The Descendants* (2005) is her most ambitious work to date need to consider their position again. It does not matter any more what the critics thought about her stance on feminism and other ideological issues; with the publication of *The Initiates*, Alkali seems to bring to the fore her ability as a creative artist to genuinely handle the craft of the novel.

Considering its impact on the reading audience, *The Initiates*, no doubt, stands out as her most realised novel to date; it is the most successful and, perhaps, the most socially relevant and artistically accomplished. It does not suffer from the representational austerity of *The Stillborn* or *The Virtuous Woman*, nor does it get overstuffed with a plethora of characters — the sheer remembrance of which tasks the reader's attention at the expense of the message they are supposed to carry — as in *The Descendants*. *The Initiates* is a compact piece, which sets out to make a social-cum-political statement and stops once that is achieved.

Alkali's concern with the girl education, early marriage and polygamy is by now tested and rested, even if temporarily, as the society has since moved forward. In the words of Charles Nnolim (2010), "the gender war is over." Having noted the transformation of the society in favour of female education, the author now tilts her attention to something else. Not that these themes are absent, but what is fore-grounded are other issues relevant to the present day society; issues that affect both men and women alike — like social responsibility and political consciousness.

The comments of Molara Ogundipe-Leslie (1987) about the commitment of the female writer in Africa are far-reaching and very relevant here. She observes that feminists have posited that the woman writer has two major responsibilities; firstly, to tell about being a woman; secondly, to describe reality from a woman's view, a woman's perspective" (p.5). This Zaynab Alkali has done abundantly in her first three novels and the collection of short stories, *Cobwebs*. As analysed here, she portrays men from this so-called feminine perspective and it is this portrayal that has often attracted critical attention recently.

The third commitment, Ogundipe-Leslie argues, is that the African female writer should be concerned with the issues of third-world realities. This refers to political awareness and the apprehension of social responsibility of each and every member of the society.

> Female writers cannot usefully claim to be concerned with various social predicaments in their countries or in Africa without situating their awareness and solutions within the larger global context of imperialism and neo-colonialism. For what is it that makes us dismally poor? What forced our individuals into such schizophrenic cultural confusion? Why are the national ruling classes so irresponsible, criminal and wasteful? Because they sold out? To whom? A deep female writer who has anything worthwhile to say must have these insights (p.12).

It is this aspect that fits Zaynab Alkali like a glove. She has those insights. Having almost exhausted all there is to say about the role of the emerging African woman in terms of social development, she now looks at issues, as Ogundipe-Leslie suggests, in a wider political perspective. The view is no longer jaundiced. She looks at how men and women, together, in the words of Li in *The Stillborn*, can walk side by side for the general progress of the society.

Zaynab Alkali has finally cleared the path of other writers like Buchi Emecheta, whose feminist stance, according to Udumukwu, is 'destructive, nihilistic or anarchic'. Emecheta is noted for consistently creating male characters that turn out to be morons. This is what leads Ojinmah and Egya (2005:67) to conclude that "some African feminist writers, it seems, are too chauvinistic in creating characters that convey their preachment." However, this observation may be true of Zaynab Alkali only in relation to her three early novels; certainly, by the time she comes to write the *The Initiates*, the novel under discussion in this chapter, the focus has changed, as indeed, her manner of presentation.

It is remarkable that for the first time, men take the centre stage in her narrative. Ordinarily, this in itself will not be an issue of significance, if the themes treated remain anachronistic or out of date. However, the thrust of her argument is political and the solution is action, which is not passive, but participatory, as in the role Samba plays to unseat a government that is corrupt and insensitive to the wishes and aspirations of its people. In this novel, Alkali has demonstrated that a woman is perfectly capable of handling male characterisation as successfully as a man can handle that of the woman. Nuruddin Farah stands out as the one African male feminist, who is able to portray women as they really are and not from the patriarchal perspective of their being objects. Alkali's experimentation in *The Initiates* is really worthy of commendation because she actually succeeds in portraying men in a positive light.

Nonetheless, her conviction that they have to be humbled before they are accepted — the thrust of this study — is still there, but downplayed. It is also pertinent to note that in this book, as in all her previous books, her reverence for the elderly is still felt. Interestingly, Tata, the eldest woman after Yamusa, Batanncha's first wife, comes out as the restless village gossip, like Maryam in *The Stillborn*. This is an exercise in realism. She does not want to over romanticise her characters, lest they look ideal, less than real and, therefore, unbelievable. This upholds the maturity of Alkali, not only as a human being, but also as a creative artist.

The Emerging Male, the Emergent Female

The central figure around whom the story in *The Initiates* is woven is Batanncha, a benevolent, steadfast elder in the village of Debro. Batanncha is highly respected and he respects those around him, particularly his friends, Batapchi and Bamusa, with whom he has lived together for over fifty years (p.156). The story begins in an air of suspense and mystery. Something bad has happened to Batanncha's son, Samba, who is a soldier in the city of Garpella. What this is, nobody knows for sure. There is a strong rumour that he is involved in a failed coup attempt and his whereabouts are not known. Batanncha is worried over this inconclusive news and nobody seems to be willing to come forward and tell him the truth; not even his friends. It seems rather late for him to learn the truth about this aspect of the human nature, but he does; and he is not happy with what he has to contend with: that even those he considers his friends are hiding something from him concerning the fate or state of his son.

> As he walked the village streets, people stopped talking, turned round and looked furtively at him or could he be imagining it? There must be something these people knew that he did not know, and his friends were not telling him (p.13).

Through the experience of this humble character, it is suggested that a calamity can still befall one, irrespective of how good one has been to one's other fellow men. The friends one has may not necessarily be true to one, unless if tested by the vicissitudes of life and they remain unwavering. So, even though Batapchi and Bamusa have heard some news about Samba, they are not willing to divulge it to his father, their friend. The action would have been right if they were doing it to spare him the pain, but it turns out later that they are simply an unreliable bunch of village gossips, just like the others. At the beginning, the novel seems to suggest that they are doing it to save him some pain, because "Samba's personal assistant had come to the village like a thief at night, and had secretly spent a few hours with only Bamusa and Salvia, Batanncha's other son", and warned that the information about Samba's state or his location, which he himself does not know in reality, should not be revealed to Samba's aged parents (p.15).

From this stage on, the story gathers momentum as the two friends advise that Salvia, Samba's brother, along with Batapchi's son and that of Bamusa, should go to the city to bring news about Samba. They go to seek for the information as directed, but in the process also lose Salvia in the city. Uncle Dogo, brother to Batanncha's late mother, is called from Ramtah-Rahi to advise on what next to be done. He suggests that the village drunk, Saji, be saddled with the task of finding Salvia and Samba. This is accepted and in the end Samba is found, alive and returns home in pomp and pageantry.

As Ojinmah and Egya (2005) observe in their seminal work, *The Writings of Zaynab Alkali*, the journey motif runs through all of Alkali's works. People are always leaving the village for the city for one thing or another, but usually to acquire more education, better life, or get work there. In *The Descendants*, it was to escape disease, poverty and superstition; in *The Virtuous Woman* to acquire education; and in *The Stillborn*, to realise a childhood dream.

In *The Initiates,* the journey motif is also there and constitutes more than a chapter in the story; it also symbolises self-awareness, discovery and growth. For all the children of Batanncha, the trip to the city is a life-changing experience, and for the better. As, indeed, it is for Saji the village drunk.

It is through this self-awareness, discovery and growth that the text makes its social commentary. Samba is not physically seen in the novel, but his presence is all-pervading. Through him also, issues are raised that affect not only the well-being of people in the village of Debro, but that of the Nigerian society as a whole. The theme of corruption in high places; materialism and economic discontent are all pursued here. It is because Samba and his general feel that the government is unjust and corrupt that they attempt to violently remove it.

> The name of Samba's general had appeared on television, in the papers and on radio as a man who had master-minded the plot on the grounds that the leadership of the government was dictatorial and corrupt, and that people were suffering from poverty (p.85).

In addition to this, there are other reasons for the coup, not the least of which is the:

> uselessness of the government that has failed to combat the rising tide of armed robbery, a situation that renders you a poor relation, because even if the roads are good, you cannot visit your next-of-kin in the village for fear. Have we not talked about at length about the drugless hospitals, and the empty classrooms, empty because the local government teachers have not been paid their salaries for six months? What about the fuel scarcity and the rising cost of living? (p.13)

These issues are, undoubtedly true; just like other references to factual subjects, like Tafawa Balewa's arrest when Samba himself was just thirteen years old (p.48). The coup and the reasons offered for it may not have been graphically treated in the novel, as, for instance, is done in the civil war novel of Festus Iyayi, *The Heroes,* but the Nigerian reader feels the event and readily associates with it because in the post-independence Africa, coups and counter coups permeate the political landscape of the continent.

Nevertheless, it is not the coup or lack of its success that is significant. Rather, it is Alkali's poignant statement here that it may be true when the leadership is corrupt, there is need for a change, but who succeeds afterwards is always the issue. If one was part of the old junta, it is doubtful if one would have any better ideas to offer to the country. This is the reason Samba's coup does not succeed. It should be recalled that a Brigadier General of that name, Samba, in *The Descendants,* also attempts to unseat the national government, fails and dies. This suggests that though the text is in support of changing bad governments, it is more concerned about who takes over when a corrupt regime is removed.

Without clearly showing so, the novel implies that Samba is as corrupt as his other military colleagues. He is showy, flamboyant and loud. By his father's admission, Samba:

> was everything else but cautious. He was never wary of the wiles of the world, impulsive, brash, pompous and over — confident. He would beat his chest with the palm of his hand, and challenge a bull to a contest... he was the type that had to poke his fingers in red flames to ascertain that it was hot (p.88).

Individuals like this are certainly not fit to be trusted with the mantle of leadership.

Besides, events in the narrative imply that Samba is also corrupt, like the description given of his father's compound, which he built into four sections. His mother, Yamusa, "pulled a weed here and a twig there among the massive flower garden in front of the fourth building. She looked around her proudly; hers was the biggest compound in the entire village and its neighbourhood, many thanks to her only son, Samba." (p.30) Without corrupt enrichment, one wonders where he gets the money to build this kind of compound. Furthermore,

> Samba always had something for someone and had touched the lives of Debro people on a personal level with personalized

> gifts, a bag of rice or salt, a tin of cooking oil, clothes and shoes...he did not leave the traditional rulers and chiefs out, royal gowns, turbans and shoes they could wear, tear and throw away, and money they could marry with on Monday and divorce on Tuesday (p.182)

It may be true that Samba is kind, as almost everybody in the village testifies to his generousity; but the source of his wealth, which is questionable, negates whatever philanthropic outlook or attitude he would have.

The suggestion here is that these are not the kind of leaders the society requires; hence, the reason their coup fails. When the government is later overthrown, by colleagues who are obviously sympathetic to Samba's cause, he is forgiven, but retired from the army. Whether those who have now taken over power are any better than the ones Samba and his colleagues wanted to overthrow is not stated. What is instructive, however, is that Samba has paid the price for his misdeeds, having come back home having lost an eye, his leg maimed and made shorter than the other and his face wounded (p.180). Having served his penance, Samba can now live among the people in the society. It is quite an irony, however, that his brother, Salvia, the twin son of Yelwa, Batanncha's second wife, the dreamer and political recluse, is at the end of the story chosen to lead the people.

This is the first consciously political suggestion in the text as to the kind of leader required to ensure the progress of the society. Unlike most of the males in Alkali's fiction, Salvia is the one portrayed without blemish and is young. The character trait he shares with other heroines of Alkali, his being a man notwithstanding, is that he is given to dreams and has a vision. In the beginning, when he was much younger, his father thought this momentary lapse to unconsciousness was a problem. He even made efforts to find a remedy for it, but the women prevailed on him, saying that when Salvia grew up, he would be able to handle his own situation for the benefit of the people. Salvia is also an avid reader, "who reads anything in print that comes his way. He knew the politics of his country like the back of his hand, but he refused to participate." (p.23)

What becomes evident is that the unending faith in and concern for education are underscored. Any person who aspires to lead the people must be thoroughly educated first and that is why Salvia turns out to be a trained accountant who works in the Federal Ministry of Finance for two years. His brief stint with the civil service goes a long way in opening his eyes to the level of corruption that obtains in the society. Unable to stand it any more, he leaves the service, afraid that he may be consumed by the system, the way two of his friends have been, only to get a different kind of reaction at home:

> "Tell me, my son, you were in town for two years. What drove you away? Did they send you home?"
> "No, mother, I left."
> "Why?"
> "I saw people taking money they did not work for."
> The old woman looked at him strangely, "Whose money, my son?"
> "Government's, mother. Taking and spending money they did not work for. It was immoral. I could not watch that."
> "So you left the city for the village only to work for free. Working for free and not taking money from it... Government's money. Who is government, anyway? (p.42)"

What comes out from the above exchange is that while Salvia attempts to explain his moral stance against corruption, the people in the village, here represented by Tata, whom he calls mother because she is old, cannot make sense of his argument. This is reminiscent of Baako in Ayi Kwei Armah's *Fragments,* who goes abroad to study and comes back home to work and finds the Ghanaian society so corrupt that he cannot fit in. In the end, he does not work and ultimately goes mad. His mother cannot understand what his arguments about it are; just as Tata cannot understand Salvia's. That is why she asks, "Who is government, anyway?"; a question Salvia is unable to answer.

The difference between Baako and Salvia is that the latter is, ultimately, recognised and acknowledged by his people, who actually give him higher office and responsibilities. He ends up in the Government House, while Baako ends up in a mad house. Through Salvia, the text makes a very positive statement about the Nigerian nation and affirms that, in spite of the present odds, there is hope in its honest, upright, selfless and visionary citizens.

Salvia personifies the positive traits of an individual destined to rule his people. He is selfless, imbued with love for the community and makes a lot of sacrifices for the benefit of the people. He does all these when he is not even aware that the people for whom he is making the sacrifice acknowledge what he is doing or care about it. At a point, they even ridiculed him. An instance is when he returns home after resigning from his job and attempts to get all the youths in his village together to organise self-help projects for the development of their community.

From this effort the villagers understand that it behoves on the society to make effort, to improve its own living standards, but not always fold its arms and do nothing because it is waiting for the government to do it for them. The people are supposed to show concern and care about their own state, even as the government does. The picture presented of Salvia, therefore, is not just that of an emerging leader, but also that of a responsible citizen, as he inculcates in the minds of the youth the culture of good citizenship and self-respect.

In her earlier works, Alkali imbues only a few young men with these attributes. Now she seems to emphasise, through Salvia, that all members of the society owe it a duty to themselves to get involved in its affairs for their overall growth and progress. When this is made impossible by the government in power that becomes the time to fight, like Salvia dreams to:

> fight whatever evil lay buried in the system...he realised that it was not just the system, but every other thing that

went with it, the entire social orientation with its misplaced priorities and perverted moral values, which had given birth to crime, corruption, armed robbery, stealing in all spheres and avoidable tragedies (p.91).

Perhaps Alkali's main problem as a creative artist is that when she sets out to moralise; she preaches; she tells the reader about the moral situation, instead of demonstrating it to him. In this regard, *Fragments* or, indeed, *The Beautyful Are Ones Not Yet Born*, are infinitely more realised works of fiction than *The Initiates*. The dream motif, which has served her well in her previous novels, weakens her plot in the current novel. It is ironical that the matter central to the theme of the work should be couched in surrealistic somnambulism at such a farcical level that even the leader-apparent abnegates his responsibilities. After the dream, divested of its symbolic essence, one comes out with the notion that not only is Salvia unprepared to be part of "the initiates", he also does not see any reason for joining them, because all he wants is his brother.

The dream, however, affords Alkali the opportunity to show in symbolic terms what she believes is really wrong with the society. What appears to be the most powerful indictment of the Nigerian leadership, represented by Magogo (perhaps taken from the Biblical Magog, signifying end times), is to be seen in the following passage:

> Actually if one looked harder, one would probably discover that the men on stage, like Magogo, were sightless, deaf and dumb. No wonder, Salvia reflected, they moved in slow motion, without focus or sense of direction. They had eyes but could not see, ears but they could not hear, and they could only garble unintelligently because they could not talk. 'God!' Salvia exclaimed. 'This must be a nightmare' (p.106).

Salvia's exclamation summarises the current Nigerian situation — a nightmare. The text suggests that where truth is caged, justice discarded and honesty ridiculed, progress must remain elusive. These ideals are represented in the novel by names like Al-Haqq, Mumini, Adll, Salaama, and so on. Incidentally, the name Salvia (which rhymes with Saviour) itself is symbolic because its feminine sound not only suggests gentleness and trustworthiness; it also represents comfort and ease as the word salve implies. So, for the society to move forward, these ideals must be realised. The leaders must eschew selfishness, reject the allure of personal aggrandisement and look at the people with salving eyes and heart of comfort.

Such a profound statement of hope should find place somewhere within the realistic actions of the characters, instead of being dwelled upon in the formless dream of a person almost psychologically undeveloped and whose circumstances of birth hardly prepare him for greater things, yet in whom the novel entrusts so much faith.

Put differently, the treatment of the theme of political corruption would have been more poignant if it were handled at a more realistic level, instead of the disorienting miasma of uncoordinated symbolism employed in the chapter dealing with the issue. Similarly, in terms of organic unity, the chapter adds very little to the plot; whether it is expunged or left as it is, the story still holds. The point is made, which is that corruption must give way if the country is to make progress; and for this to happen, some individuals must see themselves as the instrument of change. Whether Salvia expects it or not, the society has chosen him as a leader because he is perceived as capable of bringing the desired change. What this means is that the voice of the people should be held supreme. Politics, or democracy to be precise, should be at the dictate of the people, not at the dictate of the government in power.

Saji, formerly Sergeant Musa Ture, the village drunk, is the next most important male character in the novel. He is, indeed, the frog prince whom the Debro community has to kiss to bring sanity back to life. On a wider scale, Saji represents the victims of the corrupt system. He, as it were, portrays the image of those totally used and discarded by the system and, unable to come to terms with his lot, resorts to drinking. Before he became the laughing stock of the village, he was the agile village youth who led the village race and assisted Yelwa, Batanncha's wife, when she was in labour about to give birth to Salvia. He "later became a young soldier who fought to keep our country one" (p.148). The hero is now reduced to a pathetic state by the same government he served. When he was demobilised from the army, his pension was also stopped. Unkindly, BaAli, one of the village elders observed, "Saji should pull himself together. He is not the only one government has withheld their pension and gratuity." (p.79). This observation, though, is really not an indictment on Saji, much as he would like to think so, but of the whole system, which uses people when it needs them, discards them when they are not needed and refuses to honour them with their entitlements. This is injustice and there is no guarantee that everyone will react to it in the same manner.

Saji calls to mind Dogo in *The Virtuous Woman*, although Dogo is responsible for the crises that befall him. He dances to the tune of a society that unreasonably craves for male children rather than girls, even though he has nothing in particular to give to the baby. Worse, when he comes crashing down finally, the same society simply looks at him with indifference. Yet, he is able to assist his travelling companions when they are stranded in the forest, as their vehicle gets stuck in the mud, by cheering them up and giving them hope. This suggests that he is not all together useless, even though Alkali does not forgive him his chauvinism in the end, leaving him alone to take care of his infant with no female relation to help.

Saji's case however, is not as bad as that of Dogo and his final condition is essentially the fault of the government, which he had served well, risking his life to fight in the country's civil war. Curiously, even his propensity for domestic violence is handled lightly in the text. One cannot miss the point by comparing the disdain with which Madu Chimba, the village butcher, is described in *The Descendants* for incessantly beating up his wife

Peni. In Saji's case, this is almost excused as his wife loves him to the end, in spite of his attitude. The humour in the following conversation is by no means sarcastic:

> "I leave now, mother, to prepare a meal for Saji before he comes in. I need my teeth to remain intact where they are," she said with a nervous laugh.
>
> "Still the same old Saji, coming home drunk and smarting for a fight," Tata commented dryly.
>
> "Still the same, mother. Tambal fills my husband with corn beer, takes his money and whatever else, and sends him home to beat me up."
>
> "Take my advice, Adama, and bring Tambal home as a second wife. That way, Saji will not have to leave the house for a drink. If you cannot share in the money, at least, Tambal should share in the beating (p.68)."

At this level, the situation is put in a wider socio-political perspective. Saji is not inherently bad. He is a product of his own society and his wife understands this. The writer is, thus, able to look at domestic violence from the perspective of the wife who loves her husband and not the society that almost destroys him. Adama's complaint is devoid of rancor or accusation; she understands her husband well and knows that it is frustration that turns him into the kind of person he is. Still, she has hope and faith and that is why she does not, as the old woman Tata suggests, bring in Tambal as a second wife for her husband in spite of Tata's persuasive argument. In Adama, the picture is painted of the emergent traditional woman who stands by her man at all costs and refuses to bow to societal pressures. The success of her husband in the end signifies her own success too.

The novel does not sanction domestic violence, but at this stage, it does not encourage anything that would bring about unnecessary tension in a family that is already stretched to breaking point due to the injustice of the state. When Adama goes to Batanncha's house to beg for some flour for their food, the old men at the entrance of the house, including Batanncha himself, laugh at her (p.128). This attitude is disheartening and only succeeds in making the reader empathise with her, rather than take side with the elderly men who seem to have nothing better to do than gossip and guffaw when a woman passes by, like small children. Adama's actions are not accidental, but are intended to serve as a show of honour and strength, even from the wife of a drunk, against the irresponsible village elders whose vocation is only to sit and talk about others.

Saji's own moral superiority is confirmed when he comes to find the old men laughing and enquires as to the source of their merriment. Of course, they cannot tell him exactly that they are laughing at his wife for coming to the house of Batanncha to beg for food, but Bamusa cryptically responds by admonishing Saji not to ask for what makes his fathers laugh, for it may make him cry. In his drunken state, Saji still manages to say to himself that they "must be laughing at someone's expense...Nothing can make these three weirdos laugh with their thirty-two teeth, except someone's misfortune," (p.129). He staggers out and leaves them with their laughter. At this stage, though, the picture of Saji that comes out is hardly one of a messiah.

However, when Salvia is sent to the city to bring about information about his brother and he too fails to come back, matters become critical and uncle Dogo is called upon to suggest a way out of the situation. He tells Batanncha and those villagers around that they have sent the wrong persons and that Saji should have been the person to be sent in the first place. Only a man of Dogo's age and experience can see beyond the façade of drunkenness and look at the real man that is Sergeant Musa Ture. Uncle Dogo is able to see hope in "fine courageous man", where the society sees only an object of ridicule; Saji himself is overwhelmed:

> "First, he was surprised, then highly embarrassed as several people suppressed a snicker, then finally Saji was engulfed in gratitude for Dogo's faith and trust in the village's laughing stock," (p.147)

Uncle Dogo's decision proves useful to all concerned as Saji goes to the city, fulfils his mission and brings back good news to the Batanncha family, without betraying where Samba is. He himself becomes reformed and gets a job in town as a security man, which enables him to follow Samba's movements. His intermittent visits to the village and the news he brings helps the Batanncha family to keep faith, at a time when they are abandoned by virtually everybody in the village. When in the end, plans are made for Samba's return and that of Salvia and Avi Dayyan, Salvia's twin sister, it is Saji who comes out as the most important person in the Batanncha family.

> Musa Ture was a good example of the saying that the rejected stone has turned out to be the foundation of the building. Who would have ever thought that of all the people in Debro, Saji would be the man to help in the restoration of the dignity of Batanncha's family?(p.169)

He becomes more like an adviser and because old man Batanncha listens to him, the whole village comes to respect the veteran soldier. As a result of Saji's attitude, sincerity and faith, Batanncha comes to the conclusion that, "there's still love, loyalty and true friendship in this world." He mentions this with good reason because of the behaviour of his two friends, Batabchi and Bamusa, whom he discovers to be not too sincere. Through the two, Alkali discusses the theme of betrayal and materialism, underlining the fact that for fifty years, the trio have been together and Batanncha never suspected for one moment that they could be false. Indeed, Bamusa is not just a friend, but also a brother in-law, because he is a brother to Yamusa, Batancha's first wife.

Ned Sherrin (1995:132) quotes Ambrose Bierce as saying that in human relationship the future is "that period of time in which our affairs prosper, our friends true and our happiness is assured." This period in Batanncha's life happens to be just before his son attempts to stage a coup when everyone troops into his house for clothing and money; in fact, his own friends testify that even the clothes they wear are often given to them by Samba, Batabcha's son. They are still hanging around when they learn of the rumour of the coup, but as they keep coming to the house and discover that they cannot obtain the materials they used to get, they stay away. Batanncha is not surprised by the fair weather behaviour of the other people in Debro, but what stands out in his mind is the attitude of his friends – Batapchi and Bamusa.

> When his own brother-in-law Bamusa, and his best friend, Batapchi, started making excuses, it dawned on him that he was being deserted. When they finally stopped coming, the pain was intense (p.156).

But Batanncha is unheeding: "All those years, his wife, Yamusa, had warned him that the men stuck to him like bees to flower only because he took care of their financial needs. She warned him that these two men closest to him would not pass the test of friendship in hardship." (p.156) Well, in the end, they do not. Only Saji, now reformed, becomes his comfort and source of good friendship. Even at Samba's return and the planned dual wedding of Salvia and Avi Dayyan, when he allows everyone in the village to come and celebrate with him, he does so because he is a good man at heart.

The philosophy, or rather didacticism here, is that it always pays better to forgive an injury. People are generally wont to behave the way people of Debro behave, but if one perseveres, then one would be better off in the end. In any case, Batanncha's forgiving spirit pays when Salvia, his own son, is finally chosen to become the next governor of the state. The hypocrisy and betrayal of the two friends then comes to nothing since in the end he actually prospers in spite of them. It must be noted that Batanncha represents the emerging male elder in the community. Being literate, he is always depicted in front of his compound under the tree, "studiously reading from a book" (p.57), when his friends are not around. Apart from his kind-heartedness, he is also level-headed. Thus, when he confirms beyond doubt that his son is involved in a coup he says, "If my son fights for a good cause, almighty God would help him fight the battle. If he fights for an unjust cause, then like a man, he must bear the consequences." (p.88).

No doubt, *The Initiates* marks the turning point in Alkali's fiction. The concern with general societal issues, especially as they affect the wider community, is impressive. Hitherto, only inferences were made, but now it is for real. While the writer's feminist instincts are still intact, her concern seems to shift away from delineating the place of women in the society to the general condition of the people in the society. Actually, Alkali has always used the family as a microcosm of the society in her novels – Baba's family in *The Stillborn,* represents the nameless society in the novel; Baba Sani's family in *The Virtuous Woman* mirrors the changing times in the Zuma community; and Magira Milli's family in *The Descendants* reflects the transformation that has taken place in the three communities of Ramta, Makulpo and Garpella featured in the narrative. The story now in *The Initiates* is the Nigerian story, told with austere intensity.

Nonetheless, it would have been inconceivable that the writer would still fail to explore the place of the woman in all the events. Thus, it is that Avi Dayyan, the twin sister of the emerging male, Salvia, takes off where Seytu, her predecessor in *The Descendants* leaves off. She is the graduate employee of a petrochemical company; having read geology in the university. The very nature of her profession – male-dominated and unfeminine — shows that the society has really grown. Now geology is no longer the preserve of the male, just as medicine in *The Descendants* is not exclusively for men. Before then, the women hardly exceed secondary schools or teacher training colleges. The growth in education is now obvious; hence, Alkali's shift in perspective.

The first time Avi Dayyan is mentioned in the novel is by Yamusa, the first wife of Batanncha, who wonders at the odd behaviour of the twins in the family (Salvia and Avi Dayyan), as none of them cares to bring home the prospective suitors they wish to marry. "The two just carried themselves like saviours. Imagine Salvia initiating the building and mending of schools free, and Avi Dayyan picking babies from the gutter and bringing them up by herself." (p.31)

Salvia's selfless concern for his community has been discussed earlier. Avi Dayyan, his twin sister, also shares some of this love trace for the community. Hers is somewhat manifested differently, like when she picks abandoned children from the street and brings them home to rear. She works in the town, but stays mostly in the village. She is portrayed as a tireless, hardworking and conscientious woman, who takes pride in taking care of her family, even if the family members think little of her contribution. "To Batanncha, no matter how strong (she was), she was still a woman."

As Samba is incapacitated, and Salvia is not working, Avi Dayyan takes over the affairs of the house. In this regard, she is even a more realised woman than Seytu in *The Descendants,* for Seytu has no need to take care of anyone, except her immediate family; but then Seytu is a royalty and Avi Dayyan is just a simple educated woman from the village, whose brother is in the army. This makes her stand out as a pillar on whom not only her immediate family rests, but also her brother's family can lean on in times of stress. That is why she stays in the city to assist Augustina, the Calabar woman whom Samba has married.

In Avi Dayyan's character, especially that sympathetic aspect of it that is manifest in her picking abandoned children, the writer of the novel appears to probe the conscience of the society. Apparently, abandoned children should not have remained abandoned; in fact, such children should not have been abandoned in the first place, because parents should bear full moral responsibility for their children. The theme of illegitimate children, a longstanding issue in Alkali's writings, is now treated from a fresh perspective, as the current narrative does not even identify their parents. For instance, in the case of Hajjo in *The Virtuous Woman* and Bala in *The Stillborn,* their parents are known; only that the society frowns at the circumstances of their birth. They tend to get ridiculed only because their parents refuse to get married after they are conceived. When it is learnt that Sule, Li's brother, has impregnated the blacksmith's daughter in *The Stillborn*, the village concludes that he must marry her. His father, inspired by newly acquired religious values, refuses the decision, disowning the son instead, an act which leads Kaka to wonder loudly about the kind of times we now live in, when a male child would be disowned for proving his maleness.

The statement in *The Initiates* is that we are living in permissive times, but we are getting our moral priorities mixed up if we consistently condemn the helpless products of this permissiveness, instead of seeking out those responsible for the act and holding them accountable. For instance, the biological parents of Zari and Zara are not disclosed, but if the behaviour of the two youngsters Tata witnessed walking on the street is anything to go by, one can well imagine who those parents really are. What is more alarming is that the trend appears to be just beginning, Alkali is at her best descriptive when she captures the image of the two young people:

> The girl was painfully thin and skimpily dressed in faded jeans that barely covered her buttocks, a short blouse thrown on top that left her belly-button showing...The young man was not to be outdone. His trousers were tight from the waist down to the knees and loose all the way to his ankles. His shirt, tucked into the trousers, hung loosely on top, the front completely unbuttoned, exposing young hairs which signified the beginning of manhood. (p.63)

It is early evening and these young people stop right in the road hugging and kissing before the very eyes of Mama Tata. The old woman, consistent to the end, hisses: "Shameless goats. That I should live to witness such shameless times (p.63)" But Tata goes right ahead to contradict herself, "In my days such things are done under the cover of darkness (p.64)". Her point seems to be that this permissiveness is not new, but that it is now rampant and flagrant. Nonetheless, since it has become part of our culture, it is only right to put the blame on the perpetrators of the action, but not the innocent children that are the result of the unwholesome behaviour. This is Avi Dayyan's motivation to take care of a pair of twins whose mother abandons them on the street.

Avi Dayyan also is a portrait of the twenty-first century working woman who, though she desires marriage, like Glo Medina Kayes in *The Descendants,* is not in a hurry to go into it. She has a male friend, Hashim, with whom she is rather close; something her father finds curious — that a woman could become friends with a man, but because the friendship stops just short of being love, she does not marry him. In the end, she marries Hussein, her brother's close friend, when she is in her early thirties. The age is another point of difference, because that would have been inconceivable in the traditional society, where early marriage is considered a virtue. She could afford the delay for the reason that her father is literate, knowing that he will not push her out of the family into marriage while she is quite young. He might well have married his younger wife, Yelwa, when she was sixteen (p.48), but he knows that the times have now changed.

The significant point here is that Avi Dayyan marries. Marriage is given its prestige back. It is a union of love and responsibility, not the vengeful recklessness couched in contrived love displayed by Seytu in *The Descendants.* Avi Dayyan, thus, is the solid and now believable portrait of the emergent woman. Li may well have been the most popular heroine, but Avi Dayyan is the most realistic, the most realised and the most forward looking.

The fecundity in *The Initiates* lies less in the themes treated than in the manner they are treated. Nigerian writers have treated similar themes before; what is remarkable is the conclusion the writer has drawn and the deviation from the feminist norm of insisting that the man is after all as relevant to societal existence as the woman. He may need to be made aware of his own imperfections first, before he is acceptable. Thus,

Batanncha, the emerging elder, almost loses a son before he is made to fit into the society. Samba has to be turned into a one-eyed cripple before he comes to be accepted permanently in the village. Saji has to be reduced to the point of being ridiculed by all and sundry before he emerges as the saviour of the Batanccha family. Salvia, the emergent leader is given to dreams and temporary amnesia. The remarkable point is that, once they all come to terms with their lot, they get accepted, like everyone else, and are allowed to contribute their quota in the progress of the society. It is only when men own up to their own internal frailties and accept that women are equally strong that progress in the society can be made.

In *The Initiates,* there is abundant use of religious symbolism to show the extent to which the society deviates from the ideal. In the glossary (p.193), the author says that, "the names of the initiates in Chapter Seven are derived from the 99 Islamic names, or attributes of Allah (God)". This suggests that the predicament in the society is largely because people have turned away from the ways of God. Alkali has abundant faith in religion, quite unlike most feminists who believe the woman can change her lot all by herself. What to make of the religion, however, seems to be her point of uncertainty. The setting of *The Initiates* is double: it is Islamic, with the narrative dotted by the muezzin's call for prayer at dawn (p.93); but then, there is Salvia who sees salvation from a "figure that was now beckoning him to step out. Salvia wondered how it was possible for the man to walk on a mass of water as if it were land." (p.94). Earlier, his father, Batanncha of Debro has "stood erect and silent on his prayer mat in the corner of his room...and begged God for the life of his son and the protection of the Nigerian nation against principalities and powers of evil." (p.89).

In the case of Salvia, the resort to religion for succor is established; just as the role of water as a purifying element is underscored. Although a Muslim (albeit with a Christian name), he still sees the image of Jesus walking on water as a symbol of salvation. Batanncha, on the other hand, is captured standing up to pray against the principalities and powers, but standing up to pray on a prayer mat is the practice of Muslims, while principalities and powers are biblically derived concepts. The harmonisation of these dual faiths in an individual suggests that, if we could combine the salving powers of the dominant religions in the country, most of our problems would be solved. In other words, through this symbolism the text suggests that we would serve ourselves better if we look into our religions and emphasise the many things that unite us — like belief in one God — instead of the few that divide us.

There is also the use of the journey as symbol. In her earlier book, *The Virtuous Woman,* Alkali uses the journey as a symbol of human suffering and tribulations in life, the enduring of which would make humans realise their dreams, as denoted in the three girls around whom the story is woven. In *The Initiates,* the journey, which is described as a race, to the hospital where Salvia is born, symbolises the need for endurance of hardship and inconveniences, if our efforts are to yield the desired fruits. It is after Yelwa has endured this horrendous trip across the village and to the city that she gives birth to Salvia; otherwise, he would have been stillborn and only his sister would have survived. In describing this race, though, the description somewhat stretches the reader's imagination, since it is not a deliberate exaggeration as it were, but the result of poor judgement of the distance in the creative text.

As one begins to read the story, it sounds plausible until suddenly one comes to the point where it says Yelwa, caught in the spasm of labour is gently fastened to a bed and six young men are made to carry her and the bed in the middle of the night: "They had covered thirty kilometres when they met an elderly doctor, a nurse and Batanncha." (p.54). Even if the young men were twice their number, could they have really carried a woman in the spasm of labour to a distance of thirty kilometres without any incident?

Nevertheless, it should be pointed out that it is the significance of the journey that is of concern here, not the distance covered. There is a similar error of judgement when Saji is made to describe the seriousness of Samba's wound: "He had been shot in the head and that had shattered one of his eyes." (p.180) Under normal circumstances, it would not be expected that a man shot in the head to the extent of having his eye 'shattered' would survive the shooting. Nevertheless, it is easy for this anomaly to escape detection, given the racy style which the story assumes at this stage. The reader is actually gripped by the fluidity of the language, which is expressive and unpretentious.

Conclusion

The linguistic richness of *The Initiates* is enhanced by the use of proverbs, which are introduced unobtrusively to add local colour to the story. Furthermore, where these proverbs are used, they are by no means irrelevant. For instance, in describing the speed at which news of Samba's unfortunate involvement in the coup comes to the village, a well known proverb is localised with an image that gives it a refreshing stint: "Bad news travels fast like fire on harmattan grass." (p, 14) Similarly, another proverb is quoted to emphasise the place of virtue in the society: "…death is to be preferred to a shameful act." (p.15) Luckily, far from being shameful, Samba's act turns out to be actually heroic later because other people succeed in toppling the government where he failed.

In another perspective, as a reflection of the communal nature of existence in the village, a common proverb states that, "a goat in labour is never allowed to struggle alone on a tether when the owners are around." (p.10) This suggests that during the times of tribulation, no one in Debro is allowed to suffer alone. As the story unfolds though, the people of Debro do not live true to this saying of theirs, as Batanncha is allowed to suffer his loneliness without help. Nonetheless, in the beginning, the whole community shows concern and commitment, especially when everyone is involved in searching for who to send to town to bring back news about Samba. As everyone volunteers, an elder has to respond by admonishing that, "we cannot cut down all the trees in the forest to repair a single roof." (p.25). "Double sightedness is not always a sign of enlightenment. It could also be a clue of mental and emotional disorder."(p.55). It is the thought of what this proverb implies that stops Batanncha from telling the world about what he considers the special gift of his twins in being able to see deeper than most people. Batanncha reasons that in a world, such as that of Debro, "a world of distorted values and visions, where the line between the saint and the sinner is thin, there are things he could not tell the world about his twins."

The use of proverbs, thus, enhances the language in *The Initiates*. Proverbs are maximally employed to effectively weave the narrative, embolden the themes and enhance the style. This study, therefore, submits that in both form and content, *The Initiates* is the most successful of Alkali's novels to date.

REFERENCES

Primary Texts

Alkali, Z. (1984) *The Stillborn,* London: Longman.
_____ (1986) *The Virtuous Woman,* Ibadan: Longman.
_____ (1997) *Cobwebs and Other Stories,* Lagos: Malthouse.
_____ (2007) *The Descendants,* Ibadan: Spectrum.
_____ (2007) *The Initiates,* Ibadan: Spectrum.

Secondary Texts

- Abba, A. S. et al. (1997), *Creative Writing, Writers and Publishing in Northern Nigeria,* Ibadan: IFRA African Book Builders.
- Abiodun, F. (1990), "Literature and Culture in Northern

Nigeria: The Novels of Ibrahim Tahir and Zaynab Alkali" in Abdulraheem O. (ed), *Essays on Northern Nigerian Literature,* Volume One, Zaria: Hamdan Express Printers.

- Acholonu, C. A. (1995), *Motherism: The Afrocentric Alternative to Feminism,* Owerri, AFA Publications.

- Adeghe, A. (1993), "The Other Half of the Story: Nigerian Women Telling Tales" in Brown, S. (ed), *The Pressures of the Text and the Telling of the Tales,* Birmingham: Birmingham Press.

- Adimora-Ezeigbo, A. (2010), "My Snail-Sense Feminist Theory Accommodates the Menfolk", Interview granted Obafemi O. in Onukagu A.A. and Onyerionwu E. (eds) *Nigerian Literature Today No. 1*: A Journal of Contemporary Nigerian Writing, Ibadan: Kraft Books.

- Ahmed, A.A. (2005), "Stylistics and Ideological Positioning: Zaynab Alkali's Ambivalence to Feminism", A Paper Presented at the Saudi Summer School Literary Conference, Riyadh.

- Amadi, I. (1997), *Reinventing Africa: Matriarchy, Religion and Culture,* London: Zed Books.

- Amadiume, I. (1995), *Male Daughters, Female Husbands: Gender and Sex in African Society,* London: Zed Books.

- Banyiwa-Horne, N. (1986), "African Womanhood: The contrasting Perspectives of Flora Nwapa's *Efuru* and Elechi Amadi's *Concubine,* in Boyce D. C. and Adams C. A.(eds), *Ngambika: Studies of Women in African Literature,* Trenton: African World Press Inc.

- Belsey, C. and Moore, J. (1989), *The Feminist Reader,* London: Macmillan.

- Bocock, R. (1987), *Freud and Modern Society,* New York: Holmes and Meier Publishers Inc.

- Butler, C. (2002), *Postmodernism: A Very Short Introduction*, London: Oxford University Press.
- Chinweizu et al. (eds) (1980), *Toward the Decolonization of African Literature* Vol.1, Enugu, Fourth Dimension Publishers
- Culler, J. (1997) *Literary Theory: A Short Introduction*, London, Oxford University Press.
- David, L. (1992), *The Art of Fiction*, London: Penguin Books.
- El-Saadawi, N. (1980), *The Hidden Face of Eve*, London: Zed Books
- _____ (1999), *A Daughter of Isis: The Autobiography of Nawal El-Saadawi*, London: Zed Books
- Eisenstein, H. (1988), *Contemporary Feminist Thought*, London: Unwin Paperbacks.
- Emenyonu, E. N. (1991) *Studies on the Nigerian Novel*, London: Heinemann.
- _____ (2006) *New Directions in African Literature*, 25, Ibadan Heinemann.
- Gikandi, S. (ed) (2009), *The Routeledge Encyclopedia of African Literature*, New York: Routeledge.
- Hale, D. J. (ed) (2010), *An Anthology of Criticism and Theory*, London: Blackwell Publishing
- Hooks, B. (1984), *Feminist Theory: From Margin to Centre*, Boston: South End Press.
- Ityavyar, D. A. and Obiajunwa S. N. (eds) (1992), *The State and Women in Nigeria*, Jos, Unijos Press
- James, A. (1990). *In Their Own Voices: African Women Writers Talk*, London: Heinemann.

- Jatau, P. (2006), "Postcoloniality in Zaynab Alkali's Works". Paper delivered at the 3rd Conference on Literature in Northern Nigeria, Bayero University, Kano 5-6 December.
- Johnson, R. (1988), "The Social Vision of Zaynab Alkali" in *Canadian Journal of African Studies*, Vol.22, No.3, http://www.jstor.org/stable/485960.
- Jones, E.D. and Palmer, E. (eds) (1982), *African Literature Today* No.12, London: Heinemann
- Jones, E.D. Palmer, E. and Jones, M. (eds) (1987), *Women in African Literature Today,* 15, London: Africa World Press.
- Joseph, A. (2005), "The Novel in English in Northern Nigeria: Its Development and Nature (1984-1998)", Unpublished PhD Thesis.
- Mies, M. et.al. (1991), *Women: The Last Colony*, London: Zed Books.
- Miller, J. (1986), *Women Writing About Men*, London: Virago Press Limited.
- Newell, S. (1997), *Writing African Women*, London, Zed Books.
- Nnolim, C. (2010), *Approaches to the African Novel: Essays in Analysis*, Lagos, Malthouse Press.
- _____ (2010), *Issues in African Literature*, Lagos, Malthouse Press.
- Nwapa, F. (2007), "Women and Creative Writing in Africa" in Olaniyan T. and Quayson A. (eds), *African Literature: An Anthology of Criticism and Theory*, United Kingdom: Oxford University Press.
- Obiechina, E. N. (1982), "Cultural Nationalism in Modern African Creative Literature" in Jones E.D. (ed), *African Literature Today* Nos 1 - 4 Omnibus Edition, London: Heinemann.

- Ogezi, I. A. (2007), "A Celebration of Zaynab Alkali's The Descendants", http://www.africanwrtier.com/articles/
- Ogundipe-Leslie, M. (2007), "Stiwanism: Feminism in an African Context" in Olaniyan T. and Quayson (eds) *African Literature: An Anthology of Criticism and Theory*, United Kingdom: Oxford University Press.
- Ogungbesan, K. (ed) (1979), *New West African Literature*, London: Heinemann.
- Ojinmah, U. and Egya, S. (2005), *The Writings of Zaynab Alkali*, Abuja: RON Publishers.
- Onukaogu, A. A. (2009), *21st Century Nigerian Literature: An Introductory Text*, Ibadan: Kraft Books.
- Palmer, E. (1979), *The Growth of the African Novel*, London: Heinemann.
- Parrott, W. (2001), *Emotions in Social Psychology*, Philadelphia: Psychology Press.
- Peck, J. and Coyle, M. (2002), *Literary Terms and Criticism*, New York: Palgrave, Macmillan
- Schwimmer, B. (2002), "Matrifocality" http:/home.cc.umanitoba.ca.
- Shehu, H. (1987), "Feminism in the Writings of Ama Ata Aidoo and Mariama Ba", unpublished M.A. Thesis, Department of English, A.B.U., Zaria.
- Sherrin, N. (1996), *The Oxford Dictionary of Humorous Quotations*, London, OUP.
- Shotter, J. (1994), *Conversational Realities: Constructing Life Through Language*, London, Sage Publications.
- Soyinka, W. (1988), *Six Plays*, Ibadan: Spectrum Books Ltd.
- Sutherland, J. (2010) 50 *Literature Ideas You Really Need to Know*, London: Quercus.

- Stratton, F. (1994), *Contemporary African Literature and Politics of Gender,* London: Routeledge.
- *The Encyclopaedia Britinnica* (1962), 13th Edition, London: Encyclopaedia Britannica Company.
- Stevick, P. (ed) (1967), *The Theory of the Novel,* USA: The Free Press.
- Schwartz, D. C. (1973), *Political Alienation and Political Behaviour,* Chicago: Aldine Publishing Company.
- Walter, N. (ed), *On the Move: Feminism for a New Generation,* London: Virago Press.
- Wright, E. (ed) (1973), *The Critical Evaluation of African Literature,* London: Heinemann.

Chapter Twenty

Contemporary Northern Nigerian Female Writings and the Question of Blame: A Reading of Bilkisu Abubakar's To Live Again and The Woman in Me

Aisha Umar Muhammad and Abdullahi Muhammad

Introduction

In recent times gender has become one of the most sensitive and outstanding issues in the area of social and literary research in Africa, so much that it has come to occupy the attention of academics and social researchers as a vital aspect of their research effort. Writers and critics of African literature have often depicted women as docile and obedient child bearers, housekeepers, bed mates and passive members of their families and societies. This social predicament is evident, not just in the projection of the illiterate African female, but also that of the educated and enlightened women, as they confront the subjugation and challenges in their daily social experiences.

The males have usually dominated the literary field over the years, as writers and critics present the women as dormant, docile, and unintelligent members of their various societies. In Sagawa's view:

> The discussion of African Literature usually centres on the male writer and character... Rarely has the role of the women in fiction been of serious interest to the critic of African Literature [164].

This stereotypical depiction of the African woman in literature appears to had been accepted by the women and the society at large, but the early female writers in African and Nigerian literature now counter it in their respective views, as Emenyonu (2010:2) explains:

> In the articulation of gender issues in feminism, Nigerian female writers, beginning with Flora Nwapa in 1966, have taken the lead in delving into uncharted waters, infusing realism and authenticity into the portrayal of the burden of African womanhood in fiction.

The Nigerian female writers and their works fall under the third generation movement of feminism; and although Africans frown at the concept of feminism and African feminist writers, Okolocha (2012:33) argues that, "the essence of feminism in Africa is to extract concession from the patriarchal structures of society for women." The passivity of the female in a male dominated society has been in existence right from time immemorial. This informed the style of early writing and the thematic contents in relation to the depiction of women in African literature, such that these women have become stereotyped "chattels" and unimportant characters that are not expected to develop. Achebe (1958) depicts male supremacy, where the man is all and the women seen only as men's acquisition. Okonkwo's wives, especially the youngest, live in perpetual fear of "his fiery temper" (9), because he rules them with a heavy hand. Amadi (1966) depicts women as victims and destroyers. Armah (1958) presents the women as exploiters, greedy, selfish and narrow minded.

Although not all the male writers stereotyped the women in their works in similar manner; nonetheless, the early female writers "started to write ... total rejection of the images of women projected by some male writers, and others tried to glorify the roles played by women in society and thereby help to raise their status (Usman, 2006:157)." These writers and their male counterparts of similar interest, thus, began to give their female characters relevance, assigning to them crucial and challenging roles in their works, as well as putting them at the forefront of their portrayals of life, in order to "humanize them and treat them emphatically." (Nwahunanya, 2012:200). How well they are able to face the challenges, nonetheless, becomes another issue.

Furthermore, whether this really counters the previous opinion remains to be seen, but Ama Ata Aidoo (1981:81) believes that glorifying womanhood and the positive portrayal of women in fictional works is not enough. There is also the need to reveal the tragedy of women's history and portray the women fully, correctly and realistically. This is to create an avenue for critical situational analysis of the women and their place in Africa and elsewhere.

In the light of the above, Bilkisu Abubakar set out in her two novels to look at the critical issue of the effect (destructive or constructive) of societal challenges on the African woman, both at home and in the diaspora. She appears to suggest that the present social circumstances do not project much prospect for women, whether fictional or in real life. Furthermore, not all the women are able to successfully break from the shackles of societal challenges; while some make it, others get adversely affected: morally, psychologically or physically.

Emergence of Nigerian Female Writers

The earliest female writers in English in Nigeria had emerged from the South-Western region, like Flora Nwapa, Zulu Sofola and Buchi Emecheta. Others that came later included Seffi Atta, Ifeoma Okoye, Tess Onwueme, Ifeoma Chinwumba, and Kaine Agary; and, most recently, Chimamanda Ngozi Adichie and Tracia Chima Ezeajugh. For Nyitse (2010:4), these:

> Women writers have brought a new dimension to writing. In the works of these females, the traditional roles which women perform are examined so that whatever new ones they have acquired and the repercussions of this multi-tasking could be identified.

In northern Nigeria, the emergence pace was much slower, with Zaynab Alkali acting as the lone voice for many years, as her *The Still Born* champions the cause of the women. Koroye (1989:47) observes:

> From the feminist positions made familiar by novelists, like Flora Nwapa and Buchi Emecheta, an ascetic vision of the truly liberated woman informs the themes as well as the style of Alkali's novels for the image of the new woman ... a fully formed independent person, inscribed all over with the ascetic ideals of 'determination' and 'virture'.

It was to remain like that for a very long time, until in recent times several more unknown and emerging female writers, hidden in the background of northern Nigerian literature, began to attract attention with narratives of their personal experiences or observations about gender and its related issues. Indeed, many of them have been writing in languages other than English, especially Hausa, which has an old literary history that goes back hundreds of years. Notable among these writers are Asabe Kabir Usman, Fatima Alkali, Bilkisu Abubakar, Bilkisu Ahmed Funtua, Razinat Muhammad, Halimat Sekula, and Cecilia Kato.

All these attempts are geared towards identifying the position of the Nigerian woman in the socio-political and economic situation in the country. It is also a milestone in expressing the yearning and aspirations of the women in a society where they are culturally alienated and according them the opportunity to tell their own story in order to correct the wrong image of them created by the male writers, as well as inspire other Nigerian women too. The ultimate aim is to review the plight of the Nigerian woman, by dismantling all harmful traditional/cultural structures against her development and establish for her:

> --- a self consciousness of her growth as woman, of her body, her affective life and her intellectual motivation as she learns to reject male definition of women's roles as irrelevant to women's essential identity ... and her simultaneous recognition and scrutiny of the potentials in her (Dunton, 216).

Bilkisu Abubakar hails from Kaduna State; having been brought up in northern Nigeria, she is conversant with the daily experiences of the northern Nigerian woman. Consequently, she has grown committed to championing the struggle against female subjugation and marginalisation in her novels, especially *To Live Again* and *The Woman in Me*.

To Live Again tells the story of a young Hausa/Fulani woman, 'Uwani', who refuses to marry 'Alhaji', her father's choice, but marries Ahmad who she sees as "... her first and only love" (p1). Through Uwani, Bilikisu raises so many issues, such as arranged marriage, early marriage, polygamy, girl-child education, Islamic education, widowhood, divorce, child bearing, subjugation and patriarchy, which she all believes to be 'an impediment to gender parity,' because "in this new millennium, gender research would not close its eyes to aspects of traditional African culture that pose a challenge to the streaming of gender relations (Ssetuba, 2002:1)."

Uwani eventually marries Ahmad, her love and choice, as she believes that "love is all encompassing (9)", against the advice of Zainab, her step sister, who thinks that love "only breeds unhappiness when it goes sour" (10). She watches Ahmad grow from fame to fame, which eventually leads him to marry more wives, one after another. As an African (Hausa) woman, Uwani is expected to give "absolute loyalty, respect and total submission to her husband, these are the basic ingredients for a successful marriage." (18), but all she gets in return is that,

> ... he provided her with the basic things she craved for .....
> He came home ahead of time to find out how she was faring.
> And Uwani was considered lucky by other women (20).

After the birth of their two children, Yasmin and Faisal, Ahmad moves to the city for further studies and after his graduation gets a teaching appointment and moves the family to the city as well. He is pressured to marry another wife as Uwani fails to get pregnant again after the second child. The author seems to exploit the incident to challenge the influence of some traditional mothers who prevail on their married sons to patronise polygamy under the guise that they need "more grand children" (54). To Ahmad's mother and, indeed, many other women in the Hausa/Fulani society, monogamy "is not only unusual...it is also strange" (59).

Here, Abubakar is not angry with polygamy per se as an institution, but rather the humiliating way it is carried out. For instance, when Ahmad decides to marry Khadijat, one of his students, he not only delays informing the wife at home, but does so casually, only three days to the event:

> My wedding comes up after Juma'at prayer this week.
> You mean in three days time?
> ...Oh yes, insha Allahu.
> And the bride, who is she?
> You will know her; .... Khadija Usman.
> The matron's daughter you mean?
> ...You are absolutely right. (pp.64-65)

However, like the African woman that she is, "Uwani did not love Ahmad less...was something she knew could happen because it was his right." Gradually, he changes his attitude towards her and her children though and while he encourages his new wife to go for further studies, citing the importance of knowledge, he does not care to do the same for the first wife. He even gives preferential treatment to the new wife, especially by always taking her out in his car, while "most evenings Uwani stayed at home, with the children" (72). In fact, he sidelines her completely; the only time he speaks to her is when he requires something (77).

Uwani is now portrayed as a character with a strong will to survive and carry on. Thus, she quickly realises "....where her problem emanated from; her lack of western education hit her hard on the face" (80). When she voices out her desire to go to school, Ahmad ridicules her and advises her to remain at home and take care of her children. Despite the discouragement, Uwani is adamant and starts learning to read and write through the effort of Nana Mensah, a Ghanaian widow. Later, she sits for her GCE examination and passes with flying colours, although Ahmad still refuses to allow her going further in her studies or seeking for a job. However, she is content with being able to read and write; and eventually her virtues become apparent when Ahmad marries a third wife and she:

> ... became a peacemaker in the home as a result of quarrels amongst the wives, she was very diplomatic and never took sides ... She was not particular about who did what in the home. Her greatest wish was to regain the space she once occupied in Ahmad's heart and maintain peace (84).

In spite of her good qualities, Uwani is almost reduced to a piece of trash, so much that when Ahmad marries the fourth wife, "she dared not complain or question his actions though it was right for the other women to do so" (98). Eventually, she gets "the mandatory divorce," (102) and immediately, "her world crumbled completely" (102). Nana, her tutor, now proves her supportive pillar. With her encouragement and inspiration, Uwani, after her divorce, decides to go and study law in the university, where she meets Ladi, an epitome of female success outside marriage. The next time Ahmad sees her, instead of acknowledging the improvement in her personality and rejoicing in her new fortunes he attributes her success to the new male friends she must have made on campus: "Ahmad could not believe it was the same Uwani. She looked confident, calculated and beautiful, she looked quite different from how he knew her" (125). His attitude must have been borne out of jealousy and regret though, because he could not marry her again, even if she would accept him, until she marries another man, in accordance with the laws in Islam, because he had divorced her three times (*saki uku*). Subsequently, she meets and marries Captain Umar and gets the opportunity to live her life all over again.

Abubakar's second novel presents another female character, who, though she is more exposed than Uwani in *To Live Again*, fails to survive the pressure of her society and marriage. The novel describes the devastating defeat of womanhood and the betrayal of love. It sends a message of racial alienation in the face of lost identity.

Rosamond, who has been happily married to Ibrahim in England for sixteen years, suddenly finds herself in Kurmin Dusa, her husband's village in northern Nigeria, in the company of her husband and three children on a visit insisted upon by Ibrahim's mother, Inna. The children's school is interrupted, to Rosamond's displeasure.

On his mother's insistence, Ibrahim accepts not to return to England, but settles down back at home in Nigeria, a decision he keeps away from his wife until they arrive in their new home in the city where he has already secured a job. Rosamond finds it difficult to comprehend or accept the turn of events, but Ibrahim does his best to convince her and the children of the reason why they should stay; and because of the love she has for him, reluctantly decides to accept her new fate, especially when it becomes obvious that Ibrahim is not ready to allow them to return to England.

As Rosamond tries to adjust to life in Nigeria, she is hit hard by the news of her husband marrying a second wife, but she becomes unable to manage it any longer when she discovers that the new wife was her former housemaid, Zarau. Though her heart is broken by Ibrahim's attitude, "She loved him to no end and would sacrifice all she had for his sake" (33). Therefore, Rosamond accepts her co-wife reluctantly and the two others that follow later.

The influence of mother-in-laws in marital affairs is here presented negatively, as Ibrahim's mother manipulates him most of the time and controls his home. Inna cajoles him into polygamy with frequent advice from her sister, Ramatallah, under the excuse that a happy home must be filled with wives and children, thereby creating room for competition among the wives in their striving to please the husband. It is also his mother who talks him into politics and exposes him to more wealth and fame, which together seem to motivate the man to go into polygamy. His sudden interest in politics makes him more popular; "Ibrahim became a household name and the toast of several prominent people" (112). This popularity in turn earns him the love of "the Emir who offered his daughter's hand in marriage to him. She was given out as *sadaka,* as a sign of friendship" (112).

Here the author appears to bring within the focus of the narrative the traditional practice of giving out the hand of a girl child in marriage to a man. As usual, the older wife is abandoned when a new one comes in; thus, just like it happed to Rosamond earlier, "Zara'u's presence was hardly felt, since Ibrahim took another wife" (115).

On becoming the governor of the state, Ibrahim refuses to acknowledge the position of the First Lady, under the excuse that "the best a woman can ever be is a good mother and a wonderful wife" (120). In addition, his friends believe that the office of the first lady is only "an avenue for women to showcase latest fabrics and jewellery" and "also a way of intimidating other women" (120). The concern seems to be with denying women the opportunity to occupy public offices. Ironically, Ibrahim eventually neglects Rosamond and becomes preoccupied with his other wives, especially the newest Baraka, who wins him over completely, eventually becoming installed the First Lady of the state, the office he has previously denounced and refused any of his wives the permission to occupy. They now do almost everything together, spending most of their time together in the main lodge, when they are not performing any state function. It is necessary that she gives a nod to a proposal before it is approved, as she possesses him so much that everyone has to go through her to see him (153). This reflects how some men neglect their older wives and treat them unjustly, while being inconsistent in their policies in order to favour their favourite wives.

Didactically, the novel is high in emphasising that love and companionship should constitute the basis for good marriage and a happy home. Ibrahim marries four times, all for different reasons; but it is only Rosamand's that was based on mutual love and trust, which they enjoyed while it lasted back in England. His second is for money and to please his mother; that of Nana

Asma'u for fame and ambition; while the last marriage is more or less for the opportunity to showcase his wealth and acquire more fame. To such men, the women are like some kind of transient property to showcase their wealth and status.

Conclusion

Abubakar might not have intended to arouse sympathy for the heroines in her two novels examined in this chapter, but the anger she expresses towards the abuse of traditional values in the treatment of the women becomes obvious after reading the texts. Tradition, marriage and related family relationships are being deliberately exploited by some selfish men to destroy the women. For instance, in the latter text, the writer does not seem to blame the man, his mother-in-law or the society for Rosamand's plight and the role they play individually in her physical and emotional destruction as the protagonist of the story. Rather, the blame falls on her for her inability to face the challenges, accept them or run away, but not allow them to destroy her.

Although the writer seems to question the insignificant treatment meted out to women by both matrimony and the society, however, she marvels at the overt and swift way Ibrahim (and, indeed, some African men) change from the loving and trustworthy companion Rosamand had known back in England to a polygamous and egocentric man; all in the bid to satisfy his mother and society, to the detriment of his happy home. There is, arguably, the belief that environment, surroundings and society can change a man within the shortest possible time, as men do not seem to have a mind of their own in such situations. The women also believe that men lose their rationality at the slightest opportunity and forget that our attitudes determine our identity and place in the society. Rosamond eventually gets to realise who she is, but her discovery comes too late, as she does not live long enough for the ills to be corrected. One great lesson here is that, kindness, especially among spouses, should be universal, irrespective of race, ethnicity or religion. Bilkisu Abubakar emphasises in this novel, as in her first, the detrimental effects of the processes of polygamy on family life and happiness, especially on the women.

REFERENCES

- Abubakar, B. (2007), *To Live Again*, Kaduna: Zakara Communications Ltd.
- Abubakar, B. (2010), *The Woman in Me*, Kaduna: Prime Publicity Nig. Ltd.
- Achebe, C. (1958), *Things Fall Apart*, London: Heinemann.
- Aidoo, A. A. (1981), "Unwelcomed Pals and Decorative Slaves" in *Proceedings of the Internationa Conference on African Literature and English Language*. Calabar: University of Calabar Press.
- Amadi, E. (1966), *The Concubine*, London: Heinemann.
- Armah, A. K. (1968), *The Beautyful Ones are Not Yet Born*, London: Heinemann.
- Dunton, C. "To Rediscover Woman: The Novels of Calixthe Bayala", *Contemporary African Fiction*. Ed. Derek Wright Bayreuth, African Studies 42. Germany: Eckhard Breitinger Bayreuth University.
- Emernyonu N. E. (2010), "Creative Imagination and Present Day Nigerian Realities: What Else Can Literature Do?" Keynote Address presented at the International Conference on Nigeria Literature, Gombe State University, Nigeria. Nov. 1-5.
- Koroye, S. (1989), "The Ascetic Feminist Vision of Zainab Alkali" in Otukunefor, H. and Nwodo, O. (eds.), *Nigerian Female Writers: A Critical Perspective*. Lagos: Malthouse Press.

- Nyitse, M. B. (2010), "Female Writers, Sap and Globalization: An Exploration of the Novels of Kaine Agary and Ifeoma Chinwuba", Paper presented at the International Conference on Nigeria Literature, Gombe State University, Nigeria. Nov. 1-5.

- Nwahunanya, C. (2011), "Jagua Nana's Children: The Image of the Prostitute in Post-Colonial African Literature" *Ife Studies in African Literature and Arts,* No.6.

- Okolocha, H. O. (2012), "Rethinking Feminism and Nigerian Women Identity in Tess Onwueme's *Tell It to Women*", *Journal of the Literary Society of Nigeria,* Issue 4.

- Sstuba, I. (2002), "The Hold of Patriarchy: An Appraisal of the Ganda Proverb in the Light of Modern Gender Relations." A Paper presented at the Cairo Gender Symposium, 7th -10th April.

- Usman, K. A. (2006), "Gender in the Novels of Abubakar Gimba: A Critical Analysis of the Representation of the Contemporary Muslim Woman in *Sacred Apples*", in Ahmed, S.B. and Bhadmus, O.M. (eds.), *Writing, Performance and Literature in Northern Nigeria: Proceedings of the 3rd Conference on Literature in Northern Nigeria.* Kano: Department of English, Bayero University, Kano.

Chapter Twenty-One

'Identity Crises': The Dearth of Children's Literature in Northern Nigeria

Aishat Ize Yusuf, Ruth Obaude Owenmeh and Vincent Uzoma P. Agulonye

Introduction

Northern Nigeria is a region well known for its rich history, literary tradition and cultural diversity. Life is infused with cultural and religious practices and these usually form the basis on which the inhabitants of this region identify themselves as a people. It is a well known fact that the Hausa, Fulani, Kanuri and Nupe, who constitute the dominant ethnic groups in northern Nigeria, often wear their culture and traditions like a second skin. This phenomenon has sometimes evoked questions as to what could really be responsible for this love and attachment to culture, especially in this age of globalisation and rapid change in social traditions around the world. One explanation for this is the effect of the old literary traditions on the northern Nigerian peoples, especially the literature targeted at children.

Many find the task of differentiating between the literatures meant for children from those intended for adults confusing, considering their crossover appeal from both sides. Children's literature is often designed to explain the writer's world view and socialise the child readers into the religious, social, economic and political life of the adult society. This chapter will focus on the various ways in which literature for children in northern

Nigeria has been used, not just for the purpose of acculturation, but also as a means of inculcating the identity of the society into the psyche and lives of the children, who would then grow up to manifest these values and norms in their adult life.

Northern Nigeria and the Question of Identity

Northern Nigeria is geographically identified as the sprawling area lying north of the confluence of the rivers Niger and Benue, up to the borders of the Republics of Niger to the north and Chad to the northeast; and Benin and Cameroon to the west and the east; respectively. Ordinarily, anyone who hails from this geographical location should be regarded as a 'northerner', but the identity would be incomplete unless one truly identifies with the north as a living philosophy. As Ojaide (2008) explains, the concept of northern Nigeria historically evolved following colonial conquest and the establishment of the Nigerian Federation, as "a political creation that has socio-cultural, religious, geographical and other connotations." This identification is what the scholar refers to as the "Northern sensibility"; the awareness that enables writers in particular to be able to "reflect in their life, temperament, worldview, and sensibility of northern Nigeria as a distinct identifiable body..." Indeed, as Idegu (2005) expounds,

> Identity is a broad term which describes the general aspects of the individual's total personality, that is, the establishment, assimilation, or integration of, for example, societal norms, values, beliefs and standards. The individual's totality is not devoid of a collective communal or regional identity.

In order to fully fathom this sensibility, which defines the way and manner a northern Nigerian identifies with the region and is also identified with it, one has to go back into history and assess the sociopolitical history of the people. Long before colonial conquest and the influence of the West, northern Nigeria was a thriving centre of commerce, knowledge and religious interactions. It was a region interspersed with different and often competing and warring kingdoms. Despite the existence of strong traditional beliefs and religions originally, Islam gradually became the dominant religion and greatly influenced the culture of the majority of the people. Even in places where the Islamic belief was not popularly accepted or practised, it affected the way of life of the societies. Thus, the coming of the colonialists, with their worldly views and differing social practices, elicited reactions that amounted to rejecting the Western modernism, which became "synonymous with materialism, deviant behaviour, and corruption (Ojaide, 2008)". In time, this attitude, in addition to many other factors, was to influence even literary expressions, a situation that appears to have favoured the reinforcement of writing in the indigenous languages, especially Hausa, rather than in the English language.

On the other hand, as a result of these socio-cultural influences, in the north there seems to be less inclination to the individualistic tendencies found in other communities elsewhere in the country. The society has largely remained cohesive, as a result of which traditional and religious leaders are still accorded great respect and there is a collective encouragement for certain forms of behaviour and social expressions, especially with regard to the accepted modes of morality, dress, personal etiquette and the conduct of the affairs of men and women in the community. Open violation of these norms usually attracts moral sanctions, often in the form of loss of respect and dignity. All these realities have collectively helped to shape the northern identity.

Although the region consists of different ethnic and religious entities, this cultural identity of a high level of morality and accountability has been assimilated by almost all the consisting communities. That is also how the northern Nigerian identity has always been a prominent aspect of literature from that region. Literature, with its ability to acculturate and instil morals and values, has always been a highly effective tool used by individuals and societies for that purpose. The period of childhood and adolescence is the time when the individual's identity is shaped; considering the great emphasis the northern Nigerians place on their collective identity and cohesion, therefore, it is not surprising that the literature intended for their young also places much emphasis on cultivating acceptable attitudes and individuals for the upcoming generations.

To this end, participants at the Northern Nigeria Writers' Summit instituted by the northern chapters of the Association of Nigerian Authors (ANA) in 2008, had explained the objective of the summit, saying it was aimed at projecting the Northern writing within the context of Nigerian literature. Publishing their collective views in the book, *Toward Sustaining Creative Writing in Northern Nigeria* (Ismaila et al. 2009), their articles define the northern writer as that writer who shares the dreams and aspirations of the north in his or her writings, and not necessarily a writer who is a northerner by birth. It is noteworthy here that the northern Nigerian identity does not necessarily translate into ethnic identity, which is a complex matter, because "ethnic identity promotion is far from a smooth process", but is usually complicated by other more complex ssues, like migration and inter-ethnic marriages that always lead to "perforated ethnic identities (Idegu, 2005:56)". Hence, the basis for the prediction that the English language will in the future be the solution to inter-group conflicts in the country, when ethnic promotion would not be a straightforward matter any more.

The Place of Children's Literature in Northern Nigeria

The oral traditions of the region still remain the treasury house of the vast majority of the children's literature in northern Nigeria. In fact, one can easily trace the origins of Nigerian children's literary experience to the rich store of indigenous folktales, which abound in all the communities. Within the northern societies in general, prose narratives, songs, chants and recitations are associated with children, on account of their subject matter, language, structure and function (Odejide, 1991:3). These oral traditions for children serve a wide range of functions, including entertainment, relations with and socialisation into the norms of the group and the larger society.

Folk literature is broken up into myths, legends and folktales. Among the Hausa-Fulani who collectively form the largest single ethnic majority and have the most pervasive cultural practices, there is a rich tradition of folklore that has survived the ages, colonialism and even the onslaught of the electronic media in contemporary times. Folklore used to entertain and instruct the youth include:

a. *Tatsuniyoyi*: fables and tales about animals; and the magical world.
b. *Labarai*: tales of the legendary foundations of their kingdoms.
c. Youth lore for apprentice professionals, including butchers, blacksmiths, praise singers, travellers, etc.
d. The lore of young girls connected with bonding, friendship, betrothal, marriage, trade.
e. *Kacici-Kacici*: riddles.

The arrival of the colonialists had introduced a tradition of literature written in the roman script and suppressed the precolonial *Ajami* script, adapted from the Arabic alphabets, which was the medium of written expression for centuries across the region. According to Sani (1998), "The colonial British policy was to deny such literature the status of literature because it was not in a European language"; or because, in the case of oral literature, it was not "printed or published in book form." Today, we have inherited a legacy of indigenous literature written in the roman script and the phenomenon is quite prevalent in northern Nigeria. English might be the existing lingua franca of Nigeria, but has not been completely adopted in all societies, nor can it yet function in replacement of the indigenous languages. Certainly, nowhere is this more prominent than in northern

Nigeria, especially among the Hausa speaking populations. Even under the pressure of English language writing, the old literary traditions in Arabic and *Ajami* had cultivated attitudes that only gave birth to written literature in the Roman script, beginning with Abubakar Imam's *Ruwan Bagaja* and Abubakar Tafawa Balewa's *Shaihu Umar* in 1935 to the present day varieties of popular Hausa literatures. This was further encouraged by the appearance of the *Gaskiya Ta Fi Kwabo* newspaper in 1939; more recently, Tsiga (2014) reports the result of a baseline survey by Ismaila (2009) that even "the 'Kano Market Literature', jokingly referred to as the '*Soyayya* (romance) Novel', alone had produced about three thousand titles between 1984 and 2007."

Nonetheless, northern Nigeria is basically multi-ethnic and heterogenous; but it is also part of the Nigerian nation, with English as its lingua franca and the mode of instruction in all formal schools. English, therefore, plays a very important role in the development of the northern Nigerian children and the production of literature meant for them. Literature written in English may yet not enjoy the same widespread popularity as that which is written in the indigenous languages, especially in the genre of children's literature, but its production is definitely on the rise. Yusuf Adamu, a well-known northern Nigerian poet, claims to now write for children because,

> I realised that in Nigeria and Africa, we don't write for children most of the time. We only write for adults because we feel if you write for children, other writers will perceive you as an unserious writer. But writing for children is even more important than writing for adults because writing for children is likely to have more influence on the future of society than writing for adults who are already grown and who have made up their minds." Abodurin (2011:6)

Other writers like him are beginning to see the need for more literary works for children in English, although they face many challenges when they write in English at the moment. Adamu, who wrote the popular *Landscapes of Reality*, a poetry collection, also has his own take on the dominance of southern writers in Nigerian literature.

> I think it is luck. What is happening is that Nigerian literature in English is dominated by southerners but if you talk about Nigerian literature, I'm sure there are more published people in the north. More people in the north write in Hausa rather than in English because they find it easier to express themselves in their own language. One interesting thing is that they have a very large market because I can assure you my Hausa books sell more copies than my English books." Cited in Abodunrin, (2011:7)

Northern Nigerian Children's Literature in English

Northern Nigerian literature in English as a whole lags behind in relation to similar writing from southern Nigeria, or when compared to writing in the indigenous languages, especially Hausa, which currently enjoys one of the most vibrant readerships in the country and beyond. However, the situation is gradually changing, with more children being quite at home with the English language and the writers recognising the need for writing children's works in English. As these writings are also exported outside the region, it will help greatly to expose the northern Nigerian identity and sensibility to the outsiders, especially children of other sociopolitical groups. This may help to foster a better understanding of the northern Nigerian culture and world view among such children and lead to a more peaceful coexistence with others. Besides, the literature in its different sub-genres can be used to address the petty misunderstandings about the region and its people and correct the current misrepresentations.

Conclusion

The literary tradition in northern Nigeria is a thriving force, which not only serves as a means of acculturation, but also as a means of delineating the identities of the northern people. Children are the starting point on which future generations are built and, thus, need to be fed upon a rich and generous diet of literature, considering its overall influence in shaping their worldview. This will not only help them to develop a strong sense of identification with their society, but will also help them to enable them to fit into our ever-changing and evolving world.

Nigeria is a country of contrasts; and yet a country with a history of shared experiences and existence among its various ethnic and other social groups. Our literature for children should emphasise this fact, while instilling a sense of identity and belief in ethnic and universal values. Inculcating in them the value of appreciating and assimilating others can, no doubt, serve as a means of bridging the gap between cultures in Nigeria and serve as a way of developing a broader Nigerian identity.

References

- Abodurin, A. (2011), "Yusuf Adamu on Northern Nigerian Literature", Retrieved December 2, 2012 from "African Public Poets: African Poets for the World", http://234next.com/csp/cms/sites/Next/Home/5402598-146/story.csp.

- Idegu, E.U. (2005), "Identity Problematics in National, Ethnic and Regional Constructs", FAIS *Journal of Humanities*, Vol.3 No.2, p: 48-57.

- Ismaila, A. et al (2009), *Toward Sustaining Creative Writing in Northern Nigeria*, Ibadan: Kraft Books.

- Odejide, A. (1991), "The Origins, Growth and Future of Nigerian Children's Literature", *Association of Nigerian Authors Review*, October, 1991, pp. 3-27.

- Ojaide, T. (2008), "Poetry in Northern Nigeria: Challenges and Prospects", *Poetry and Poetics*, Proceedings of the 5th Conference on Literature in Northern Nigeria, pp. 1-13.

- Sani, A. A. (1998), "Colonialism and the Transition from Orality to Literacy in Northern Nigeria: The Instance of Hausa Narratives", *Work In Progress*, Department of English Ahmadu Bello University, Zaria, Vol.10, pp: 112-122.

- Tsiga, I.A. (2014), "Re-Defining Minorities, Federalism and Politics in Nigeria: The Death of Minority Languages and Implications for the Future" in Egwemi, V. T. Wuam and C.S. Orngu (eds.), *Federalism, Politics and Minorities in Nigeria*, Lagos: Bahiti and Dalila Publishers, pp. 36-54.

Index

INDEX

Aafa Adama, Al-Ilori
   – praise of, 219
Aami (Arabic script), 159
Abanger, Emmanuel 259
Abbas, Idris Isah 163
Abbas, Marwan 164
Abbasyd Dysnasty, 132
Abduallah Al-Qadi Al-Hajj 26
Abdu, M. 35
Abdulkareem, Idris 59
Abdullahi Smith Research Centre, 42
Aboriginal Yorubas, 208
Abu, Eugenia 43
Abubakar Bilkisu 341-351
Academics and Educationists, 41-42
Achebe, Chinua 60, 195-196, 288-289, 303
Adamu, Ladi 43
Adamu, Yusuf 60, 358
Adelodun, Ibrahim 181
Adidie, Ngozi 343
Aernyi, J.T 259
Affirming National Identity, 194
Afonja (Aare Onakakanfo of Yorubaland), 177-178, 184, 208
African
- female writer, 312- 313
- feminist writers, 342
- folktales, 124
- imaginative writing, 14
- languages, 200
- Literary artist, 238
- literature, 22, 196, 220, 341
- Magic
   - channel, 256-266, 268
- films, 268, 271-275
- movies, 265-278
- male feminist, 313
- Muslim society, 103
- novel, 295
   - tradition, 224
- novelists, 225
- woman in writings, 28
- women in literature, 342
- Writers, 195, 238, 288
   - English language writing, 288
   - Series (AWS) 288-289
Agary, Kaine 343
Agbaji families, 179
Agbe, 176
- calabash drums, 183
- Ensemble-Nupe Origin, 182
Agbekoya uprising, 89
Age of globalization, 353
Age-old tales, riddles and songs, 169
Ahamadu Bello University, 30
Ajami ,198
- script,198, 357-358
Ajami, Hausa 76
Ajani Ogun (Yoruba), 253
Akiga, Benjamin 28
Alasalatu musical groups of Ilorin, 185
Alaya family, 179
Alfa Alimi 178
Alhaji Abubakar Imam (1911-1981 A.D.) 130-132
Ali Hauwa 290
Ali, Maryam Ali 290
Alimi, 208
Aliyu, Kamal 290
Alkali, Fatima 344

Index

Alkali, Zaynab 196, 201, 290, 294, 311-335, 344
Al-Qasim Hariri, Abu Muhammad 106
Al-Tahir Aliyu, Muhammad, 80
Ameh Ooni, the Great
– sustaining hegemony through ritual death, 80-83
Aminu, Jibril 42
Aminu, Saira 301
ANA (Association of Nigerian Authors)
- Kano branch, 61
- National Library in Lagos, 61
Analysis, 303-308
Ancient folkloric traditions, 158
Animal fables, 103
Anthology of
- fairy tales, 103
- short stories, 63
Anthropological autobiography, 27
Anti-colonial
- battle, 142
- fight in Nigeria, 152-153
- struggle, 151
Anti-Semitism 122, 125
- narrative, 122
Apala, 176
Arab-based citizens, 182
Arabic
- and Islamic studies, 216
- heritage, 129
- language, 129, 130, 132, 216
    - and literature, 132, 138-139
        - as source of indigenous literary writing in northern Nigeria, 138
    - heritage, 138
    - literary, 132
    - writers, 137
- literacy, 137
- literary
- structures, 133
- texts, 136
- tradition, 136
- literature, 134, 139
- memoir, 24
- orthography, 129
- poem, 19
- Rhythmic prose, 132
- scholars from Ilorin, 215
- story book, 136
- tradition, 129
- Tales 13
- writing, 136, 198
    - and literature, 129
Arabs scholars, 204
Artistic
- Attahiru, 93-94
- Celebration of Attahiru's Heroism, 95-97
Artists and literary writers, 36
Ashuaibu, Malam 28
Association of Nigerian Authors (ANA), 64, 227, 35
Atiku, Abubakar Dan 29
Atlantic slave trade, 76
Attah, Seffi 290, 343
Attahiru-mortydom in the protection of the Caliphate, 76-80
Aural-visual production, 261
Authorial ideology, 68
Autobiographical writing, 18
Autobiographicals genre of literary writing, 16
Autobiographics, 17
Autobiographies or memoirs, 141
Autocratic political institution, 151

B aalu
- female *Dadakuada,* 182
Baduku, Ahamadu 227-230, 232
Baikie, Adamu 42
Balewa, Abubakar Tafawa 32-34, 153, 355, 31

Balogun, Ola, 253
Baluu, 176
   - music, 175
Bank of the North, 43
Bargery, Dr. 27
Barthes, Roland 195
Baruba, Hermit, 177
   - family, 207
Bauchi
   - Discussion Circle (later the BauchiGeneral Improvement Union), 149
   - General Improvement Union (BGUI), 149, 152
Bauchi, Abubakar 159
Bayajida story in Hausa, 2
BBC Trust rating its Hausa service, 40
Belgore, Justice 41
Bello, Ahamdu 15, 31-32, 34, 42, 44, 153
Bello, Muhammad 24
Bello's Character, 24
Bend down bookshops, 64
Bennywood-Benue landscape, 254
Binanci, Usman Adamu 61
Biography
   - as historical revision, 33
Biographies of famous Nigerian nationalists, 141
Boko (Roman script), 159
Boko Haram, 83
Bond FM Lagos's Kukan Kuraiya, 164
Bond FM. 163
Book
   - fairs and exhibitions, 64
   - reading programme, 169- 170
Books of fiction, 200
Borno Empire, 58, 130
Boundaries of ethnic groups, 252
British
   - Broadcasting Corporation, 162
   - colonial
      - administration, 108-109, 160
      - authorities, 84
      - conquerors, 96
      - conquest,19, 185
      - translations bureau in Nigeria, 104-109
   - colonialism, 91
   - colonization, 75
   - conquerors, 92
   - conquest of the Sokoto Caliphate, 143
   - imperial powers, 198
   - rule, 28, 76
   - West Africa, 160
Broadcast languages, 161
Broadcasting
   - in the Hausa language, 160
   - Law, 161
   - news, 161
Grimm Brothers' collection, 109
Grimm Brothers' collection of fourteen stories, 102
Bulama, Mohammed, 43

Clever Gretel story, 114-115
Caliphate frontiers, 144
CG for Clever Gretel, 109-116
Chia, Suemo 260
Children's literature, 353
Chinuwumba, Ifeoma 343
Chiroma, Adamu 18
Christian
   - missionaries, 186
   - missionary education, 67
Chronicle of
   - Abuja, 28
   - Kano, 29
   - Katsina 29
   - Sokoto 29

Index | 367

- Zaria 29
Citizens Association of Kano, 149
Civil War, 34-37
- and Northern Nigerian Life Narratives, 34-36
Clark, Trevor 32-33,75
Classical theoreticians, 299
Clever Gretel (CG) 112
- original German version translated into English, 110-111
Code
- mixing 257
- switching, 257
Collection of
- Arabic occasional poems, 216
- narratives, 36
- stories, 135
Collective
- cultural identity, 194
- destiny, 15
- identification, 193
- identity, 13
- memory, 28
Colonial
- authorities, 90-91
- bondage, 3
- conquest, 354
- education/literary projects, 285
- Government, 146
- hegemony, 197
- heritage 287
- history, 58
- language, 226
- objectives, 143
- rule, 143
- power's 94, 98
- projects, 285
- rule, 26, 76
- system, 96
Colonialism, 26, 73, 77
Colonialist historiography, 57

Comedic narratives, 124
Commemorative writings, 40
Communal wars, 208
Communicative
- practices, 267
- resources 267
Community
- ethics, 6
- morality, 5
Conservative
- Islamic tendency approach, 146-147
- Northern outlook, 292
Constitution of the Federal Republic (1999), 58
Construction of history, 58
Contemporary
- life narratives in Northern Nigeria, 36
- life writing in Northern Nigeria, 36-43
- literary theory, 101
Creative
- writing, 130
- writers in English, 216
Cross-cultural connectivity, 256
Cultural
- activities, 180, 187
- and literary identity, 136
- and political Associations, 147
- and religious
  - practices, 353
  - values, 73
- arrangement, 5
- artifacts, 181
- Associations, 147, 149
- contestations and crises in northern Nigeria, 57
- forms of colonization, 202
- harmony, 7
- history of the North, 129
- hybridity, 225
- hybridization, 251

- identity, 355
- imaginings, 14
- imperialism, 225
- incorporation, 198
- Indices (Language),176
    - as historical source of Ilorin Music, 183-184
- monuments, 16
- mutations, 14
- plurality, 215, 220
- practices, 180, 209, 256
- references, 2
- representation, 198
- study, 16
- transformation, 266
- tutelage, 199
- violence, 198

Culture
- clash, 240
- conflict, 290

Custodian of humane cultural behavior, 7

Dabino, Ado Ahmad Gidan 169
Dadakuada, 176,186, 215
- Northern Islamic music origin, 182-183

Danfodiyo, Abdullahi 24
Danfodiyo, Nanan Asma'u Usman (1793-1865), 22
De Naeyer, Jacqueline 114
Decolonization, 57
Diction
- in Drama, 300-301
- language, 300

Digital
- life story, 17
- Satellite Television (DSTV), 265

Dikko, Muhammadu 29
Dikko, R.A.R. 147
Discursive formations, 290

Domestic
- disputes, 77
- violence, 324

Drama, 98, 159
Dundun
- drums,181, 183
- Oyo origins, 182
- *Sekere music, 176*

Earliest female writers, 342-343
Early marriage, 312, 345
East, Rupert M. 104-105,114, 130, 137, 198-199, 200
Ecobiography, 17
Edowood-Edo language film, 254
Education of the Nomads, 42
Eid el-Fitr, 178 184
Eid El-Kabir, 178 184
Elegy, 215
- For
    - Abd Allah 23
    - Bello, 240
    - Gidado,23

El-Zakzaky-led Muslim Brotherhood, 83
Emecheta, Bauchi 343-344
Emergence of Nigerian Female writers, 343-350
Emergent female, 314-334
Emerging male, 314-334
Emila, 177
Emir Aliyu Abdulkabir , 218
Emirate
- Authority, 146
- political structure of Northern Nigeria, 181

English
- language, 201,216, 355-356, 359
  writing, 358
- novel, 295
- translations, 125

Epics 58
Ethnic
    - and
        - cultural identities, 19
        - religious entities, 355
        - universal values, 360
    - consciousness 260
    - group, 22,75, 178,180, 208-209, 246, 252, 257, 259, 353
    - identity promotion, 356
    - nationalities, 57
    - origins, 179
    - promotion, 356
    - regional and
    - national identity, 259
    - world communities, 251
Ethnomusicologists, 175
Eugenia Abu's collection of essays, 40
Eurocentirism, 225
European
    - and African audiences, 124
    - civilization, 2
    - language, 220,221,357
    - powers, 78
    - stories, 103
    - tradition, 113
    - writings, 227, 231
Evolution of life writing in Northern Nigeria
    - civil war, 19
    - colonial 19
    - contemporary,19
    - independence,19
    - periods of,19
    - pre-colonial ,19
Evolution of literature, 69
Eyinla or Ayinla,207
Ezeajugh, Tracia Chima 343

Falke, Umar 20
Falsetto voices, 176

Family relationships, 350gender parity, 345
Farah, Nuruddin 313
Feature programmes, 161
Federal
    - Department of Culture, 160
    - prose books, 160
    - Radio Corporation of Nigeria, Kaduna, 162
Female
    - heroism, 89
    - writers, 342-343
        - in African,312
        - and Nigerian literature, 342
Feminism in Nigerian Literature, 238
Figurative language, 308
Figures of speech, 308
Film
    - as a Genre of the Mass Media, 266
    - industry , 254
    - Production in the Tiv Society – background to, 256-257
Filmic adaptation of books, 102
Films
    - and Construction of reality, 266-267
    - and Gratification of Matrimonial Needs 267-270
First Republic, 38
Folklore, 256
Folkloric
    - genres, 157
    - traditions, 158
Folktales, 103, 357
Forceful incursion of the Roman alphabet, 198
Formal diction, 300
Freedom *Radio,168*
    - Kano, 163
French classicism, 194

Fuji, 176,185-186
   - musicians, 185
Fulani, 208
   - descent, 179
Full scale radio programmes, 161
Function of language in drama, 303
Funtua, Bilikisu Ahmed 344
Funtua, Garba 199

Gaa hamlet 17
Gambari group, 208
Gandoki, 196
Gara, Tafida Ibrahim, 61
Garba, John 147
Garba, Mohammed T. 290
Gaskiya Corporation, 17, 114, 159, 226
   - Zaria 69, 130
Gaskiya Ta Fi Kwabo, 38, 130, 162
   - newspaper 285-286,358
Gbagyi literature, 196
Gender war is over, 312
Geo-political zones, 57
German
   - cultural heritage, 103
   - Romantics, 194-195
Germanic folktales, 103
Gestures, 301
Ghanaian
   - language (Ewe and Twi), 160
   - society, 319
Gidado, Waziri 28
Gidan Ilori, 216-220
Gimba, Abubakar 201, 290, 294
Girl
   - education, 312
   - child education, 345
Giwa, A.T. 290
Global
   - crises, 74
   - culture, 293
Globalised literature, 108

Globalization, 62,251, 353
Gombe, Aliyu 61
Good Bargain
   - original German version translated into English, 116-118
Gowon, Yakubu 30
Grand Khadi of Northern Nigeria, 42
Grimm Brothers'
   - stories, 102-103
   - Tales, 113-114,122
   - in Africa, 109-110
Grimm, Jacob Ludung 102
Grimm, Wilhelm Carl 102
Group identity, 283, 288
Gumi, Sheikh Abubakar Mahmoud 42
Gwarzo, Muhammadu 159

Hafsatu, Hajiya 44
Hamisu, Muhammad Salisu 164
Hasan, Aliyu 61
Hassan, Malam 28
Hassan-Tom, Usara 290
Hausa
   - and tradition 158
   - Boko (modern writing in Roman alphabet) literature, 104
   - Book
      - literature, 200
      - reading sessions, 168
      - writing competition, 160
   - books of prose fiction, 164
   - City-states, 58
   - comic scripts, 115
   - creativity, 200
   - cultural theory, 5
   - culture,159,200, 305
   - dictionary, 27
   - fiction texts, 165

- fictional books, 162
- films, 299
- folkloric genres, 159
- Fulani
    - community, 294
    - culture, 181-82
- language, 136, 138, 162
    - for communication, 105
    - radio in Nigeria and Africa, 162
    - writers, 138
- listeners, 162
- literary
    - critics, 199
    - development, 105
    - language, 137
    - movement, 55, 61
    - works, 170
- literature, 107, 137, 159, 196, 202, 212
    - and English, 204
    - and identity, 193-204
- naming conventions, 124
- Northern
    - literature, 200
    - setting, 199
- Novel, 61
    - and Radio Programmes, 162-164
- oral traditions, 158
- performing artistes, 105
- poems, 216-220
- poetics, 6
- prose
    - books, 163
    - Fiction
        – overview of the emergence of, 159-160
    - narratives, 162
    - publications, 160
    - reading programme, 163, 169
- radio

- journalism, 40
- programmes, 158, 162
- rhetorical
    - and literary corpuses, 5
    - expressions, 5
- Roman script version of some Arabic texts, 104
- service (of BBC), 162
- Service of Radio France International, 164
- society, 158, 169
- writers, 137, 169
- Writing, 201-202
    - competition, 286
- written
    - literature, 170
    - sources, 162
Hausanized English Language novel 287
Heinemann
    - Education Books (HEB) 289
    - Series, 290
Hikaya, 163
Historical
    - accounts of cosmopolitan organization of Ilorin, 176
    - and comparative linguistic analysis of vocabulary, 183
    - Attahiru, 91-92
    - Development of prose, 282-295
    - Events, 87
    - fiction, 3
    - materials of Ilorin music, 176
    - narrative, 96-98
    - origins of some musical styles, 182
    - records, 286
    - sources of Ilorin music, 176
    - Truth versus Artistic Truth, 87-91
    - wars, 182
Historicism, 90

Historification, 68
Historiographic Survey of Ilorin Music, 175-187
Historiographics of other towns, 29
History
- and artistic recreation, 95
- and Identity, 197
- definition of, 1-2
- of Ilorin music, 186
- of the development of Ilorin music, 187
- of Yoruba-land, 22
Home video film productions, 254
Horizon of continuity of self-projection, 291
How literature portrays identity, 4

I_{bo}
- culture, 289
- novel 288
- writers, 289
Ibrahim, Kashim 32
Identity
- conflicts, 239
- crises, 240
- cruises, 353-360
- Feminism and Nigerian Literature, 238-239
Ideology of tribalism, 34
Igala
- Kingdom, 58
- Literature, 196
Iin da Ranka Sunday magazine, 163
Ikpilakaa, Samuel T. 259
Illustrations and Visual Iconography of
- KDK, 114-116
- KMW, 122-124
Ilorin
- a multi-ethnic cosmopolitan city, 181
- community, 176
- culture and language, 209-211
- Emirate, 177, 179, 181, 184, 209, 216, 220
- historical formation, 207-209
- literary tradition, 220
- music history, 175
- music, 175
- oral song, 7
- people, 177-181
- Praise Poetry, 216
- Yoruba dialect, 210-212
Imaginative writing, 196
Imam, Abubakar 61, 69, 102, 104-107, 109, 113-114, 121-122, 124-125, 130, 133-135-137, 147, 199, 358
Imam, Hauwa 43
Imamanc i, 106-107
- *for Imam, 199, 200*
Imperial powers, 96
Imperialism, 77, 180, 225
In Da Ranka of Freedom Radio Kano, 170
Independence Life Writing in Northern Nigeria, 31-34
Independent couples, 269-270
Indigenization of the broadcasting services, 161
Indigenous
- African
  - audiences, 108
  - Languages Cinema, 255
- Cinema in Nigeria
  - early attempts at, 253-254
- folktales, 356
- initiatives, 105

- language
  - Cinema (ILC) 255-261
  - film, 254, 260-261, 355, 357, 359
- literary writing in Northern Nigeria, 138

Index | 373

- literature, 109, 357
- musical practices, 186
- societies, 251
- theorization in Film production 261

Indirect Rule, 75
Individual and collective identity, 13
Informal diction, 300
Ingawa, Ahmadu, 199
Interaction with invisible Beings, 134
Inter-ethnic marriages, 356
Inter-group conflicts, 356
Internal conflicts among Tiv communities, 258
International
    - languages, 203
    - Publishing
        - House, 288
        - outfits, 289
    - radio stations, 162
Interpretative dialogue structures, 124
Inter subjectivity, 101
Intertextual
    - Interpretation of
        - TGB and KMW, 121-122
        - CG and KDK, 112-114
    - relationships, 102
    - theory, 101
Islamic
    - belief, 84, 355
    - celebrations, 185
    - culture, 185
    - doctrine, 178, 209
    - education, 345
    - festivals, 178
    - influence 287
    - law, 20
    - leadership hierarchy and values, 179
    - leadership, 21
    - missionary, 184

- musical genres, 185
- proclivity, 292
- religious festivals, 184
- revolutionary tendency, 146-147, 150
- scholarship, 105
- sensibility, 220
- societies, 22
- system of values, 293
- tenets, 208
- tradition, 209

Istanci, 105,199
Iyayi, Festus, 316

Jafaru, Alhaji (Emir of Zazzau), 142
Jibia, Aliyu 290
Johnson Samuel, 207-208
Johnson, Dul 290
Journalists, 40
Juju, 185
Julde, Malam 147
Jumare, Malam 147
Junaidu, Alhaji, 204

Kacici *–Kacici 357*
Kaduna State Radio, 162
Kagara, Abubakar Iamam 102, 159
Kaita, Isa 161-162
Kalala da Kalalatu (KDK), 112-113
Kallywood-Hausa language films, 254
Kanem Borno Empire 19
Kankara, Musa Muhammad, 163
Kannywood, 254
    - Films, 299-308
Kano
    - AM and FM, 161
    - Market Literature, 160,200, 358
    - State Agricultural and Rural Development Agency (KNARDA), 158

Kano, Aminu 33-34, 153, 142
Kano, Dan 290
Kano, Mamman, 162
Kanuri literature, 196
Kanuri origin, 183
Katibanmu in, 970s, 163
Kato, Cecila 344
Katsina Native authority Information Service, 226
Katsina, Ahimadu 199
Katsina, Wazirin 162
KDK for Labarin Kalala da Kalalatu, 109
Koki, Mahmudu 27
Koko, Ahmad Isah 163
Kongi's Harvest, 253
Koranic education, 286
Kristeva, Julia 136
Ku Karkade Kunuwanku, 163-164, 168
Ku Matso Ji, 2004, 163
Kukan Kuraya, 163
Kunnenka Nawa, 163-164
   -programme, 169
Kur Muhammed, Colonel 34
Kwa, Williams, 260
Kwadayi Mabudin Wahala (KMW) (Greed Leads to Hardship)
   - the Good Bargain (TGB) in Hausa, 118-120
Kwaggh-hir drama performances, 256
Kwararafa Empire 58

Labarai 357
Labarin Kalala da Kalalatu, 109

   - Clever Gretel in Hausa, 111-112
Labo yari and His Works, 226-227
Laderin family, 208
Language
   - and culture, 252

   - in drama, 299, 300-301
   - of films and drama 305
   - use, 307
   - Cultural Aesthetics and Indigenous Film, 252-253
Lantern, 290
Largema, Colonel 34
Large-scale solidarity, 15
Lawyers and Judges, 41
Legends, 357
Lexicographic enquiry, 183
Life
   - Narratives, 14, 27-28, 35, 37, 41,
   - of Traditional Rulers, 39
   - of Professionals, 39-43
   - writing
   - activities, 19
   - In Northern Nigeria, 16-19
   - Pre-colonial Northern Nigeria, 19-26
   - scholarship, 19
Linguistic
   - enquiry, 183
   - culture, 184
   - groups, 253
   - misoneism, 201
   - richness, 334
Listener survey, 168
Listening culture, 158, 169
Literary
   - activities, 55, 63
   - and written literature, 159
   - association, 64
   - communication, 251
   - competitions, 104, 285
   - corpus, 125
   - critics, 61
   - enterprise, 63-64
   - expression, 19, 355
   - Literary fiction, 3
   - genres, 215, 283
   - heritage, 105, 136

- historians, 143
- landscape 287
- narrative, 132
- programmes, 163
- representation, 295
- resources, 2
- scholars, 282
- skills, 170
- Society of Nigeria (LSN), 64
- style, 104
- technique, 107
- theories, 5
- theory and criticism, 202
- trade, 229
- tradition, 209, 220, 255, 288, 353, 359
    - in Ilorin, 212-216
- transition, 207

Literature
- and Identity, 195-197
    - in Northern Nigeria, 193-204
- Bureau, 104, 107
    - objectives of, 104
- for children, 360
- in Northern Nigeria, 62-69, 196-204
- tradition, 130

Lives of politicians, 36

Local
- African traditions, 5
- languages, 160, 256

Love of young girls, 357
Lugard, Frederick, 75-76, 78-80, 92

Madhu (Eulogy), 215
- *poems, 23*
- *poetry, 23*

Magaji Kuntu 179
Magana Jar ice 1-3, 135-138, 168, 196, 199
- Volume III, 134-136

Mahdi group, 83
Mahmud, Aisha Bello 168
Maimalari, Colonel 34
Maitatsine of the 2000s, 83
Malthouse 290
Manian trasmutative strategy, 106
Mao's Cultural Revolution in China, 3
Maqamah, 132
Material culture, 181
Maulud Nabiy 178, 184
McMillan 290

Media
- forms, 266
- literary commentary, 63

Medical Doctors 40-41
Migration, 356
Military conquest, 180
Mission schools, 186
Mnenga, Tersoo 34

Modern indigenous language
- and dialogue with the National Cinema, 255-256
- cinema 256
- films, 254

Modes of recreation, 260
Mohammed, Idris 40
Moorland, Colonel 78-79
Moremi myth, 89
Mother tongue, 203
Muffet, F.J. 81
Muhammad, Razinat 344
Multichoice subscribers, 265
Munkaila, Muhammed 61

Music
- as cultural artifacts, 181
- of Islamic origins, 185

Musical
- activities, 187
- genres, 182-183, 186
- history, 187

- instruments, 181
- practices, 187
- styles,175
    - in Ilorin, 182
- *types 176*
Muslim
- faithful, 92
- Hausa community, 113
- Hausa in Northern Nigeria, 104
- of West African,131
- scholars, 106
- *Ulama class, 145*
Mythical story, 177
Mythology, 256
- of his people, 231
Myths, 357
    - and legends, 2

Nagogo, Usman 29-30
Nana Asma'u (daughter of Usman Danfodiyo), 22-23
Napoleonic Wars, 103
Narrative
- style, 108
- of Politicians, 37
- of Public officers, 38
Narrativisation of the transcendent, 291
Nasal voices, 176
Nation-building and development, 57
Nation-ness and Identity, 14-16
National
- Cinema, 255-256
- film industry, 255
- identity, 194, 292
- in Northern Nigeria, 61
- languages, 62
- policy, 61
- Qur'anic competitions, 185
Nationalism, 14

Native
- Authority (NA), 146, 149
- languages, 226
NCNC,Lagos, 152- 153
Neo-classical period, 284
Ngugi wa Thiongo 289
Ngugi, James 289
Nigeria Broadcasting Corporation, 161
Nigerian
- anti-colonial history, 142
- Broadcasting Service (NBS), 161
- Children's literary experience, 356
- Civil War, 28,83,226
- Female writers, 342
- film
    - makers, 253
    - traditions, 255
- *films in indigenous languages, 253*
- Folklore Society, 64
- historical plays, 89
- identity, 355
- languages, 60
- literary elite, 56
- literature, 356
- National
    - Communication Policy, 266
    - Novel Tradition, 288
- novel 288
- political history, 32
- writers, 331
NKST Media services. 259
Nollywood, 254
Non
- African audiences, 124
- Arabic system of writing, 29
- Islamic traditional
    - practices, 185
    - festivals, 184

- Nigerian women married to Nigerians, 239-240
North and Northern Nigeria, 57-59
Northern
- Elements Progressive
  - Association (NEPA), 150
  -Union (NEPU), 34, 83, 150-153
- ethnics, 292
- fiction, 202
- General Improvement Union, 147
- history and identity, 35
- languages, 209
- Life Writing in the Colonial Period, 26-31
- Literature Agency, 159
- Nigeria
  - and the Question of Identity, 354-356
  - Before Colonialism, 75-76
  - Literary tradition, 223
  - Writers Summit, 35
- Nigerian
  - Children's Literature in English, 359
  - culture, 359
  - Female writings, 3412-351
  - heritage and identity,138
  - life narratives, 43
  - Literary heritage, 129
  - literature,196-197, 201, 344
    - in English 288
  - musical elements, 176
  - Novel, 291, 293
  - Publishing
    - Company, 159-160
    - Corporation, Zaria, 226
  - writers, 290,295
    - in English, 223
  - writing, 231
- People's Congress,(NPC), 83, 149
- perspective, 292
- politics, 153
- Region Literacy Agency (NORLA), 285
- sensibility, 354
- subjective, 14
- traditional leadership, 29
Northwestern University, Evanston, Illinois, U.S.A. Library, 20
Norwegian literature, 226
Novel in English, 295
Novels on the Radio
– current context of, 165-168
Nupe Kingdom, 58
Nwapa, Flora 343-344

Obafemi, Olu 290
Oboni, Ameh 80-82
Odes, 22-23
Ogbele -Music –Ekiti origin, 182
Ogundipe-Leshe, Molara 312-313
Ojbara family, 179
Ojo Isekuse, 177-178, 207
Okoye, Ifeoma 343
Old
- emirate system, 146
- literary traditions, 358
Olufadi, 208
One North Phenomenon, 15,19
Onwueme, Tess 343
Opam, Colonel 34

Oral
- compositions, 186
- form of communication, 252
- (literary) , 251-261
  - in Ilorin, 212
- literature, 159, 212
- means of communication, 251
- narrative, 103,255

- performer, 7
- production, 252
- singers *(mawaqa or alulu gbomi eko)* 2
    - or writer, 8
- sources, 157
- theory, 5
- tradition, 3, 109
- traditions, 356-357
    - of Africa, 2
- world 257

Orature and written literature, 131
Orin Omo Oba, 215
Orthographies, 61
Osofisan, Femi 75, 89
Osundare, Niyi 63
Oyo Empire, 179

Pagan communities, 184
Panegyrics, 58
Pankeke-Jihad war songs, 182
Pan-Nigerian solution, 152
Peaceful reforms, 149
Pedagogical Traits, 133-134
Penal code, 84
Peoples Redemption Party, 37
Performing Musicians Association of Nigeria, 185
Place of Children's Literature in Northern Nigeria, 356-359
Playwright, 93, 95,98
Plurality of voices, 196
Poem, 217-218
    - of Homer(The Iliad and the Odyssey), 2
Poetic
    - composition, 283
    - genres, 215
    - language, 101
Poetics, 283
    - license,91,96, 125
Poetry,58,159

- collection, 358
- in Hausa 61
- writing, 229

Political
- activities 153
- agitation, 152
- configuration, 144, 291
- corruption, 322
- demarcation, 209
- image, 153
- landscape, 317
- organizations, 153
- Parties,149
    - and the Emergent Nationalism, 147-151
- status of Ilorin, 220
- structure, 179

Politico-cultural institutions, 75
Post-colonial
- meaning of, 225
- studies, 225
- theory, 226
- writings, 224

Postmodern literary ideologues, 5
Power
- imperialism, 84
- of language, 308

Pre-colonial
- education system of northern Nigeria, 131
- writers, 25

Pre-Islamic
- belief system, 29
- Hausa-Fulani cultures, 292

Private
- Sector 43
- citizens, 36

Process for apprenticeship, 195
Professionals (journalists, medical doctors etc), 36
Prose ,159,215
    - and identity in Northern Nigeria, 281-295

Index

- fiction writings, 157
- narratives, 157, 356
- reading programme, 164
- style, 284
  writing, 158
Prototype characters, 58
Public officers (including bureaucrats), 36
Published accounts of 1966 coup plotters, 35
Pyramid Radio's Ku Matso Ku ji, 164
Pyramid Radio, 163

Qadiriyya, 83
Queen Amina of Zazzau
  - story of, 2
Quintessential Sa'adu Zungur, 151-154

Racial and national identities, 253
Radical Islamic tendency, 149-151
Radio
  - And Television Kaduna, 161
  - Broadcast
    - as Influence on the Literary Works, 169-170
    - in Africa, 160, 162
  - Broadcasting in Hausaland
  - Centres, 161
  - Distribution -Service (RDS), 161
  - Kano AM 163-164
  - Kano FM's Ku Tara Biyu, 164
  - Kano, 163
  - Kano's Kunnenka Nawa, 168
  - Lagos, 163
  - Listening, 158
  - Nigeria 3
    -Kaduna, 163
  - overview of history of, 160-162
  - services, 160
  - station broadcasting in Hausa in Niger Republic and Ghana, 164
Rahama Radio Kano, 163
Rai Dangin Goro programme, 168
Raji, Remi 219
Ramadan, 185
Rao Dangin Goro, 163
Readership, 63
Reading
  - audience, 31
  - formations, 290
  - Reading programmes, 169
  - programmes of radio stations, 165
Re-emergence of Indigenous Nigerian Cinema, 254-255
Regional
  - broadcasting houses, 161
  - radio stations, 161
Religion, 176
  - as historical Source of Ilorin Music, 184-185
Religious
  - allegories, 103
  - communities, 75
  - conflicts, 83
  - festivals, 209
  - history of Ilorin, 184
  - leaders, 42
  - symbolism, 332
  - values, 330
Republic of Biafra
  - declaration of, 34
Resistance literature, 28
Rima Radio AM and FM
  - in Sokoto state, 161
Rima Radio Sokoto, 163
Riwan bagaja 130
Roman
  - orthography, 136, 138

- script, 159, 198, 200, 357-358
Romanised Hausa script, 105
Rotimi, Ola, 75,90
Royal musical instruments, 181
Ruma Radio Sokoto's Hikaya, 164
Rural communities in Northern Nigeria, 158
Rustic farces, 103
Ruwan Bagaja 104, 104-105, 107, 130, 133-134, 137-138, 157, 159, 196, 358

Said, Edward 68
Sanusi, Wazirin Zazzau 147
Saussurean and Bakhtinian theories of language and literature, 101
School literary associations, 68
Second
    - generation of Hausa writers, 199-200
    - Republic, 37
      - in Nigeria, 161
Second World War, 40, 160
Sekere, 183
    - Music –Oyo origin, 182
Sekuila, Halimat 344
Self
    - government, 15, 31
    - identity of the woman in Soulmates, 240
    - migrants, 179
    - migration, 179
    - narrative, 25, 27
      - of Artists and Literary Writers, 38-39
    - publications of Northern writers, 290
Self-help projects, 320
Senwele, 176, 215
    - adaptation of Baalu 182
Separate couples, 270
Shafa Labari Shuni 162
Shagari, Shehu 37

Shaihu Umar (Hausa), 253
Shariah law, 84
Shehu Alimi 184
Shehu, Emman Usman 290
Sheikh
    - Abubakar Mahoud Gumi's autobiography, 42
    - Al –Torodi 25
    - Alimi, 208-209
    - Muhammad Al-Sabbagh Al-Kashinawi (Katsina Schola) a.k.a Dan Marina, 20, 22
    - Uthman Danfodiyo 24, 184
Sheme, Ibrahim, 61
Sholagbey compound, 183
Situational code-switching, 307
Skinner, Neil 27
Slave
    - trade, 157, 180
    - trade expedition, 180
Slavery (war refugees), 179
Smith, Mary. F. 27
Social
    - activities 176, 209
    - and literary research in Africa,. 341
    - commentary, 316
    - composition, 187
    - construction, 267
    - effects of colonialism, 27
    - group, 89, 251, 281
    - history of Ilorin society, 187
    - institutions, 187
    - intercourse, 179
    - order, 27
    - responsibility, 312
    - structure of Tiv Society, 28
    - subjectivity, 194
    - values of (Ilorin) people, 209
Societal
    - ethics, 25
    - responsibility in Ilorin society, 220

Society of Nigerian Theatre Artists (SONTA), 64
Sofola, Zulu 343
Sokoto
- Jihad, 130,198
- caliphate, 22, 25, 58, 75-76, 87, 97, 143-144, 145, 184
- scholars, 19
- Youth Social Circle, 149
Solagberu, 208
- family, 179
Solomon, Anjira 260
Source of
- His stories, 131
- Ilorin Music, 181-183
Southern
- Nigerian Literature, 20
- writers in Nigerian literature, 359
Sowande, 75
Soyayya
- Novel, 358
- soft fiction, 200, 202
Soyinka, Wole 60, 75, 89, 195, 292
Stevenson, Robert Louis 237
Stockholm syndrome, 89
Stories of British royalty, 3
Storytelling, 157-158
Style of
- Northern Nigerian aristocracy, 30
- non-Western music, 175
Sudanese Arabs, 179
Sufi brotherhoods, 83
Sule Mohammed 290
Sule, Egya 290
Sultan Attahiru, 77-80, 82, 87, 91-93, 95-98
Sultan of Sokoto, 91
Survey of Ilorin Music, 175
Swahili language, 108
Synopsis of
- Soulmates, 239-240
- the play, 301-303
System of hereditary succession, 150
Systematic dissociation of identity, 197

Tahir, Ibrahim 201, 290
Talakawa, 150
Tarka, J.S. 32
Tarka-Ti case, 34
Tatsuniyoyi, 357
Taura Biyu 163
Techniques of writing, 130
Textual migration, 101,102
Theory of language, 6
Tijaniyya, 83,145
Tiv
- communities, 258
- culture, 256
- ethnic group, 257
- independence politics, 34
- indigenous language films, 259
- language
- Cinema 259
- films, 256
- Literature, 196
- lore 28
Tivwood/Tiv films –Tiv – language production, 254
Traditional
- beliefs and religions, 355
- couples, 269
- institutions, 39
- leaderships institutions, 29
- life narratives, 17
- music, 184
- of literature, 357
- practice, 349
- rulers, 36
- society, 331
- sociology, 98
Tragic ideological conflict, 37

Translation
- and Literature Bureau, 159
- Bureau, 104-105, 107
- of foreign literature, 109
Transmutation of transnational literature, 106
Travel literature, 215
Tribal
- and religious conflicts, 75
- or local level political leadership, 34
Tukur, Muhammad 23
Tukur, Tijjani 61

Uga, Ada 290
Ulama, 144-146, 150
Umaru, John Tafida 159
Unegbe, Lt. Col. 34
Unique racial genius of a people, 194
United Islamic State of West Africa, 76
Universal subjecthood, 194
UPGA, 152
Use of
- Arabic works, 176
- figures of speech, 308
- gratification approach, 267
- language, 300
   - in two film, 302-303
- proverbs 335
- Syntax, 300
Usman, Adamu Kyuka 290
Usman, Asabe Kabir 290, 344
Uthman Danfodiyo, Sheikh, 76, 79, 184

Value assessment 260
Values and identity of African culture and society, 196
Verbal
- and non-verbal utterances, 303

- phrase and musical phrase, 181
Vocality as identify of the woman in Soulmates, 245-249
Voice of Nigeria, Lagos, 163
Voicelessness as identity, 240-245

W*aka, 176, 185- 186, 212*
   - adaptation of Were, 182
   - music, 175
   - themes of prophets of God or Muslim Scholars, 214
   - in Ilorin, 212-216
Were, 176, 185,214-215
   - Music adapted from Islamic festival of Ramadan, 182
Western
   - cultural form, 288
   - cultural practices, 186
   - education, 129, 131, 138, 151-152, 186, 286, 288, 290, 293-294
      - as historical source of Ilorin Music, 185-186
      - on these musical types, 176
   - ideal of culture of literature, 195
   - modernism, 355
   - style schools, 159
Whiting, Mr.l. 104
Willcocks, Colonel 78
Women in African literature, 342
Women writers, 238
Words and expressions peculiar to Ilorin Yoruba dialect, 210-211
Work of drama and literature, 299
World languages, 203
World War II, 162, 202
Writer's world view 353
Writing
   - modern self narratives, 25

Index

- of Arabic, 129
- of Hausa stories, 129-130
- /creativity, 95

Writings of Nigerian women, 239
Written (literary) in Ilorin, 212
Written literature, 215
Wurno, Mai, 79

Yagba Land, Kogi State, 180
Yakubu, Balaraba Ramat 290
Yakubu, Mukhtar 142
Yari, Labo 226-227, 232, 290,293
Yari, Muhammadu Uban (Emir of Katsina) a.k.a (Karyagiwa), 20-21
Yollywood –Yoruba language films, 254

Yoruba
- language, 208, 220
- films, (Yollywood), 254
- settlement, 177
- *Ulama* 22

Youth love for apprentice professionals, 357

Zamfara Radio, 163
Zango, Nasiru 70
Zare da Abawa of Pyramid Radio, Kano, 163
Zaria Zumunta Association, 149
Zoy radio station, 161
Zungur, Sa'adu 141-154
Zurke, Malam 132-133

www.ingramcontent.com/pod-product-compliance
Lightning Source LLC
Chambersburg PA
CBHW051347290426
44108CB00015B/1915